The Lessons of History

The

Lessons

of

History

MICHAEL

HOWARD

Yale University Press

New Haven & London

Designed by Sonia L. Scanlon
Set in Galliard type by
Brevis Press, Bethany, Connecticut.
Printed in the United States of America
by Vail-Ballou Press, Binghamton,
New York.

Library of Congress Cataloging-in-
Publication Data
Howard, Michael Eliot, 1922–
    The lessons of history / Michael
    Howard.
        p.   cm.
    Includes index.
    ISBN 0–300–04728–2 (cloth)
           0–300–05665–6 (pbk.)
    1. History, Modern—20th
century.   2. Military history,
Modern—20th century.   3. World
history.   4. Military history.
I. Title.
D431.H68   1991
909.82—dc20   90–37654
                                        CIP

A catalogue record for this book is
available from the British Library.

The paper in this book meets the
guidelines for permanence and
durability of the Committee on
Production Guidelines for Book
Longevity of the Council on Library
Resources.

10 9 8 7 6

Contents

Introduction / 1

1   "The Lessons of History": An Inaugural Lecture given in the University of Oxford, March 1981 / 6

2   Empires, Nations and Wars / 21

3   Prussia in European History / 49

4   Empire, Race and War in pre-1914 Britain / 63

5   The Edwardian Arms Race / 81

6   Men against Fire: The Doctrine of the Offensive in 1914 / 97

7   Europe on the Eve of the First World War / 113

8   1945—End of an Era? / 127

9   Ideology and International Relations / 139

10   Churchill and the Era of National Unity / 152

11   War and Social Change / 166

12   Military Experience in European Literature / 177

13   Structure and Process in History: A Valedictory Lecture given in the University of Oxford, May 1989 / 188

Attributions / 201

Notes / 203

Index / 209

Introduction

The pieces collected here were mainly written during my tenure of the Regius Chair of Modern History at Oxford between 1980 and 1989. The wide responsibilities of this Chair, which extend in principle from the end of the Roman Empire until the present day, compelled me to reflect both more broadly and more deeply than I had yet done about the purpose and nature of historical studies in general, especially as they were carried on in my own university. The Inaugural Lecture which opens this collection deals with the perennial problem of teaching history at Oxford. The final Valedictory Lecture reflects the conclusions I had reached after forty years about the nature of historical studies and their value in training not only political but ethical judgement. To the general reader the first lecture may appear parochial, the last idiosyncratic. If so, they can safely ignore both and concentrate on what lies between.

Most of these pieces have a common focus. They reflect an interest not so much in the study of war, with which I have been concerned throughout most of my academic career, as in those deeper processes of historical change from which the wars of the nineteenth and twentieth centuries originated. In particular they deal with the evolution of 'nations' and of nationalism in nineteenth-century Europe, and the relationship of that evolution to the transformation of agrarian into industrial societies; that process of 'modernisation' which, beginning in Western Europe in the eighteenth century, was by the end of the twentieth to encompass the entire world, and whose effects trouble us still. The frenetic nationalism which led to the First World War; the bellicist Fascism which precipitated the second; the creation and conflict of new nations which followed the collapse of the old European empires after 1945; all can be traced to the growing pains of industrial societies, the conflict of ideologies to which these gave rise, and the development of new political organisms and at-titudes as mass communications and universal education raised and trans-formed the level of political consciousness throughout the world. This was the political womb, to use Clausewitz's analogy, within which the embryo of twentieth-century warfare was incubated. We must study this process if we are to understand why these wars occurred at all and why they took the form that they did.

I have published two earlier collections of occasional pieces: *Studies in*

War and Peace (1971) and *The Causes of Wars* (1983). The introduction to each quite consciously reflected the concerns of the moment. The first was strongly (and adversely) affected by the utopian turmoil of the students' revolt of the late 1960s. The second was written during the debate over the installation of Intermediate Range Nuclear Forces in Europe, when Western governments were trying to keep their heads among the clamorous ululations of the Campaign for Nuclear Disarmament in Europe on the one hand and the Committee on the Present Danger in the United States on the other. Rereading them makes me realize how impossible it is for historians to detach themselves from their environment. Our agenda is set by current controversies, whether we wish it or not. If we take part in them, we have no right to claim that our historical studies provide a kind of inner light denied to lesser mortals. Historians are as prone as anyone else unconsciously to formulate conclusions on the basis of temperament, prejudice and habit, and then collect the evidence to justify them. It would be dishonest to pretend otherwise.

Historians, further, find it as difficult as anyone else to distinguish between the significant and the transitory in contemporary affairs: to determine whether an event is purely fortuitous or indicative of a long-term trend. The challenge today (and I write in May 1989) presents itself in a particularly fascinating form with the contemporary developments in the Soviet Union. In various places I have stressed the cultural distinctiveness of Soviet society, the historical background which has produced a social structure favouring the community against the individual, state power against 'human rights', centralised *dirigisme* against local initiative. I have suggested that whatever our moral distaste for such a regime, there was no need necessarily to see it as a threat, and that we could and should learn to cohabit peacefully with it; but that there was no reason to expect any fundamental change in the nature of a political system based on the historical characteristics of Russian society.

This diagnosis has now been called in question in a fashion that no one ever anticipated. Mikhail Gorbachev and his colleagues in the Soviet Union have turned their backs on their historic traditions on the highly pragmatic grounds that, whatever its ideological and cultural justification, the communist system, as it developed in the Soviet Union out of the previous czarist despotism, simply does not work. Without renouncing Marxism-Leninism as such, they condemn its consequences and look to the despised bourgeois West to provide remedies. Open debate at home on the basis of freely-available information; friendly intercourse with the rest of the world; liberation of the East European satellites to find their own way to prosperity and freedom; drastic reduction of armaments: who, ten years ago, could have predicted anything of the kind?

The reaction of some historians is to wag their heads sagely and say they have seen all this before. In the eighteenth century Peter the Great and Catherine II imported Western technology and concepts to enable their Empire to compete on equal terms—not least military terms—with its European rivals. In the nineteenth century Alexander II liberated the serfs in the aftermath of defeat in the Crimean War in order to develop a market economy. In the pre-1914 era Counts Witte and Stolypin initiated a crash programme of industrialisation and land reform so as to keep pace with the fast developing West. None of these measures changed the fundamental nature of Russian society. All led to bleak authoritarian reaction. Is there any reason to suppose that Gorbachev will do better?

The question can be answered only if we understand not only the structure of Soviet society but the processes operating within it; a distinction elaborated in my valedictory lecture. If Gorbachev were no more than a single gifted and courageous individual, his chances of changing the system would be no better than those of his predecessors. But if he is himself symptomatic of systemic change, a representative of a whole generation of politically-disillusioned technocrats as ready to jettison the irrelevant lumber of Marxism-Leninism as were the bourgeois elites of Western Europe in the nineteenth century to jettison the dogmas of the Catholic church, then we may be witnessing a transformation which makes historical analogies irrelevant. In the Soviet Union, as elsewhere throughout the world, the imperatives of modernisation may override both ideological commitment and cultural conditioning, whatever political strains they may cause in the process.

Instant judgement always tells us more about the person judging than the situation judged. There are those whose perennial optimism leads them to see the Soviet Union transformed overnight into a civilised partner willing to abide by all the Western rules of the international game. Others, who have a visceral or a professional need to consider the Soviet Union as a permanent and transcendental adversary, regard Gorbachev as at best a transient phenomenon, at worst an enemy all the more dangerous for his rational discourse and his smiling face. My own view, and one which is at least compatible with a study of the historical process, is that Gorbachev is symptomatic rather than exceptional and that in consequence the changes he has initiated will ultimately be irreversible. But they will be slow to take effect, and the process will be dialectical rather than continuous. Further, whatever happens, the Soviet Union will remain a major power whose military strength and political culture will continue to present major difficulties for the West. We must look for evolution rather than transformation, and not expect too much too soon.

The events of the past decade however suggest that the fundamental problems of the twenty-first century will not be those of traditional power confrontations. They are more likely to arise out of the integration, or disintegration, of states themselves, and affect all actors on the world scene irrespective of ideology. The emergence of centrifugal nationalism within the Soviet Union has presented Gorbachev with complications neither he nor anyone else anticipated. They have led gloomy analogists to see the Soviet Union not as a new Third Reich but as a latter-day Habsburg Monarchy, increasingly unable to control its subject nations and equally liable to provoke a world war in its efforts to do so.

The problem in the West is more subtle. Apart from foci of fanatical nationalism such as are found in Northern Ireland or among the Basques, our long-term challenge is that of maintaining cohesion in increasingly heterogeneous societies where traditional national loyalties are widely regarded as anachronistic or irrelevant. Throughout the Western world social tensions have been sharpened. First, the dislocation caused by economic change has created large minorities of unemployed and unemployables; and second, global mobility, by making possible mass emigration, has eroded the cultural cohesion of older communities, called in question fundamental institutions and attitudes developed in, and for, homogeneous societies, and presented developed capitalist economies with unprecedented problems of adjustment and assimilation. It is significant that even in the United States, that classic melting pot, little more than half of the population regard themselves as sufficiently part of the political community to vote in presidential elections.

The tone and content of the Churchill Memorial Lecture which I gave in London in the autumn of 1984 reflect the anxieties of a particularly tense moment in industrial relations in the United Kingdom—a moment which passed but left much bitterness behind. It is true that national cohesion may not be an unmixed blessing. Intense patriotic sentiment was a condition if not a cause of the two world wars, and there was a very ugly side to the jingoism which swept Britain during the Falklands campaign and the United States during the Grenada episode. But its waning has left us with problems to which neither constitutional democracy nor Marxism-Leninism provides ready-made answers. Without some degree of conscious national commitment and consensus, states become ungovernable.

As for the highly heterogeneous collection of states which make up the so-called Third World, the difficulties of simultaneously creating viable political communities and carrying out effective modernisation have defeated all but the most talented or the most fortunate of their leaders. Revolutionary socialism may be a powerful recipe for social mobilisation, but it is disastrously inadequate for long-term economic development. On the other hand free-market capitalism creates horrifying inequalities and widespread corruption, which in their turn inhibit economic growth and breed social and racial tension. For most countries in the world the road to economic prosperity and political stability will be long and hard.

We are left with a West whose wealth provides no relief from anxiety and turbulence; a socialist world which has now recognised with astonishing unanimity that its God has failed; and a Third World which nothing can spare the strains and conflicts inherent in modernisation. These are not exactly the 'broad, sunlit uplands' of which Winston Churchill once spoke, but the least that historians can do is to remind the world that there *are* no such uplands—or rather that when we do find them, we will find also deeply shadowed valleys full of misery and despair. Each new generation is presented with new problems and new challenges, and analogies drawn from the past are likely to be more of a hindrance than a help in solving them. If the past has anything to teach us it is *humility*—and suspicion of glib formulae for improving the lot of mankind.

Yet at risk of appearing complacent, we can say that we have not done too badly over the past forty years. There remains shocking suffering all over the world, but we are developing techniques and resources to alleviate it. We have avoided nuclear war—indeed major war of any kind. Standards of living and life expectancy throughout the world have continued to improve, if faster in some places than others. If we are no happier than our ancestors (and how are we to judge?) the fault lies in ourselves rather than in our circumstances. And as one whose conscious political experience now extends over half a century, I can say that I would rather be living in 1989 than in 1939—or indeed at any date between the two.

1

The

Lessons of

History

There are countries where it is taken for granted that university professors should be appointed by the State. This has not prevented the universities in question from maintaining their eminence in scholarship or even their independence of political pressure, but no one would regard this as a practice that we in this country should wish to imitate. The appointment of a handful of professors by the Crown, a tiny and usually eccentric minority in a national professoriate whose present numbers I dare not even attempt to compute, is tolerated here as an amusing anachronism. It is not regarded as a serious infringement of academic freedom, so long as the professors in question behave themselves. Speculation about their appointment enlivens the tedium of academic and even metropolitan life. Nobody really objects very much to the appointment itself, whatever views they may hold about the successful candidate.

The founding of this Chair in 1724 by King George I was attributed by unsympathetic contemporaries to the desire of the incoming Hanoverian dynasty to get their man into a nest of unregenerate Toryism, and I have no doubt that they were right. But the explicit argument advanced for it was perfectly reasonable. The King pointed out that in neither Oxford nor Cambridge was any provision then made for the study of Modern History or Modern Languages 'the knowledge of which is highly necessary towards compleatly qualifying the Youth committed to their care for Several Stations, both in Church and State, to which they may be called'. It was for that reason that His Majesty had resolved 'to appoint two Persons of sober Conversation and prudent Conduct, skilled in Modern History and the Knowledge of modern languages . . . to be our Professors of

An Inaugural Lecture given in the University of Oxford, March 1981.

Modern History . . . who shall be obliged to read Lectures in the public schools at such times as shall hereafter be appointed'. The universities in fact were expected to make themselves socially useful or, as some would say today, 'relevant'. A knowledge of history was considered necessary for those members of the public service whom it was the function of the university to train; and the Crown exercised its authority, by these as by other Regius appointments, to indicate what, in its view, universities should be doing for the common weal.

Two and a half centuries ago, universities were even less responsive to demands for social relevance than they are today. Over a hundred years were to pass before a Regius Professor was appointed who was able to make the slightest impression on the university, or indeed on anyone else. The first to do so was the redoubtable Dr. Thomas Arnold of Rugby, whose lectures in 1841 (one enviously reads) drew audiences of three hundred or four hundred at a time. In one of them he apparently gave 'a most striking account of the blockade of Genoa, at which the Master of Balliol is said to have wept.' But Arnold was a brilliant comet flashing all too briefly across the dark Oxford sky; within six months of delivering his Inaugural Lecture he was dead. A decade later the school of Modern History was founded, or rather a joint school of Law and Modern History. But paradoxically it was then that the tribulations of the Regius Professors began. For the corpus of college tutors resolved that, whoever might now superintend the teaching of history in Oxford, it would not be the Regius Professor. The German model of professorial superintendence was rejected. No less a man than Dr. Edmund Pusey wrote a pamphlet showing that in Germany infidelity and immorality were the direct results of the professorial system. So the Oxford history school developed in its own inimitable way, leaving the unfortunate Professor high and dry.

Interestingly enough the way the school did develop was very much that intended by the royal founder of the Chair; as a liberal education for the governing class, or as one Regius Professor, Goldwin Smith, put it, as a means 'to win the landed aristocracy and gentry to study'. The Regius Professors did not like this at all: 'an easy school for rich men', sneered Professor Edward Freeman. At a time when the great History Schools were developing in Germany, in France and in the United States, under professorial direction if not dictatorship, in Oxford men of the calibre of Goldwin Smith, William Stubbs and Freeman found themselves lecturing to classes of half a dozen, if that. No provision was made for graduate study or scholarly training. All Freeman could hope for, he lamented in his Inaugural Lecture in 1884, was to be 'the helper, if need be the guide,

of any, old or young, . . . who . . . between the frenzy of amusement and
the frenzy of the examinations can still find a few stray hours to seek
learning for its own sake'. Twenty years later Sir Charles Firth gave an
Inaugural which he described as 'a plea for giving future historians a
proper professional training in Oxford, and therefore an attack on the
system of historical education which renders it impossible'. His tutorial
colleagues were so nettled by this that two dozen of them wrote an open
letter arguing that the object of the Oxford History School was *not* to
train professionals but to provide a humane and liberal education for 'the
ordinary man'; whom they defined as 'one capable subsequently of being
a Cabinet Minister, a Bishop, an Ambassador, Viceroy of India, or one of
the Permanent Under Secretaries of the Civil Service'. There are still those
among us who, mutatis mutandis, would hold the same view.

But in the twentieth century the situation changed. This was due partly
to the hard work of Firth himself, who developed that greatest of undergraduate special subjects, the Great Rebellion, later to develop into the
Commonwealth and Protectorate, in which so many distinguished Oxford
scholars were to win their spurs. But yet more was it due to that formidable
trinity of medievalists who succeeded one another in the Chair between
1925 and 1957: Carless Davis, Maurice Powicke and Vivian Galbraith.
All were Oxford men trained under T. F. Tout in Manchester, who brought
back to the enervating air of their own university the invigorating rigour
of the North, and created a graduate school in their own field that was
rapidly emulated in many others. Since then, graduate courses and semi-
nars have multiplied; undergraduates are taught to use primary material
at an early stage in their courses; and most important of all, no scholar
can hope to be elected a Fellow of a College, or given a tenured post on
the staff of any History Department in this country unless he has shown
evidence of considerable achievement as a professional scholar. Professor
Galbraith indeed in his Inaugural Lecture in 1948 no longer thought it
necessary to address any more appeals to his colleagues for the encouragement of research. He directed his fire against the government, demanding that more of the taxpayers' money be spent on making more
materials available for the cohorts of research students who were now
descending on the Public Record Office.

The pendulum had indeed swung so far that my predecessor Hugh
Trevor-Roper (now Lord Dacre) devoted his own Inaugural Lecture to
giving it a hefty shove in the reverse direction. Research, he agreed, was
all very well; but if professional historians produced studies that were of
interest only to one another, they would rapidly kill their subject stone

dead. Unlike the sciences, he argued, the humanities 'owe their title to the interest and comprehension of the laity; they exist primarily not for the training of professionals but for the education of laymen; and therefore if they once lose touch with the lay mind they are rightly condemned to perish'.

For of course the tutors were, and are, right. Only a tiny minority of students come to universities to learn how to be professional historians, and it is not primarily for them that our History Schools should be organized. The state now provides the money, and students are encouraged to find the time to read history—the three most formative years of their lives, when they could be learning a trade or a profession far more lucrative, of far more immediate 'relevance' to social needs—because it is still believed that a knowledge of the past is prerequisite to an understanding of the present; an understanding equally necessary to the élites who conduct the business of the state and the electorate to whom they are responsible. It is still believed that an understanding of the past is a necessary part of that self-awareness, that understanding of ourselves, that is the true object of a liberal education. To know the way in which our society came to be formed, to have some understanding of the conflicting forces within it, is not only an advantage in the conduct and understanding of public affairs: it is indispensable. No amount of technical expertise, no degree of professional competence, can ever take its place.

This understanding is of so broad, so general, and often of so incommunicable a kind that social scientists often and understandably lose patience with historians who are reluctant to translate it into precise recommendations or formulate from it specific laws, and themselves seek to provide more direct techniques of guidance. Often their insights have brilliantly illuminated our understanding of both past and present: Max Weber, for one, did not write as a historian, but no historian, of any era, can now afford to neglect his work. But in formulating laws that will be either predictive or normative social scientists have been no more successful than historians; for the number of variables is so incalculable, the data inevitably so incomplete. The theories they formulate are at best explanatory or heuristic. They can never be predictive. Even the most convincing of their theories should be regarded as tentative hypotheses to be critically re-examined as new data become available. Even the most persuasive will eventually be displaced and relegated to the museum of historiographical curiosities. They may illuminate our judgement, but they can never take its place.

As a historian specializing in military affairs I was beset at an early age

by sheep hungry for food that I did not feel competent to provide. I had
to deliver, to a class of young army officers, a lecture on the Italian campaign of 1943–5. I sketched as best I could its rationale, its course and
its consequences, with some deeply felt comments on the quality of the
leadership on both sides. At the end there was a silence which I correctly
gauged to be disapproving. It was broken by a young man in the front
row asking impatiently, 'But what were its *Lessons?*' And well might he ask.
What was the point in all this if it did not have a direct professional
relevance? They were busy men. But it was a question that nothing in my
historical training here or in the University of London had equipped me
to deal with and which I deeply, and absurdly, resented having to answer.

In fact of course one could derive many 'lessons' from that campaign
for the military professional, who was likely to be confronted again with
comparable if not identical problems of tactics, supply, intelligence and
morale; and sharply focused questions directed to such specific issues could
indeed produce valuable answers. But as a historian I was conscious above
all of the unique quality of an experience that resulted from circumstances
that would never, that *could* never, be precisely replicated. The lesson that
most of those involved in the campaign on either side would agree about,
is that if one wants to conquer Italy, the southern end of the peninsula is
not the best place to begin. But the historian now knows that when the
Allies landed at Salerno no such campaign was visualized and no such
object intended. The Allied leaders were responding to the unforeseen
circumstances created by the collapse of Mussolini's regime in the only
way that seemed open to them; and the only 'lesson' that a historian would
be justified in deriving from these events is that in war, in *any* war, this is
the kind of thing that armed forces may find themselves having to do; not
necessarily through the miscalculations or the stupidity of their leaders,
but because all other options seem to be foreclosed or appear demonstra-
bly worse. Subsequent generations of historians will deepen our understanding of the circumstances that shaped the decisions and set them in
their social and economic framework. The Allied obsession with firepower
and air power, the reluctance to accept heavy casualties, their lack of combat skills in comparison with their adversary, the excellence of their supply
and welfare services and the determination to maintain them at whatever
cost to mobility: all this may, in the long run, be of greater interest to the
historian than the events, or even the outcome of the campaign itself. But
what lesson can this teach, except that armed forces reflect the societies
that produce them, and within the limits these impose on them they can
only be expected to produce a finite range of results?

It is safer to start with the assumption that history, whatever its value in educating the judgement, teaches no 'lessons', and the professional historians will be as sceptical of those who claim that it does as professional doctors are of their colleagues who peddle patent medicines guaranteeing instant cures. The past is infinitely various, an inexhaustible storehouse of events from which we can prove anything or its contrary. Do arms races always end in war? The longest and perhaps the bitterest arms race in modern history was that between the French and British navies between 1815 and 1904, a period of 90 years in which peace was successfully preserved between two powers who had for 125 years before that been engaged in virtually continuous official or unofficial conflict. Does 'appeasement' never pay? It paid off handsomely enough when the British settled their differences with the French in Africa in 1904 and with Russia in Central Asia three years later. Does neutrality, or non-alignment, enhance national and international security? The example of Switzerland and Sweden argues one way, that of Belgium, of Holland, and of the smaller Italian states in the eighteenth century quite another. In short, historians may claim to teach lessons, and often they teach very wisely. But 'history' as such does not.

The trouble is that there is no such thing as 'history'. History is what historians write, and historians are part of the process they are writing about. We may seek for what Jakob Burckhardt described as the 'Archimedean point outside events' which would enable us to make truly dispassionate judgements and evaluations, but we know we cannot find it, and I am afraid we mistrust those of our colleagues in the social sciences who believe that they can. We know that our work, if it survives at all, will be read as evidence about our own *mentalité* and the thought-processes of our own time rather than for anything we say about the times about which we write, however careful our scholarship and cautious our conclusions. We also know—or ought to know—how incomplete at best our knowledge of the past is bound to be: either because we have so little to go on or, for more recent times, because we have so much and have to be rigorously selective if we are going to make any sense of it at all. New evidence is constantly suggesting fresh perspectives and fresh conclusions, and historical controversies normally end because the participants are tired of them rather than because a consensus has been reached on which all can agree and which provides a firm platform for the proclamation of reliable conclusions. Was there, or was there not, a general crisis in the seventeenth century? Were the governing classes of the Second German Reich or were they not determined on world war? On these great questions no certainty has been reached and none can be expected. But how much better we understand the past because they have been so exhaustively discussed!

The professional historian thus tends to be impatient of the layman who seeks guidance from him in dealing with the questions of his own day, let alone the future. His time is cut out trying to discover as best he can, not only what 'really happened' in the past, but, increasingly, what the past was really *like;* in recreating the intellectual and social structures which will enable him to 'explain' events; trying, for example, to understand the social and intellectual framework that made the war of 1914 or the Revolution of 1789 *possible,* rather than tracing the course of events that led to them or allocating 'responsibility' among the participants; much less generalizing from them about wars and revolutions in our own day. And this, for the layman, is maddening. He looks for wise teachers who will use their knowledge of the past to explain the present and guide him as to the future. What does he find? Workmen, busily engaged in tearing up what he had regarded as a perfectly decent highway; doing their best to discourage him from proceeding along it at all; and warning him, if he does, that the surface is temporary, that they have no idea when it will be completed, nor where it leads, and that he proceeds at his own risk.

Well, the road works have to be done, and of course they are never complete. Even if no new evidence about the past, archaeological or documentary, compelled us to review our ideas about it; even if technology provided us with no new tools; the continual reshaping of our own minds by the events and social processes of our own times would make us ask new questions and discard earlier interpretations as inadequate if not false. None the less all this work must have some object, some aspiration in view. It cannot be simply the study of the past 'for its own sake', for outside the minds and writings of historians the past has no independent reality. If we as historians demand considerable sums of public money and battle for our quota of students it is not to enable us solipsistically to cultivate and refine our own perceptions and sensibilities. It is because we can, and should, claim to serve a more fundamental social purpose; and if we do not fulfil it things can go very wrong with our society indeed.

I am very well aware that the argument that historians have a social function—indeed a social obligation—is likely to be no more welcome among scholars today than it was when the first holder of this Chair was appointed over two and a half centuries ago. Professor Galbraith himself sounded from this very rostrum a trumpet blast against the conversion of the study of history to 'mere propaganda, resting on a narrow basis of civic usefulness', and we know what he meant. 'Socially useful' or 'relevant' history, whether consciously or unconsciously selected or tailored to meet contemporary social or political needs, has no place in a university or anywhere else. But there is a danger that this is the kind of history that almost automatically would get taught, or at least learned, if the historical profession did not exist to prevent it. For all societies have *some* view of the past; one that shapes and is shaped by their collective consciousness, that both reflects and reinforces the value-systems which guide their actions and judgements; and if professional historians do not provide this, others less scrupulous or less well qualified will. Far more than poets can historians claim to be the unacknowledged legislators of mankind; for all we believe about the present depends on what we believe about the past.

Certainly the historian cannot escape from the present. The more ambitious he is in attempting to create great comprehensive patterns of historical development, as did Marx, or Toynbee, or Spengler, or Sorokhin, the more evidently will he betray the moods and preoccupations of his own day. But he can, even within the limits imposed by his own cultural environment, ensure that our view of the past is not distorted by fraud, by evident prejudice or by simple error. Our primary professional responsibility is to keep clear and untainted those springs of knowledge that ultimately feed the great public reservoirs of popular histories and school text books and are now piped to every household in the country through the television screens. It is not an indifferent matter, or one of purely scholarly interest, to choose examples from recent history, if it is widely believed that Adolf Hitler had no special responsibility for the Second World War; or that 120,000 people were killed in the Allied bombing of Dresden; or that Churchill connived in the murder of General Sikorski, or deliberately allowed Coventry to be bombed in order to protect the ULTRA secret; or that the United States deliberately destroyed Hiroshima and Nagasaki, not in order to forward their military operations against Japan, but as a demonstration intended to overawe the Soviet Union. Such beliefs about the past, however indirectly, shape attitudes and guide judgement for the present. It is important to be sure that they are correct.

So the first lesson that historians are entitled to teach is the austere one: not to generalize from false premises based on inadequate evidence. The second is no more comforting: the past is a foreign country; there is very little we can say about it until we have learned its language and understood its assumptions; and in deriving conclusions about the processes which occurred in it and applying them to our own day we must be very careful indeed. The *understanding* of the past, particularly of the beliefs and assumptions that held societies together and determined those activities on the level of high politics that are normally regarded as 'history', is the most rewarding, as it is the most difficult, of the historian's tasks. And it is here that he needs that quality of imagination so properly called for by my predecessor in his valedictory lecture. Yet it is a quality best used, not in creating alternative 'scenarios' of the past, but in recreating the structure of beliefs that determined action and perhaps made some actions more likely than others. It would indeed be fascinating and not illegitimate to ask what would have happened if Hitler had shown more interest in sea power; or had spared more resources for the Mediterranean theatre; or had above all shown more knowledge and understanding of the United States. But perhaps it is more useful to understand the prejudices and the order of priorities likely to exist in the mind of an autodidact whose formative years were spent in Vienna, where the great issues of the day related not to the rivalry of distant seaborne Empires but to the clash between Teuton and Slav, between German and Czech, between Western and Russian power and—with horrible implications for the future—between Gentile and Jew.

For this quality of historical imagination is needed as much in dealing with the recent as it is with the more remote past. No one can be under any illusions about the difficulties of comprehending the world of Charlemagne, or of Frederick Barbarossa or even of Napoleon Bonaparte. But is it really any easier for us today to understand the world of High Victorian Imperialism or of Edwardian England? And how many historians can claim to have comprehended, not so much the motives and intentions of Adolf Hitler, over which so much ink has been spilled, but the world-outlook and the value-systems that held the Third Reich together and kept the entire German people working and fighting until the very framework of their society had been destroyed over their heads? It is only if we have achieved such an understanding that we can plausibly answer such hypothetical questions as, whether the Second World War could have been averted or curtailed if we had 'stood up to' Hitler sooner; of if we had given greater encouragement to the clandestine opposition within German; or if we had not demanded unconditional surrender. What was the *society* that we were dealing with, and how could it have reacted to these events?

If it is difficult for historians in retrospect, with all the wisdom of hindsight and all the time in the world, to comprehend the complex processes that went to the creation of the Third Reich and the nature of the society to which it gave political expression, we should not be too quick

to condemn those contemporary British statesmen who so tragically misunderstood the phenomenon in their own day. For their perceptions were
also constrained by their cultural framework. Neville Chamberlain and his
closest colleagues had been brought up in the England of Queen Victoria
and were middle-aged when the First World War began. Their world was
that of the British Empire. The problems posed by the Congress Party in
India, by the Wafd movement in Egypt, and by the relations of Briton and
Boer in South Africa were more immediate to them, more real, more
urgent, than were the racial antagonisms of Central Europe. How could
they be expected to see the significance of that populist nationalism, fuelled
invariably by anti-Semitism, that was seeping up everywhere in the Continent like so much sewage through the cracks in the old order; the *anomie*
that ravaged societies where traditional values had been destroyed by war
and revolution? The works on European history on which they had been
brought up had been written before the turn of the century in a spirit of
optimistic liberalism, seeing in the unification of Germany and of Italy the
happy climax to a long struggle for freedom and self-expression and taking
little account of anything that had happened after that. Even those of their
Foreign Office advisers who saw the dangers of National Socialism saw
them in traditional terms: the revival of the power and the pretensions of
the German, indeed the *Prussian* state, which they had known in their
youth. Few if any comprehended the full challenge posed by the 'Revolution of Nihilism' which enabled the Nazis to find willing collaborators
in every country they conquered; and made of Nazism a popular, indeed
a *populist* movement, of a kind that both liberal and Marxist historians
have found difficult to explain away.

When we consider the insularity of our attitude to our continental
neighbours after 1945, the patronizing aloofness displayed by so many
British statesmen and senior civil servants towards the birth of the European Community, their reluctance to give that lead in the remaking of
Europe which was for so many years ours for the asking, we may wonder
how far this attitude was rooted in a historical consciousness nurtured by
university history teachers who for generations had seen the Continent as
an area of concern for specialists, the study of whose problems was an
interesting option but no more. It is significant that in the Oxford history
syllabus in the 1920s there was only one special subject available in modern
continental history—that on Congress diplomacy between 1815 and
1822. Others available included British rule in India, the development of
Canada and the revolt of the American colonies. Admirable as it was that
the horizons of undergraduates should have been extended to the other

side of the Atlantic, the contribution that the Oxford History School made to our understanding of our nearest neighbours was, for that generation, notably small.

And this perhaps indicates that the value of history as a training of the judgement and of the imagination is very limited if it is exercised only in recreating our own past, with little reference to the total context within which our society developed and, more particularly, the often very divergent structures of other societies whose development may have been of yet greater importance to the making of the world in which we live today. If it is, indeed, one of the major functions of the historian to explain the present by deepening our understanding of the past, then a study simply of our own society will not get us very far. Our awareness of the world and our capacity to deal intelligently with its problems are shaped not only by the history we know but by what we do *not* know. Ignorance, especially the ignorance of educated men, can be a more powerful force than knowledge. Ethnocentrism in historical studies, whatever its advantages in scholarly training, is likely to feed parochialism in the societies which those historians serve; and such parochialism can have pretty disastrous results.

Am I now suggesting that the history taught in universities and schools should, in spite of all I said a few moments ago, be 'relevant', and guided by some criterion of civic usefulness? In a sense I must admit that I am. But we must distinguish between *how* history is studied by the professional historians and *what* history is taught to the laity. The range of the historical profession must be universal, and universities exist to make possible that universality. In the eyes of the scholar, as in the eyes of God, all ages are of equal significance. It is as important to understand Byzantium as it is to understand the Soviet Union (and unless one understands Byzantium how can one understand the Soviet Union?). It is as important to understand the pre-Columbian societies of Central America as it is to understand Moghul dynastic rule in India, or the system of land tenure in fifteenth-century Franconia, or the development of municipal government in Leeds. The past is a vast chain, every link of which must be kept in good repair. The links that lie chronologically or geographically near us can claim no special priority from the professional historian, and one of the things we have to teach the laity is that this is so.

But if our object in teaching history to the laity is to enable them to understand the present by explaining the past, and we have only three years in which to do this, then we cannot avoid making hard decisions about what we are going to select from the illimitable range offered by

past; what aspects of it we allocate for the compulsory and what for op-
tional study. If a valid definition can be given to the term 'Modern History'—and I sometimes doubt whether it can—then it must be the history
concerned with the world in which we live today and with the processes
that have gone to form it. We are therefore justified in asking how far the
subjects we prescribe for study will enhance that understanding, and in
giving some priority to those for which a case can most easily be made.
Of course it is true that for a full understanding of the contemporary
world it is as important to understand the causes of the decline of the
Roman Empire as those for the rise and fall of the Third Reich. The
academic snobbery that disdains the history of the recent past precisely
because it relates so obviously to the present is as indefensible as the lay
impatience with a remote past because on the face of it it does not not.
But the layman has every right to ask the historian, not how his own
researches contribute to our understanding of the contemporary world,
but how do the studies that he, the layman, is required to pursue? And
there is a certain obligation on our part to provide a convincing answer.

In the eighteenth century the world of classical antiquity provided a
model whose 'relevance' to contemporary issues was unquestioned, or only
just beginning to be questioned. In the nineteenth century the historian
was expected to show only how his society had reached its existing state
of perfection or—for the less easily satisfied—might be expected to progress to a future state of perfection. But the demands of our own tumul-
tuous century have been more complex. To explain 'the modern world',
the historian has to involve himself and his pupils in the study of societies
sometimes very different from his own. And he may find himself forced
to adopt a standpoint, from which the history of his own society will
appear to be of secondary importance.

The range of the Oxford History School has been commendably extended since the Second World War. Special Subjects and Further Subjects
have splendidly proliferated, bringing every corner of the world within the
purview of any student who wants to take advantage of them. But the
Anglocentric core remains—and I use the prefix 'Anglo' advisedly. The
Irish dimension is still peripheral, studied only in so far as it affects the
fortunes of the political parties in Westminster; and again one may wonder
how far its absence has contributed to the neglect shown by the British
public and the incompetence displayed by successive British administrations in dealing with the Irish problem over so many years. It is still
possible here to study nothing that has happened beyond these shores save
for a period of 'General History' covering a couple of centuries; which

effectively means the history of Europe and of Western Europe at that; and woe betide the naive examiner who demands any broader knowledge from the candidates who take this paper! As for the history of the United States, a society which more than any other is likely to shape our lives if not our deaths, that is regarded as a matter for specialist study, and the great bulk of undergraduates leave the Oxford History School as ignorant of it as they were when they arrived.

If we are properly to educate the laity it is not enough to awaken an interest in the past to provide them with an agreeable leisure occupation. It is not enough to provide for them scholarly exercise in the handling of evidence on which they can sharpen their wits. We have to teach them how to step outside their own cultural skins and enter the minds of others; the minds not only of our own forbears, enormously valuable though this is, but of those of our contemporaries who have inherited a different experience from the past. And important as is the contribution of our colleagues the geographers and anthropologists, on whose insights we increasingly draw, the study of history alone can teach how to do this; history and the subject so properly associated with it when this Chair was founded: modern languages. As Burckhardt said, we cannot know too many languages. We need them not so much in order to make ourselves understood but in order to understand. Without knowing the languages that shape and express their thought our comprehension of other cultural communities will be dim and unreliable, however great in the abstract may be our knowledge of their past. Lord Dacre, in his farewell to his colleagues, congratulated us on having resisted up till now the general decline into 'monoglot illiteracy'. If we do not continue to resist it, and more, if we do not fight hard to reverse it, we shall find our range not being extended but narrowed, and our contribution to the understanding of both the past and present reduced to the level of parochial trivia.

And this is the third 'lesson' that historians must teach: the importance of comprehending cultural diversity and equipping oneself to cope with it. Much has properly been made of Neville Chamberlain's failure to understand Hitler, as of Roosevelt's failure to understand Stalin; but these disastrous misunderstandings are often depicted as cases of honest men being outwitted by crooks. Alas, the misunderstanding was at a far deeper level than that, and it is one that is constantly recurring as new elites, almost boastfully ignorant of their knowledge of any world save their own, acquire authority in some of the most powerful states in the world. We have seen so much of this since the Second World War: people often of masterful intelligence, trained usually in law or economics or perhaps in political science, who have led their governments into disastrous decisions and miscalculations because they have no awareness whatever of the historical background, the cultural universe, of the foreign societies with which they have to deal. It is an awareness for which no amount of strategic or economic analysis, no techniques of crisis-management or conflict-resolution and certainly no professed understanding of 'the objective historical process of the international class-struggle' can provide a substitute. Such miscalculations are always dangerous. In our own day they may be lethal on a very large scale indeed.

This brings me to the last and most sombre 'lesson' that the study of history has to impart; and that is, how vulnerable may be the social framework which permits the historian to ply his trade at all. I am not referring to the fact of which we are all uncomfortably aware, or should be; that if the statesmen of the world do not conduct their affairs with prudence, I might well be the last occupant of this Chair. Our own generation knows from experience that no society has a dispensation from catastrophe, and that history provides no sure formula for avoiding one. This knowledge is in itself the beginning of wisdom. But there are other, more subtle, dangers to which societies have succumbed; dangers which, by destroying the insights that historical studies can provide, could make catastrophe more likely. Sir Maurice Powicke, one of the most learned and humane scholars ever to hold this chair, once proclaimed confidently, 'Nobody can abolish the past'. Today if he attended many International Historical Congresses, he might be less sure. There are countries in the world where it is precisely the duty of historians to abolish the past, and their own professional survival depends on their success in keeping it abolished and erecting in its place a socially convenient myth which it is their function to defend, embellish and generally keep up to date.

Such a role is nothing new for historians. In most societies, in most eras, they have received official countenance only on condition they subscribed to and reinforced the reigning dogmas. The emergence of bourgeois liberal societies in which historians are free to publish what *had* 'really happened' in the past, at whatever embarrassment to the authorities of the present, to demolish myths rather than create them, is only a few centuries old. Such 'bourgeois objectivism' does not flourish in totalitarian societies, nor is it very helpful to the nation-building élites in the Third World. The freedom of historians to teach, study and publish as their scholarly instincts dictate, and to treat professors intruded by the Crown with the genial tolerance they deserve, is itself the result of historical circumstances which historians themselves should understand very well;

as they can understand how fragile and fortuitous these circumstances can be. And this is a matter of which no historian can afford to be simply a dispassionate chronicler and analyst. However great his intellectual and moral detachment, in the last resort he is committed to the values, and to the society, that enables him to remain so detached. He is a member of the polis and cannot watch its destruction without himself being destroyed. However impatient the historian may be of lay requirements for guidance, however diffident he may be in claiming a wisdom he knows he does not possess, this is the one thing he *should* know. This is the one 'lesson of history' he must never allow himself to forget.

2

Empires,

Nations

and Wars

The death of Yigal Allon in 1980 was mourned as deeply by his many friends in Britain as it was by the entire nation of Israel. Shortly after the war of 1949, in which his own achievements did so much to secure victory, Allon came to Britain, the land of his former imperial over-lords, to perfect his English and to complete an education in the academic aspects of the politics of which he had already so much direct experience. He made many friends during his time at Oxford, and his circle in Britain was further enlarged by the close relationship of mutual affection and esteem that developed between him and the British strategic thinker B. H. Liddell Hart, in whose company it was my own privilege to meet him. It is not too much to say that Allon acquired for Britain and her peoples an affection second only to that devotion to his own land to which his entire life bore witness. Some of us in England came to see him as a statesman in the tradition of Jan Christiaan Smuts, who had also made his reputation as a daring guerrilla commander defending his South African homeland against the British with courage and skill, and who had also, after the eventual settlement of that dispute, emerged as one of the greatest and closest friends this country ever had.

In commemorating Yigal Allon it has therefore seemed appropriate that I should reflect on some of the main factors in world history that shaped his life and his career. First there was the existence, for good or ill, of the British Empire, which had made possible the establishment of that Jewish national entity in Palestine out of which the nation of Israel was to develop. Secondly, there was the concept of national independence that nurtured Allon and so many others in their struggle against what they saw as alien

The Yigal Allon Memorial Lectures in the University of Tel Aviv, March 1982.

oppression. And finally there is the activity of war in which he showed himself such a master: an activity that both creates States and destroys them; and one that could today destroy mankind.

Empires

Let us first consider how the British Empire came into being; both in general and in the Middle East. This can be done only by short-circuiting the mass of theorising about 'Imperialism' that has characterised the past century of political thought, and oversimplifying to the point of dogmatism. I do not want to deal with the abstract concept of 'Imperialism', but with the concrete phenomena of Empires, and particularly the British Empire. The crude economic reductionism of the earlier part of this century that equated imperial expansion with the needs of a developed capitalist system tended to ignore not only the first three centuries of European overseas expansion but also the imperialist expansion of land powers, from the great Empires of classical antiquity including the Roman, up to those of modern times such as the empires of the Habsburgs, of the Ottoman Turks, and not least that greatest of all land Empires that survives so formidably into our own epoch; that of the Soviet Union. The causes for imperial expansion are too complex to be reduced, as the English economist J. A. Hobson reduced them in his influential study *Imperialism*,[1] to a single 'tap-root'. They can include the pressure of scarce resources, a simple warrior gratification in dominance and conquest, or zeal for religious conversion; all sometimes combined. But I propose to deal with the three elements that appear to me to have been fundamental in determining the growth of the British, and perhaps all the European seaborne Empires: *trade, settlement* and *security.*

About the first I shall say little. It was the search for wealth, made possible by the development of marine technology and to some extent of weapons, that led the peoples of Western Europe to establish their global trading systems in the sixteenth century; first the Portuguese and Spanish, then the Dutch, finally the British and the French; systems focussing on the Caribbean and Central America, or India and South-East Asia, though with many extensions and entrepôts elsewhere. But it was not trade that brought the British to the Middle East. Certainly the British partook, from the late sixteenth century onwards, in the great trading system between the Levant and Western Europe that had survived in spite of all disturbances since the days of the Phoenicians, but it was not until the late nineteenth century, and then for quite other reasons, that the British established a foothold in what was then known as the Near East.

Nor were the British brought to Palestine by that second great incentive to imperial expansion, settlement; a process which created the first British Empire in North America that was lost two hundred years ago, and a little later, when steam transport made mass emigration possible, founded those white British dominions that in my childhood sprawled so splendidly red over the map of the world. But the British did not occupy Palestine in order to 'colonise' it, in the old sense of the word. No more than any other area in the Near or Middle East was it seen as an appropriate area for British settlement. British occupation of Palestine was motivated by the single, simple, if on the face of it slightly ludicrous, consideration of *security*.

Lord Salisbury, the British Prime Minister at the beginning of this century, once said in exasperation about his military advisers that if they had their way they would garrison the moon to protect us from an attack from Mars. Certainly if one examines it the 'security imperative' appears at least as significant an element in the growth of the British Empire as the 'economic imperative'.[2] In speaking to an Israeli audience, I need not labour the point, how fundamental the 'security imperative' is to so many decisions in international affairs, and always has been. The absence of any consideration of this dimension in so much Marxist thought is understandable to students of the sociology of knowledge: early Marxist thinking was developed entirely by men with neither direct nor indirect experience of the conduct of state affairs—an innocence that blinded them to much in human history even if it enabled them to see further than their predecessors in other directions. In fact the political and military leaders responsible for the expansion of the British Empire in the latter part of the nineteenth century were (with a few notorious exceptions) little concerned with profit, even if many of their countrymen were. But they were increasingly obsessed with security.

By the middle of the nineteenth century the three original trading establishments that the British had established in India two centuries earlier—Calcutta, Madras and Bombay—had gradually extended over the mainland by a process of osmosis, seeking greater security against their French rivals or hostile native political authorities, until they joined together in a single hegemony extending from Ceylon to the Himalayas, for which the British government assumed political responsibility after the last great convulsions of 'the Indian Mutiny' in 1857. Already there was an increasing obsession with the protection against foreign attack on the communications with India both by land and sea. *Points d'appui* had to be established on the coasts of South and East Africa, and their protection involved expansion into the hinterland. The Ottoman Empire had to be propped up as a protection against the threat posed by the encroaching Russian Empire in the Middle East. When that position was abandoned as politically untenable, influence and ultimately dominance in Egypt had to be secured. To ensure the peaceful occupation of Egypt, British rule had to be extended into the Sudan. And a few years later, when European-financed railway schemes in the Ottoman Empire threatened to bridge the Sinai desert and bring Egypt within reach of hostile land attack, some British officials began to consider the desirability of a pre-emptive occupation of Palestine, even before the events of 1914–15 turned the threat into a reality.

The British were thus determined to retain control of Palestine, once they had conquered it, for reasons neither of profit nor of settlement, but of security: in the short run, to keep out their immediate rivals the French; in the long, to strengthen their position in a region deemed vital to the defensive system of the entire Empire. The decision in October 1917 to establish a Jewish National Home there, on the small scale originally envisaged, was not seen to run counter to this object, but it was not taken purely because of the persuasive talents of Chaim Weizmann. It was expected also to pay considerable short-term dividends, encouraging the Jewish population of a Russian Empire whose will and ability to continue to fight in the First World War was rightly seen as tenuous, and of a United States whose commitment to that war could not as yet be taken for granted. But at least one British statesman glimpsed the long-term costs. As Sir Robert Cecil put it to his Cabinet colleagues, 'There is not going to be any great catch in it . . . we shall simply keep the peace between the Arabs and the Jews. We are not going to get anything out of it. Whoever goes there will have a poor time'.[3]

We may note that it was in the same spirit of weary resignation that some British statesmen thought it necessary to establish British rule, not only in Palestine and Iraq, but also in Persia and trans-Caucasia. It may be in the same spirit that the Russians apparently find it necessary to extend their rule over Afghanistan (something the British frequently contemplated) and then, perhaps Baluchistan.* The greater one's possessions, the more insecure they are likely to appear and the more pressing the requirement to take whatever measures are necessary to secure them. These

*Written in 1982.

measures, almost invariably, involve expanding one's defence perimeter rather than contracting it. It is a phenomenon not confined to world Empires: it can happen in quite small states as well.

As the maritime Empires of Western Europe expanded, they passed through three stages. The first, which lasted from the fifteenth until the second part of the seventeenth century, was one of simple intercourse with the indigenous societies on a basis of cultural equality.* For the most part the European traders or settlers were lodged precariously in coastal settlements within reach of the guns of their ships or protected by forts, unable or unwilling to penetrate deeply inland and largely dependent on the good will of their hosts. By the end of the seventeenth century however the military and organisational skills developed in Europe were enabling the settlers to penetrate into the interior, to deal with native authorities on superior terms, to defeat numerically superior armies—as the British and French did in India—and dictate advantageous and exploitative treaties. The Europeans thus entered upon a second stage of conquest, one of hegemony without direct control. Still numerically enormously inferior, they depended for their survival on their capacity to manipulate or dominate the native élites.

The final phase, that of direct rule, began in the nineteenth century with the rapid industrialisation of Europe and the European-settled eastern shores of North America. Steamships became available to take Europeans to their colonies in enormous numbers, and to open up the great inland rivers. Railways opened up the hinterland. Advances in medical science enabled Europeans to survive in climates where malaria and yellow fever had previously made settlement impossible. Above all, breech-loading firearms and ultimately machine-guns produced a crushing military superiority. It was a combination that gave Europeans a total dominance almost wherever they went, so self-evident as to be accepted without question even by their victims. By the end of the nineteenth century 'the white man' had assumed a natural superiority that gave him a 'right to rule'—a right that he did not hesitate to exercise; sending out to his colonies not simply traders and soldiers but bureaucrats and officials, who took with them all their domestic habits, administrative processes, ethical norms and social assumptions, on a scale that added up to a massive transfer of their

*From this one must of course make a major exception of the behaviour of the Spaniards in Central America, who succeeded in exterminating or enslaving much of the native population.

cultures. Within their Empires, Englishmen and Frenchmen, wherever they went, could feel 'at home'.

This improvement in communications and living conditions continued at an accelerated pace even after the end of European rule. Air travel and air-conditioning was to open up the entire world to Europeans and Americans—and not simply their élites, but massive sections of their peoples—who took their life-styles and social expectations with them wherever they went. The result has been to reveal to the disappointed leaders of the 'Third World' that the removal of European military and political control was not enough to produce equality between the former imperial powers and their subjects. That control had been made possible by cultural advantages which they could not rapidly imitate and which seemed to become ever greater as technology progressed. 'The Political Kingdom' sought by Kwame Nkrumah in Ghana has produced few of its hoped-for results. That is not the least of the causes of the continuing tension between the European societies and their former colonial subjects.

It was only towards the end of the nineteenth century that the Europeans saw any need to *justify* their conquest and rule. Conquest was, after all, a perfectly normal historical process and always has been. Where territory was, or seemed to be, unoccupied, the European settlers took possession of it in the name of their own sovereigns. Where it was occupied, they dictated terms to the conquered inhabitants. Nor did there seem anything unusual about it to the inhabitants themselves, most of whom had conquered or been conquered often before in their history. They accepted their new rulers, for the most part, as clearly possessing what the Chinese called 'the Mandate of Heaven'. Moreover as European societies in the eighteenth and nineteenth centuries developed new standards of cleanliness, health, social efficiency and technical achievement, there was added to this traditional right of conquest an assumption of cultural superiority that made such imperial dominance appear to the conquerors not only natural and inevitable but in a deep ethical sense *right*. Indeed it came to be seen as an obligation, a *mission civilisatrice*, to open up the dark places of the world, as they were seen, to the light. Anti-imperialists have written much in disparagement of the trader with his whisky bottle and the soldier with his machine-gun, but against these archetypes must be set the doctor and the missionary, who were quite often combined in the same person. Only if one ignores an entire dimension of Victorian England can we regard this element in imperial expansion as a superficial and hypocritical top-dressing concealing deeper motives of greed for economic exploitation. There was, in the generation of Victorian Empire-builders, a deep sense of rectitude and obligation, a belief that from those to whom much was given, much was also required. It has been inherited by the idealistic young people of the West who today concern themselves so passionately with the problems of the Third World; even though they do not take kindly to being reminded how much they share in common with their imperialist great-grandfathers.

So to the right of conquest, and a sense of cultural superiority so strong that we would not hesitate to condemn it today as 'racist', there was added a sense of obligation, which often appeared at its most intense in such countries as Egypt and the Sudan, from which no profit whatever was to be drawn. It was this sense that enabled even those liberal Englishmen and women who believed most strongly in democracy and national self-determination, those who looked to Mr. Gladstone or his memory as their mentor, to accept and even endorse the desirability of imperial rule. The belief in unilinear human progress that both the liberals and the Marxists of the nineteenth century had inherited from the Enlightenment enabled them to see the white races as being simply further along the road that all mankind was treading, with a consequent obligation to help those less fortunate than themselves to catch up. So while conservatives justified the Imperial mission in terms of upholding law and order—both of them visualised according to a purely European model—the liberals saw it as preparing peoples who were still *in statu pupillari* for eventual self-rule; which they also conceived of as a European-type polity, however much it might be adjusted to suit local circumstances. As Lord Milner put it in his widely-read study *England in Egypt,* 'We do not want to stay in your country for ever. We don't despair of your learning to manage decently your own affairs. [But] you need to be shown what to do, [and] you also need to practise doing it. You need energy, initiative, self-reliance'.[4]

Some people might be ready for self-rule sooner than others, but few Englishmen before 1914 believed that they would see any of them making the grade in their own lifetime. This was the problem of the Jews in Palestine: they *had* made the grade. Culturally they were self-evidently equal to their rulers. Colonial officials posted to Palestine from other parts of the Empire had a very difficult adjustment to make, and it is not surprising if not all succeeded in making it.

There was also among British and French Imperialists during the first three decades of this century a strongly-held if naive belief that membership of the Empire ought to be a more attractive option than independence outside it—that nationalism was all very well but supra-nationalism was better, and that wealth, status and opportunity would be enhanced for all by belonging to a world-wide Empire, by being able to say, *civus Romanus sum*. The British did not attempt, as did the French, to elevate their subject peoples by bringing them in to a homogeneous cultural community in which all shared identical rights of citizenship and were all regarded, whatever their origin, as being *Frenchmen*. On the contrary, the British were encouraged to take pride in the very diversity of their Empire, the wide range of religions and races it embraced, seen at its apogee at the Diamond Jubilee of Queen Victoria in 1897 when a dazzling array of princes and potentates from the ends of the earth paid tribute to the Queen Empress, subjection to whom did not diminish but rather enhanced their status with their own peoples.

For a time the magic worked. Where, as in India, British rule could be imposed over existing hierarchies without disturbing them, not only was it cheap and acceptable—one British Resident at a Maharajah's court could virtually govern millions of his subjects—but it did provide for indigenous élites the possibility of moving in a wider world, both socially and, increasingly, educationally, of mixing with the ruling classes of the metropole on equal or near-equal terms. The preservation of existing hierarchies was thus important for ease of control. But it was also considered desirable, by many officials in the Colonial Office in the early part of this century, as the growth of anthropological knowledge induced an increased respect for indigenous cultures, and a general reaction set in against the simple confidence of the Victorians that the institutions and the values of the metropole would provide, always and everywhere, an acceptable model.

But if indigenous cultures were preserved, what happened to that zeal for 'progress', to that diffusion of Western values, to that bringing of light to the dark places of the earth that had inspired liberal imperialism? How were standards of living to be improved without an increase in productivity brought about by capitalistic exploitation that was often totally disruptive of indigenous social structures? Indeed as indigenous élites absorbed Western values through travel and education, they often showed little appetite for retaining habits and relationships they had come to regard as antiquated and absurd. Was the Empire to be a great organ of social and economic transformation, as Marx himself saw and applauded it for being, or just a vast anthropological museum?

It was not a decision that could be made in London, or even Paris. Once the world was opened up to European enterprise, trade and exploitation, the transformation was going to happen anyway. There was indeed a strong element of *socialist* imperialism, represented by the Fabian Society, that desired to extend political control in imperial territories in order to protect indigenous societies against the effects of uncontrolled economic exploitation. And it was a transformation which ultimately destroyed the Empires that effected it. By opening up these territories, by creating a two-way traffic with the metropole, by educating local élites in the skills needed to staff their offices and run their businesses, to say nothing of disseminating their own concepts of justice and equality, the Europeans were undermining their power as fast as they were extending it. Theodore Herzl himself when he visited Egypt in 1903 found the British achievement 'superb': 'Letting in air and light, breaking up old tyrannies, destroying abuses; but by teaching freedom and progress, sowing the seeds of revolt. English colonial methods would either destroy the Empire or lay the foundations for world domination—one of the most fascinating alternatives of our age—we would like to see, 50 years hence, how it turns out'.[5]

This was the ultimately fatal paradox of the European, especially the British, Empires. They prided themselves on having introduced law, order and stability; and if this had been *all* that they had done, they might have lasted as long as their Roman and Ottoman predecessors. But this law and stability was introduced not for its own sake, but to make possible economic development. Economic development brought social change. Social change brought political aspirations—aspirations naturally modelled on those developed within, and for, the metropole. These aspirations were, imprecisely, termed 'nationalist'. They took many forms, but all were rooted in a sense of identity based on alienation. They were specially bitter among those indigenous élites which, having been educated and socialised in metropolitan value-systems, still found themselves humiliated and excluded by their imperial masters. Membership of the wider imperial system had certainly opened wider vistas as to them, but they were vistas of independence; of self-government; and, if need be, of revolution.

Nations

The concept of self-government is one that in our own time seems so natural, so self-evident, that the problems it caused, as it spread across the world in the nineteenth and twentieth centuries, have often been misunderstood. The central difficulty was often not the apparent one, of the need to overcome the resistance of those groups who remained attached to feudal or monarchical concepts of authority, or who asserted the kind of 'right to rule' that we considered above. Even more profound was the problem implicit in the phrase itself. Who, or what, was this 'self' that was being governed?

Initially there was no need to ask the question. The concept of 'self-government' was clearly applicable to the inhabitants of an existing political community who had become conscious of a common identity in confrontation with a government whose legitimacy they had ceased to find acceptable. Leaving aside its more remote medieval origins, we note that the concept of 'popular sovereignty' appeared in a complex form in England in the seventeenth century and in a comparatively simple and straightforward one in North America and then France in the eighteenth. The idea of the 'nation', initially interchangeable with that of the 'people', emerged from a perceived conflict between government and governed, and from the doctrine that the former derived its authority ultimately from the latter. 'The principle of sovereignty rests essentially in the Nation', proclaimed the Declaration of the Rights of Man in 1789; 'no body of men, no individual, can exercise authority that does not emanate expressly from it'.[6]

The principle expressed in that declaration of independence from feudal and dynastic obligations has now become so self-evident as to be almost a platitude. Only in certain monarchies in the Islamic world are such obligations still considered valid. In the Western world and the cultures derived from it their last vestiges were swept away in 1918. Where monarchies survive it is because of their success in transforming themselves into symbols of 'the nation', exercising a precarious charisma derived from their success in focussing popular affection, and from their evident abnegation of political authority. Now all governments, however dictatorial—and indeed especially the dictatorial—claim to derive their authority from 'the nation' or 'the People'; in the case of communist states, a people emancipated not only from feudal but from capitalistic exploitation. There is no other acceptable justification for political independence, for the rights of statehood, other than a claim to represent the will of the population of the territory concerned;* which leads on to the difficult questions, What is that will, and how is it expressed?

The statesmen of the French Revolution assumed that France was a natural unity, and by a natural extension that all other 'nations' were the same. They had inherited from the old monarchy a political framework remarkably coherent politically and—at least so far as its élites were con-

---

*Two interesting exceptions have recently arisen, in the instances of the Argentine claim to the Falkland Islands and the claim asserted by certain Israelis to Samaria and Judaea. In both these cases historical claims to the territory are held to override the wishes of the present inhabitants.

cerned—monolingual. The Abbé Siéyès could plausibly define a Nation as 'a body of associates living under one common law and represented by the same legislature'.[7] There were inconvenient anomalies, in particular the Bretons, but they could be overlooked or if necessary crushed.

It was not so easy, however, for that other politically coherent and monolingual nation, the British, to overlook the comparable anomaly within their own borders, the Irish, although they did their best to crush them. At the time of the French Revolution the Irish were governed (and one does not have to look far for comparable examples today) virtually as a conquered people without political rights. Since they constituted a permanent base for possible foreign invasion, the English thought it too dangerous to grant them independence. Confronted by the French ideological challenge, the British tried to solve the problem by bringing the Irish 'under the same law and legislature' as themselves by the Act of Union of 1801. But the Irish were still effectively excluded from the franchise by the maintenance of existing disabilities on Roman Catholicism, the creed that particularly distinguished Irish from British culture, then as now. When, a quarter of a century later, this position became politically untenable and the exclusive religious 'tests' were abolished, the Irish used their newly-acquired status as full members of the political community in order effectively to dissolve it; which after nearly a hundred years they succeeded in doing. But there remained in the north of their island a minority that wished to retain their status as members of the community of 'the United Kingdom', and within that minority there was, and remains, a further minority that wanted, and wants, to join the Irish Republic; all of which has presented the British with problems that we show no signs of being able to solve. A majority of Ulstermen firmly maintain that they belong not to the Irish nation but to the British. A minority insist that the British are alien interlopers and that they belong to the Irish. In this instance the territorial approach to nationality that regards all the inhabitants of a given region as belonging to a single nation, 'living under one law and represented in a common legislature', has broken down, and the problem is one too complex to be solved by the simple expedient of secession.

In spite of this standing example to the contrary, the 'territorial' approach to the question of nationality, the assumption that all the inhabitants of an area within which a common political system has been established effectively constitutes a 'nation', worked well enough where the ethnic structure was homogeneous and the culture was distinguished by a single common language. In Britain and France at the end of the eighteenth century this could be taken for granted. The development of a common language as a necessary medium for administration, law and literature had been a necessary element in the state apparatus constructed by the French and English monarchies in the later middle ages, and the meticulous refinement of the French tongue by Boileau and other seventeenth-century scholars was a significant aspect of what today we would call 'nation-building'. Community of language as a foundation for political community was so basic that Siéyès did not consider it necessary even to refer to it in his definition of 'a nation'.*

East of the Rhine however, where political and linguistic boundaries rarely coincided, this territorial concept of nationality was found unsatisfactory. Political communities ranged from minuscule duchies to the vast and amorphous Holy Roman Empire; neither of which could provide the kind of focus for national self-consciousness that lay so ready to hand for the French and the British. If identity could not be found in political structures it had to be sought elsewhere—in the community of *language*. The use of a common tongue indicated at least a cultural unity, a kind of collective subconscious, a community pre-existing and more 'natural' than the 'artificial' political loyalties that divided it. Already before the French Revolution Johann Herder and his German contemporaries were exploring and praising the cultural diversity inherent in the variety of European languages. Consciousness of this diversity became acute when the armies of France crossed the Rhine, the Alps and the Pyrenees, proclaiming the Rights of Man in distinctly foreign accents. The experiences of the revolutionary epoch pointed, for the generation of Johann Gottlieb Fichte and Ernst Moritz Arndt, the contrasts between the scope and power of German culture and the divisions and impotence of her political structures. For them the creation of a state structure to give expression to this latent nationhood became a moral imperative.

Where the Germans led, others followed. The achievement of 'nationhood', the creation of independent political entities corresponding to cultural communities defined by language became the great aspiration of the young idealists of the nineteenth century. The Italians, the Poles, the Irish, the Hungarians were only the first in a long queue. Their leaders were the precursors of the social revolutionaries who were to dominate the later part of the century, but their appeal was the more powerful for being more

---

*Though we must always remember that the community of which he wrote, both linguistic and political, was still one of élites. It is doubtful whether the peasants of Brittany, Provence or Languedoc would have understood one another, much less what was being said and done in their name in Paris.

widely spread among all classes of society. Their messianic vision, of the natural harmony of nations once these had been brought fully into being, was, like all such visions, as powerful as it was naive.

The trouble is that all 'nations', even if we consider them as cultural and not political communities, are the result of complex and usually brutal historical processes. All have involved amalgamations and suppressions. The apparently homogeneous nations of Western Europe had digested older cultural communities with greater or lesser success. France had absorbed Normans and Bretons and Provençals and the people of Languedoc; with such success, indeed, that there seemed no reason why she should not extend her range further and absorb Algerians, Senegalese and Annamites, turning them equally into Frenchmen. Spain had digested Basques and Catalans. The English had digested the Welsh and a greater part of the Scots and at least some of the Irish, to produce the amalgam known as 'British', which optimists believed would one day absorb the stubbornly resistant Frenchmen of Quebec and the Dutchmen of the Transvaal. All these 'nations' were in fact *empires* in miniature, and the chain-reaction of nationalism would one day split them as well; Basques, Bretons and Welsh discovering long-buried identities that some of them preferred to assert in preference to continuing as subordinate members of a greater whole.

If the old and apparently solid nations of Western Europe were thus vulnerable, what hope was there of more coherent ones emerging East of the Rhine? Would a united Germany include those ethnic Poles or Bohemians who had for so long been assimilated into German-dominated political communities? If the Poles achieved nationhood once more, would their state include the Ukrainians who had once formed part of historic Poland? If Hungary had a right to independence, did not the Slovaks and Ruthenians and Rumanians and Croats who formed part of her traditional domains have a similar right? If in fact the states-system of Europe was to be remodelled to give effect to German and Italian aspirations to national unity, what about the Slavic peoples further east, to whom history had given an even rawer deal? Then there was the greatest Slavic community of all, the Russians. How far would their boundaries extend, east and west, in the new nationally-determined order? And finally, what about those communities which in terms of historical continuity and cultural cohesion outdistanced all their competitors and which, as their host communities rediscovered their national identity, were becoming apprehensively conscious of their own isolation: the Jews?

When the German nationalists discovered, as they did in 1848, what a

Pandora's box they had opened, they tried to limit the damage by asserting that only 'historic' nationalities had a right to independent political existence; which was as much as to say that only peoples with a past were entitled to a future. But this was a challenge to discover a past, if necessary indeed to invent one; and many of the great historical projects of the nineteenth century, with German scholars in the lead and Czechs, Poles, Bulgarians, Serbs and Russians crowding thick and fast behind them, were set on foot to establish the title-deeds of nations to that historical identity that would entitle them to political independence. Professors of history found themselves, or made themselves, significant political figures. So also did lexicographers and professors of language and literature. It was of the highest importance to show that the national tongue—Gaelic, Basque, Czech, Serbo-Croat, Ruthenian—was not just a local dialect or a *patois* fit only for the peasantry, but a rich, flexible and precise medium of communication that could be used in law and administration and should be taught in schools and universities—especially in universities, which was where the governing classes were trained. Languages could perhaps exist without nations, but a nation without a language was a contradiction in terms—as the Belgians found from the moment they established their independent kingdom in 1831.

So the spread of universal education throughout Europe during the second half of the nineteenth century developed, in the multi-national regions of Central and Eastern Europe, into a struggle for political dominance, in which those national cultures that prevailed suppressed those that did not. Germans and Russians suppressed Poles, Poles suppressed Ruthenes, Hungarians suppressed Croats and Rumanians, and Italians, a little later, suppressed Slovenes. In much the same way further west Spaniards were suppressing Basques, English were suppressing Welsh, Scots and (less successfully) Irish,* and further west still British Canadians were suppressing French. The dominant culture saw the suppression, if not the elimination, of these local variants as a necessary part of 'nation-building', of the creation of homogeneous political communities and smoothly-running bureaucratic structures. The same went for the suppression of such political discontents as this process caused.

The sinister consequences of this search for homogeneity, for cultural purity, do not need to be stressed before a Jewish audience. If only one linguistic culture could prevail in a nation, then the others must be suppressed or extruded. The same applies, a fortiori, when the cultural dif-

*Or so the Welsh, the Scots and the Irish tended to believe.

ferences are religious. As national self-consciousness grew and was inculcated through the state educational process, so minorities were seen as decreasingly tolerable, more of a threat to the kind of national unity to which European states competitively aspired. This threat was all the more menacing when these minorities enjoyed the support of powerful and hostile forces beyond the frontier, as the south Slavs in the Habsburg Empire enjoyed the support of Serbia and her patrons in St. Petersburg. The result was a vicious spiral of suppression and conspiracy that culminated in the assassination at Sarajevo with all the disastrous consequences that flowed from it.

For a European the main interest of these developments must lie in their contribution to the causes of the First World War—and indeed the Second, for which the immediate cause was also the struggle between German and Czech and German and Pole that had been foreshadowed a century earlier. For an Israeli their significance is, perhaps, different. It was the 'nationalisation' in the 1880s and 1890s by the German Empire of its Eastern territories and the Russian Empire of its Western, the assertion of cultural and political dominance by Berlin and St. Petersburg over the minority cultures and groups in these border regions, that made life for the Jews in those areas more and more difficult. This growing oppression, in which government policy was reinforced by popular prejudice, resulted in those major emigrations, mainly to the United States, but of which a small proportion were finding their way, even before the close of the nineteenth century, to Palestine. It also led Herzl to the conclusion that in a world where, increasingly, nationality was the only passport to political legitimisation, Jewry could survive only if it possessed its very own 'nation-state'.

I need not linger over the long-term consequences of this (at the time) amazing aspiration. To the great body of Jews in Western Europe, who had for a couple of generations been liberated from their ghettoes and were occupying positions of increasing influence and responsibility within their host communities, the idea appeared insane. Nevertheless the anti-Semitism that everywhere accompanied the rise of nationalism was, by the first decade of this century, beginning to exert such pressure, not only in Eastern and Central but even in Western Europe, that the Zionist ideal began to appear, not as the absurd aspiration of a handful of fanatics, but as the only escape from a situation becoming increasingly intolerable. Even so, so long as the United States remained open to unrestricted immigration from Europe, even those who sympathised with the Zionist solution saw no great urgency about implementing it.

That the seeds of a Jewish State ever came to be planted at all was the result, as we saw in the first part of this chapter, of a temporary coincidence of British imperial interests, the exigencies of wartime policy, and Zionist aspirations. The subsequent coincidence between the curtailment of immigration into the United States and the terrible developments in Europe in the 1930s and 1940s, when the zealots of national purity were able to impose their principles regardless of the cost in human life and dignity, made the establishment of that State seem a matter of sheer human survival, whether it suited British imperial interests or not. It was then that the young men of the Haganah like Yigal Allon had to turn their weapons against those British authorities whose power had made the establishment of a 'Jewish National Home' possible in the first place. Thanks largely to their efforts, Herzl's dream was realized and the Jewish State was established at a cost transcending the loss of Jewish, British and Arab lives that it entailed. For as had happened in Europe, nationalism bred counter-nationalism. The Arabs living in Palestine had not been conscious of a Palestinian nationality before the establishment of substantial Jewish settlements in what, with some reason, they regarded as being 'their' country. Now they became aware of an identity and a lost homeland. Israeli nationalism created, with tragic inevitability, Palestinian nationalism. The explosive chain reaction that had spread in the nineteenth century from Western into Eastern Europe had now been carried into the Middle East.

The establishment of the Jews in Palestine was only one of the conduits that carried European ideas of nationalism beyond the confines of that continent. Turkish nationalism had been aroused at the beginning of the twentieth century by the successive humiliations inflicted on the Ottoman Empire by the repeated intervention of European Powers on behalf of client nations in the Balkans, whose causes they sponsored with a mixture of idealism and self-interest. Egyptian nationalism had been stirred even earlier by European intervention in the domestic affairs of that country. Further East, direct imperialist pressures evoked a national movement on the Indian sub-continent with the foundation of the Congress Party, and in a more violent form in China with the Boxer Rebellion. But this spread of national self-consciousness, initially arising from resentment at alien repression, carried with it the same problems that had perplexed the Europeans. What was the 'self' that was being governed? Did India comprise the Moslem minorities—or Ceylon? Did China comprise Tibet? What were the 'nations' of Africa, where the Europeans had drawn frontiers to suit their own convenience, taking little account of existing tribal divisions? In sub-Saharan Africa there were no 'nations' in the European sense of coherent cultural communities aspiring to political self-expression. The nation had to be created *after* independence, to clothe the administrative skeleton bequeathed by the European Empires with political flesh and blood.

Still, the concept of 'nationality' made possible in the Third World, as it had in Europe, a degree of social mobilisation and political participation that could probably never have been achieved by other means. The worst expectations by the former colonial powers of the chaos and inefficiency that would follow their departure, were only too often to be realised. None the less it was a necessary chaos, ultimately more likely to produce a peaceful order under popular control than the efficient administration of law and order by an alien minority according to alien principles. Yet in the Third World, as in Europe, the evil effects of nationalism were rapidly to become evident, as inconvenient minorities were extruded (like the Indians in Uganda) or suppressed (like the Ibos in Nigeria). The quest for purity, for homogeneity, that had nearly destroyed Europe was to become evident elsewhere, often with no less shedding of blood.

The tragic horror of the Holocaust quite rightly commands our attention as the final, nightmare consequence of this quest for national purity in Europe. But there was another result, less horrifying certainly, but yet deeply sad. It was the *impoverishment* of national cultures that resulted from their drawing apart from one another, from their search for purity of self-expression. It had, after all, been the cross-fertilisation of national and cultural traditions that had created the astonishing richness of European civilization during the half millennium between the fifteenth and the twentieth centuries—the intermingling of Italian and French and Spanish and English and German to constitute a common European cultural core. It was a richness that reached its culmination in the nineteenth century when for the first time the Jews began to play a full part in the cultural life of the communities in which they had lodged so long as tolerated but not always welcome guests; rising quickly to the head of the learned professions, distinguishing themselves as scientists and thinkers and musicians as well as men of affairs and patrons of the arts. It is not too much to say that the elimination of the Jews has created a barrenness, a sterility in European culture that is at its most evident in the country that was most thorough in extirpating them—Germany. The same could be seen on a very much smaller scale a few decades ago when the French made a brief attempt to insulate themselves from American culture, or on those occasions when the Germans have tried to exclude the French. It is a process of self-starvation, almost of self-castration. No culture is complete and adequate in itself. Deprived of constant cross-fertilisation, it loses all creativity.

The vigour of American culture today is the result of its eclecticism, its variety, and not least the hospitality that the United States has offered to immigrants of the Jewish race for the past hundred years. Hitler is reported to have dismissed the United States as a serious factor in world affairs with the contemptuous phrase 'Das ist kein Volk; das ist nur ein Mischung' (That is no people; it's just a mess). Ironically he failed to appreciate that it was precisely in that *Mischung* of peoples and cultures that the enormous and flexible strength of the United States lay; and that by expelling those members of its own community who did not measure up to their absurd standards of racial purity, the National Socialists had crippled their country, perhaps fatally. The Jewish scientists who were compelled to flee from Nazi Germany made a truly formidable contribution to Allied victory in the Second World War.

Today Israel can draw on the same multiple sources of strength. To insist on some abstract concept of primal purity, whether that is gauged by race or by religion, to exclude from one's community anything that appears adulterated or alien, is a recipe for weakness, as it is for isolation. It is the acceptance and the domestication of the alien that have provided the strength of all the truly great cultures of the world, the constant enrichment of one's heritage through fresh contributions. During the Diaspora the Jews developed a diversity and acquired a range of insights denied to more territorially rooted peoples. Their gathering together in Israel has created a nation unique in its range and potential. Even more than the United States can Israel take as its own the motto E Pluribus Unum.

All this is very fine, I can hear some of you say, and we do not deny that it is very desirable. But what matters in the end is the unity of the *unum*; and how do you achieve it, *e pluribus*? How do you reconcile a diversity of cultures with the necessary singularity of loyalty? How can one tolerate these diverse cultures without their rendering the state ultimately ungovernable—as they did the Habsburg Monarchy? How many official languages can one tolerate? What values, what religions, does one inculcate in the national schools? Does not the historical record suggest that diversity is tolerable only within a framework created and imposed by a single dominant culture that maintains its dominance—as the original Anglo-Saxon culture of the United States has remained dominant in spite of the infusion of countless other races and traditions?

To this question there can be no simple answer or formula; only a continual dialectic. Diversity must not extend to the weakening of the state structure that makes it possible; but the state that eliminates diversity in the interests of homogeneity and cohesion is likely in the process to destroy the social basis of its strength. And how diverse, how multicultural can a state afford to be if it is going to meet the ultimate test of survival in war?

Wars

I referred above to the belief held by Mazzini and other nationalists in the early part of the nineteenth century, that the assertion and fulfilment of the principle of national self-determination would eventually bring about perpetual peace. But they accepted that the peace to which they looked forward so confidently was only the light at the end of a tunnel of violent and inevitable struggle—much as their successors, the social revolutionaries, believed that the just social order to which they aspired could be achieved only by violent and, if need be, bloody revolution.

From the very beginning the principle of nationalism was almost indissolubly linked, both in theory and practise, with the idea of war. For Hegel, for Fichte and Arndt, those Prussian thinkers whose ideas were to be archetypical for so much nineteenth-century nationalism, war was the necessary dialectic in the evolution of nations. As one deputy at the Frankfurt Assembly of 1848 put it, 'Mere existence does not entitle a people to political independence; only the force to assert itself as a state among others'.[8] In nation-building as in revolution, force was the midwife of the historical process.

The terrible thing is that, historically speaking, these thinkers were right. It is hard to think of any nation-state, with the possible exception of Norway, that came into existence before the middle of the twentieth century which was not created, and had its boundaries defined, by wars, by internal violence, or by a combination of the two. These wars, in many cases, had been fought not between peoples but between princes asserting juridical claims to what they regarded as their personal property; but they were none the less decisive in the creation of these coherent political units out of which 'nations' were to evolve. Indeed such dynastic wars could in themselves create national self-consciousness, as the Hundred Years War did certainly for the English and to some extent the French.

The true national content of such early struggles is hard to evaluate. Later generations have enveloped them in so impenetrable a fog of historical myth that such figures as Henry V and Joan of Arc sometimes seem as legendary as King Arthur and his knights of the Round Table. For as

nations came to define themselves and trace their origins, the history of
their conflicts with one another became a central part of this process of
definition, and the concept of the 'nation' became inseparably associated
with the wars it had fought. British nationalistic history is the history of
its battles—Bannockburn, Creçy, Agincourt, the Armada, Waterloo; wars
fought for the most part by a monarchy, but a monarchy which through
the sheer process of fighting (and more important, winning) them, became
a focus for national sentiment. For France the wars and victories of the
old monarchy were to be almost obliterated by the victories more directly
associated with the French *people*; Marengo, Austerlitz, Jena, Wagram, battles won by conscript armies commanded by officers who had risen from
the ranks. For Germany the foundations laid by the Wars of Liberation in
1813–15 were to be crowned by the military achievements of Sadowa,
Gravelotte and Sedan—wars won not by princes but by great popular
armies. For the United States the nation was moulded by the War of
Independence and united by the result of the Civil War, whose climactic
battle of Gettysburg has entered deep into the national myth. Such battles
were decisive acts made possible only by the mobilisation of national resources and the exercise of the national will. They epitomised national
solidarity and self-sacrifice. But yet more important were the political consequences that flowed from them, the part they played in creating a power
structure in which some nations survived and flourished as independent
entities and others disappeared, some for centuries, some for good.

It is a chastening exercise to recall the states that have disappeared as
the result of unsuccessful wars—or have never succeeded in coming into
being. There were the crusader kingdoms of the Middle East. Rather
nearer home for me, and nearer our own time, there was the Duchy of
Burgundy, which contested the hegemony of Western Europe with the
Kingdom of France in the middle of the fifteenth century and under more
skilful leadership might have obtained it. In Eastern Europe there is, or
was, the great principality of Lithuania. Further south the ethnic blocs of
the Ukraine and Armenia struggled for centuries and in vain for political
self-expression. The Kurds struggle still. In the Mediterranean a different
turn of history might have produced for us a wealthy and independent
Kingdom of Catalonia. In Africa we have in our own time witnessed the
establishment and disappearance of the state of Biafra. And most interesting of all, and most significant in its consequences for the history of
the world, in North America there briefly appeared in the middle years of
the last century, with every appearance of permanence and economic advantage, the Confederate States of America. One could draw an interesting

map of the world depicting these defunct or still-born states, or indicating how the frontiers of existing states would differ if they had lost some of the wars that they won. The harsh fact is that the state structure of the international system as it exists today is not the result of peaceful, teleological growth, the evolution of nations whose seeds have germinated in the womb of time and have come to a natural fruition. It is the result of conflicts that might, in very many cases, have been resolved differently.

Herein lies the fascination of, and the justification for, the study of military history. The military historian has to examine those situations where the destiny of a people, and the ultimate course of world history, seems to be determined for generations by the decision of a single man, the fortitude of a single army, the efficiency and skill of a particular group of military specialists. We now know that these situations cannot be considered in isolation and that the outcome of military operations will be powerfully affected by social and economic considerations that determine the nature of military equipment, the state of morale and training of troops, the professionalism and status of military leaders. Seldom do armies confront one another drawn from societies so similar in every respect that the outcome of the conflict will not be influenced, however marginally, by factors deriving from the difference in their social background. Armies are microcosms of their societies; often indeed their core.

Up till our own century, then, war has been a principal determinant in the shaping of nation-states. That there have been other determinants goes without saying; the growth of wealth, the emergence of a regional élite alienated from the existing authorities, the incidence of economic oppression, the collapse of traditional centres of power; these are only some of the most obvious. But whether these contributory causes will effectively result in the formation of a new political unit, sovereign within its own territories, will almost invariably be determined by the use, or the effective threat, of armed force. It is true—and indeed it is one of the few blessings of our disturbed century—that within the past thirty years well over fifty new sovereign states have achieved independence without the use of violence; but that independence was the indirect result of the defeat, or the exhaustion, of their former imperial masters in the Second World War, enhanced by the successful example of those peoples, in South-East Asia and elsewhere, who had successfully fought for their independence. For reasons touched on in the first part of this chapter it became clear to the rulers of European empires that the day when they could maintain suzerainty over distant dependencies with a minimal use of military force had long since disappeared. Now the cost of maintaining imperial rule outweighed any possible benefits. For Britain, the traditional problem of 'Imperial Defence' ceased to be one of maintaining order in subjected territories, and became one, no less difficult and not particularly welcome, of protecting those dependencies, whether as close at hand as Ulster or as distant as the Caribbean or the Falkland Islands, which for reasons of their own wanted to *remain* British.

Interestingly enough the new nations that have achieved independence without having to fight for it are no less militant in their outlook than those who did. Indeed in the successor states of sub-Saharan Africa where the transition to freedom took place under the most peaceful circumstances imaginable—Ghana, Nigeria, Uganda—the military rapidly achieved a political dominance that owed nothing to any contribution they might have made to any struggle for independence. In fact in states where such a struggle really had taken place, however, such as Yugoslavia, Algeria and Vietnam, it is not evident that the military enjoy either social prestige or political power. The effort that peacefully-born successor-states devote to their armed forces, to say nothing of the strident tone of their discourse in international affairs, suggests that they feel almost a sense of guilt that they should have escaped the usual bloody *rites de passage*.

Such wars for freedom, or for national self-determination, are now the only armed conflicts generally held to be legitimate, or 'just'; apart, that is, from simple wars for self-defence. In the nineteenth century Europeans on both sides of the Atlantic considered that they had a self-evident right to settle in territories they found agreeable and to subjugate any native inhabitants as might offer resistance. This claim based on cultural superiority was to be used in our own time by the Third Reich, to justify their wars in Eastern Europe and their grotesque attempts to 'colonise' Poland and the Ukraine—history repeating itself, not as farce but as nightmare. That was the last imperial war. No one has yet shown any inclination to imitate it.

In fighting to preserve their old Empires, or perhaps to carve out new ones, states have justified themselves in different ways. The French justified fighting to maintain their presence in Algeria by claiming it as part of the metropole. The British justified their operations in Kenya and Malaya by claiming that these were intended to pave the way to peaceful self-rule; as indeed they most successfully did. The Russians justified their entry into Afghanistan, as into other places before that, by the professed need to suppress those subversive elements which were preventing the true voice of the people from being heard. The United States likewise justified its intervention in Vietnam by citing the need to establish political conditions of order that would make it possible for the true wishes of the people to be consulted. The popular will has everywhere displaced dynastic right as the accepted criterion of legitimate government, and at least lip service has to be paid to it. Those states which continue to exercise control over territories in open defiance of the wishes of the population find themselves the objects of universal condemnation.

But this rhetoric does not answer the question posed above: What is this 'self' that is being governed? What is the popular will, and how is it to be ascertained? In all too many countries which have successfully liberated themselves from alien rule, power now passes from hand to hand among military groups who no longer even bother to legitimise themselves by holding, and if need be rigging, elections. The magic words 'in the name of the people' are in themselves regarded as sufficient sanction for their rule.

Yet the fact that this criterion can be abused and manipulated, both by internal and external seekers after power, does not invalidate it. Self-determination, the right of any political community to determine its own structure and exercise sovereign power within its own territories, remains the foundation of any free society, and willingness if necessary to defend that right by force is the only guarantee that such societies can continue to exist. The objective *need* for their existence is by no means self-evident. Great powers have always found it difficult to take claims for self-determination when voiced by small peoples very seriously, and their authorities normally regard those who voice them as unrepresentative trouble-makers. 'What makes a people happy?' asked the Austrian military governor of Lombardy in the first half of the nineteenth century: 'It is not to form an extensive and populous nation. It is good laws, the preservation of ancient traditions and a thrifty administration'.[9] The same was said in slightly different words by the British in India, in Egypt and indeed everywhere within their huge empire. Even-handed justice and low taxes were as much as any people could expect from government, and indeed considerably more than they had been in the habit of receiving in the past. There would always be malcontents unwilling to accept these blessings at the hands of alien rulers and who believed, in spite of all evidence to the contrary, that their peoples would not be happy until they were 'free'. Such peoples were a nuisance, and best locked up.

It is not fashionable to express sympathy with those imperial administrators who regarded the preservation of order as the ultimate criterion of justice, the greatest boon that governments could bestow on the governed. But the question must arise, at what point does this fissile process of self-determination stop? Wars of National Liberation have proceeded in a chain reaction around the world during the past two hundred years, and the fuse that was lit by the American and French Revolution is not burned out yet. After each fresh upheaval, whatever settlements may be reached, there are always likely to be dissident and extremist groups or *groupuscules* who maintain that they alone represent the popular will (or what would be the popular will if 'the People' had not been so corrupted and misled) and that they are therefore justified in using violence to disrupt the government and create conditions favouring a fresh upheaval. Because such beliefs owe more to subjective psychological factors than to objective social ones, such groups will exist in any society, and will always be a nuisance. Governments are normally justified in not taking their political pretensions seriously, however much trouble they may cause to the police. They are likely to achieve little unless the government loses its nerve and either surrenders or over-reacts. Only if these rebels can show themselves to command a wide measure of popular sympathy and can act as a catalyst for more general social and economic discontents do they attain political significance; and it is often only by promoting armed rebellion that they can discover whether they command such sympathy or not.

The early, pathetic attempts by Mazzini and his contemporaries, like the more sinister manifestations in our own time by the Baader-Meinhoff Gang and the Red Brigades in Europe, merely showed that no 'objective revolutionary situation' (to use the Marxist jargon) existed. But on the other hand many of the nationalist leaders in the Balkans might have been forgotten, or remembered only as local *banditti,* if they had not been able to exploit the discontent of the peasants against landlords who happened to be alien. Then social and national factors merge. Was a rising of Serb peasants against Turkish landlords, or one of Irish peasants against English landlords, a *national* phenomenon? If it did not begin as one, it could rapidly become so. And once the element of nationalism is introduced, the matter at issue is no longer one of peasants demanding just treatment from their landlords, but of the right of the landlords to own that territory at all. A *jacquerie* becomes a struggle for national liberation.

Such a struggle need not initially take the form of a 'war' in the sense of an armed conflict between sovereign states, although in international law once the insurgents have established effective political control of a substantial territorial area they are entitled to belligerent rights. But such insurgency is more likely than not to attract outside support, which can lead to major conflict between great powers. In 1859 French support for Italian nationalism led to war with Austria. In 1877 Russian support for

Bulgarian nationalism led to war with Turkey. In 1914 Serbian support for Bosnian nationalism, and Russian support for Serbian nationalism, triggered off the First World War. Nor should we forget that it was German support for their countrymen first in Czechoslovakia, then in Danzig, that provided the excuse for the Second.

Obviously in all these cases the casus belli provided the occasion rather than the cause of the war; but it was an occasion that legitimised, in terms of accepted international morality, the longer-term and more complex intentions of the powers concerned. And as has so generally been the case, a pattern of behaviour established in Europe has now been extended to the rest of the world. It might have no less tragic results. In Latin America we see Cuban support for El Salvadorian resistance against what is seen as an American-dominated government, with Soviet support for Cuba. In South Africa we see Angolan support for SWAPO forces in Namibia against the South African administration, with further global implications for stability both within and outside that region.* And I need hardly emphasise the example that must today be in everyone's mind; the resistance of the inhabitants of the West Bank region to Israeli military occupation, with the overt support of the great mass of Arab countries beyond the border—a situation alarmingly similar to that Austrian occupation of Bosnia-Herzegovina which contributed so powerfully to the instability of the Balkan region before 1914 and was to have such catastrophic consequences. Mazzini and his followers were right: the path of national self-determination was to be marked by long and bloody struggles. But so far from producing an ultimate resolution based on universal justice, each struggle, in a continual dialectic, has thrown up fresh problems as impossible to resolve by peaceful means as any in the past.

Once wars have begun, what then? I concluded the previous section with the question, how well does a multi-cultural community stand up to the test of war? Here the historical record provides slightly more comfort. War is, at least initially, a great solvent of internal tensions; so effective indeed that historians have sometimes accused governments of beginning them deliberately in order to solve their domestic difficulties—a charge as difficult to document as it is to refute. In 1914 Britain was rent by social strife, and over the issue of Northern Ireland seemed to be approaching the brink of civil war. These problems disappeared overnight in a great burst of patriotic enthusiasm. The Russian Empire had barely survived one revolution and seemed to be lurching towards another. In Germany,

*Written in 1982.

France and Italy society was polarised between factions that were barely capable of communicating with one another. In all these nations war created a degree of national unity and social integration as unprecedented as it was unpredictable. Even within the Habsburg Empire the internecine conflicts that had paralysed the monarchy for a generation, the struggles between German and Czech in Vienna, between Hungarian and Croat and Rumanian further East, were suspended, and all fought loyally together under the Imperial flag. Only after two years of military disaster did the structure begin to disintegrate and collapse. Had the war ended victoriously for the Central Powers before 1916, the Habsburg Empire might have emerged from it strengthened, at least in the short run, by the sense of common pride and achievement that always attends on military success. It is interesting to speculate as to what Europe would have looked like—what indeed the world would have looked like—if there had been a clear victory for either side before the end of 1916; before Russia collapsed in revolution and the United States entered the war.

The fact that there was no clear victory for either side before the end of 1916 cannot, however, be attributed to purely contingent circumstances, to 'the fortunes of war', or the presence or absence of military skill on one side or the other. The conflict was not one that could be settled by simple military victories. The armies were no more than the cutting edge of embattled peoples whose manpower and resources could be drawn upon by their governments to produce a continuous effort transcending victories and defeats such as, in earlier wars, would have produced clear decisions. Even governments like those of the Habsburg and Romanov Empires that had no claim to embody popular nationalism could survive casualty rates running into six figures and still continue to fight. And when these societies began, after two years, to show signs of strain, they were sustained by their West-European allies, Germany, France and Britain, whose governments could with some reason claim to represent a truly 'national' will and which fought on until one of them collapsed through total economic exhaustion. Nor was that the end. At the end of the First World War, first Russia and then the Central Powers disintegrated, militarily and politically, under a prolonged strain too great for their societies to bear. Yet within a generation all were engaged in another and yet more terrible war, the result of which was to establish the Soviet Union as one of the two greatest powers in the world and to re-establish a politically divided and transformed Germany in a position of foremost economic advantage. As Adam Smith once put it, in discussing some of the more unrealistic assumptions about economic warfare, there is a great deal of ruin in a nation.

Under the conditions that prevailed during the first half of this century, then, war, terrible as it was, still served as a remarkably effective instrument of political cohesion. Even the element in it that had been so dreaded in prospect and proved so dreadful in reality, the air bombardment of civilian populations, contributed to this cohesion by destroying the distinction between front line and base, even between government and governed, bringing the whole of society equally under threat. In Britain at least, the experience of common danger and deprivation created a degree of national unanimity that makes many of my countrymen look back on the wartime years with a certain degree of nostalgia. Today Israel lives under a comparable threat and has done so ever since the foundation of the state in 1949. The country is a beleaguered garrison in which everyone is equally at risk, and where the distinction between the armed forces and the civilian population is one simply of function. You have your share of domestic difficulties and divisions, but I find it hard to believe that the continuing dangers under which Israel lives are not an integrative element in your society, and that the removal of those pressures might not result for you in more problems than it would immediately solve.

A threat to national security is normally a factor producing national integration, since it can usually be met only by a degree of social mobilization that in itself can be achieved only by a high degree of social conciliation and consensus. But that situation has been transformed by the advent of nuclear weapons. The threat these pose to national security is not one that can be countered by popular mobilization, by the creation of nations in arms. Writing at the beginning of the nineteenth century, Clausewitz described how war, which for a century past had been an occupation for princes and professional armies, had now become an affair of peoples; how war had been, as we would put it today, 'nationalized'. Without popular mobilization and participation, wars could no longer effectively be fought at all. Today in Western Europe and the United States we are seeing a reversal of that process. War is now seen as being a matter for governments and not for peoples; an affair of mutual destruction inflicted at remote distances by technological specialists operating according to the arcane calculations of strategic analysts. Popular participation is considered neither necessary nor desirable. As in eighteenth-century Prussia, the function of the civilian is seen as being to provide the money to enable his government to purchase the weapons and hire the specialists needed to defend him. This is not a recipe for national solidarity, and in my view much of the malaise in Western Europe today, much of the general support for the more extreme manifestation of the anti-nuclear movements with their implicit neutralism, arises from precisely this divorce between the people and the mechanism for their defence. Nor do I believe, incidentally, that it is a very effective recipe for national defence. If Europe were to be attacked by the Soviet Union, it would have to be defended, at least in the first instance, by its own peoples; not by nuclear weapons under the control of a transatlantic ally.

Even in the nuclear age, the obligation on the citizen to fight in defence of the community that embodies his values seems to me to be absolute, and the more fully he is a citizen, the more total that obligation becomes. This ugly skeleton of military obligation for the preservation of the state can become so thickly covered with the fat of economic prosperity and under-exercised through the skilful avoidance of international conflict that whole generations can grow to maturity, as they have in Western Europe today, without even knowing that it is there. Fortunately or unfortunately, you in Israel are under no such illusions. But with the obligation to fight if necessary to defend one's community there goes the duty, no less absolute, to fight in such a way as will so far as is possible avoid the slaughter of the innocent; as it is to ensure that the defence of one's own rights does not involve, if one can possibly avoid it, the denial of the rights of others. If one ignores these obligations, the security one purchases by force of arms may be tenable only on a very short lease. With patriotic commitment and military skill, if these are not to be wasted and perverted, there must go also political wisdom; and a fundamental humanity.

In Yigal Allon all these qualities were finely blended. He was a great soldier; courageous, inspiring, resolute, fertile in ideas. He was a wise statesman; one whose loss his country and the world as a whole could ill afford. And more than either of these, he was a deeply humane and humble man.

I am deeply grateful to you all for granting me this privilege of celebrating his memory. Long may it endure, in this land that he did so much to build.

3

Prussia

in European

History

On February 25, 1947, the Allied Control Council of the four victorious powers occupying Germany decreed that the Prussian State, 'which from early days has been a bearer of militarism and reaction in Germany' was, 'with its central government and all its agencies, abolished'.[1] In fact this decree was less a legal enactment than the exorcism of a ghost. 'Prussia' in the sense described by the Control Council as 'a bearer of militarism and reaction' had disappeared in the revolution of November 1918, with the exile of the Hohenzollerns and the destruction of the privileged status of the old landed classes. The coup de grace to the independence of the Prussian State had been administered by the measures of *Gleichschaltung* (integration) carried through under the Third Reich. None the less, 'Prussia' was considered by the Allies to have borne as much responsibility for the Second World War as she was generally believed, in Anglo-Saxon countries, to have had for the first. If there was no longer a living political organism, there was, it was believed, still a spirit that had survived it; a spirit of militaristic aggression based on *Kadavergehorsamkeit* (corpse-like obedience), on a rejection of liberal values, on a contempt for democracy, and on the worship of blind force. In order to destroy this spirit, the Allies still thought it necessary to exhume the corpse and drive a stake through its heart.

One cannot expect from peoples and governments, in the immediate aftermath of a war in which they had suffered so grievously, cool analytical judgement based on profound historical learning, and it was only to be expected that Allied statesmen allowed their actions to be determined by a commonly held myth. Only a pedantic minority questioned the identification of Nazism with Prussianism, or were concerned to analyse which features of National Socialism derived from the Prussian tradition and which did not; or considered whether there were aspects of that tradition which were admirable in themselves and whose disappearance might be a misfortune for Western civilization. The evidence of Prussian guilt seemed self-evident: indeed the bulk of it was to be found in the writings and speeches of those who had been concerned to glorify Prussian ideals, from Friedrich Jahn through Heinrich von Treitschke to Moeller van den Bruck. The verdict was not surprising; but was it just?

Certainly the whole course of Prussian history over the past three hundred years had gradually set the Prussian State apart, in a curious way, from the others of Western Europe; a political process which nurtured both a social and an intellectual tradition which was in many respects alien, and which became increasingly hostile, to those of the societies developing west of the Rhine. But this consciousness of alienation was a development purely of the nineteenth century. In spite of the claims of Droysen and Treitschke, I know of no evidence that the Great Elector Frederick William saw himself as set apart, in any fundamental cultural respect, from the other princes of Central Europe in the seventeenth century who were struggling for survival and self-assertion. Certainly Frederick the Great saw himself as a full member of the European family, and aspired to play a leading role in it. The foreign contemporaries of the Hohenzollerns in these centuries saw them as different from themselves only in the greater skill and success with which they performed in the game which they were all playing, the consolidation and extension of State power. 'Vous êtes,' wrote Mirabeau to Frederick the Great in 1786, 'le seul souverain de l'Europe qui, loin d'avoir des dettes, ayez des tresors; vos troupes sont excellentes; votre nation est docile, fidèle, et bien plus douée d'ésprit publique qu'on ne devrait attendre de sa constitution servile'.[2]

This admirable performance was generally considered to be the result of wise statesmanship and prudent administration; certainly not, as Heinrich von Treitschke was to suggest eighty years later, the manifestation of qualities first developed by the Teutonic Knights whose discipline and ruthlessness had enabled them to subdue Prussia in the fourteenth century.

> Who [enquired Treitschke] can understand the innermost nature of the Prussian people and the Prussian State unless he has familiarised himself with those pitiless racial conflicts whose vestiges, whether we are aware of them or not, live on mysteriously in the habits of our people? A spell rises from ground which was drenched with the noblest German blood in the fight on behalf of the name of Germany and the most sublime gifts of mankind.[3]

Sentiments such as these would have made no sense whatever in the Berlin of Frederick the Great, let alone the Königsberg of Immanuel Kant. The very name "Prussia" derived simply from an administrative expedient: it was the only available royal title that could legitimately be bestowed by the Emperor upon his loyal supporter the Elector of Brandenburg in 1701. Certainly no one yet considered that the tap-root of the "Prussian" State, comfortably situated as it was in the middle of Germany with its prosperous provinces on the Rhine, lay in those arid eastern lands which contributed so little to the wealth of the monarchy and whose origins in conquest had long been forgotten.

Yet Prussia's characteristic as a *military* monarchy, if not yet a militaristic state, was already well established in the eighteenth century. This owed little if anything to the traditions of the Teutonic Knights; everything to the methods used by the Great Elector to build up and consolidate his power; to the almost pathological passion of Frederick William I for things military; and to the adventurous ruthlessness with which Frederick the Great used the military forces he had inherited to make Prussia one of the great powers of Europe.

The Great Elector was certainly not unique in using the defence requirements of his sprawling territories to consolidate his internal power by establishing a fiscal system independent of the representative bodies of his estates. The symbiotic relationship between military forces, bureaucratic administration and royal power was a general characteristic of European political systems in the later part of the seventeenth century. But the achievement of the Great Elector was distinctive in two ways which were to prove of decisive importance for Prussia's future in Europe—and indeed for Germany's position in the world.

The first was this. All the great nations of Europe were consolidated as states by their reigning dynasties. The Hohenzollerns did for Prussia what Capets, Valois and Bourbon did for France, Normans, Angevins and Plantagenets for England, Habsburgs for Spain and Austria, and the Romanovs for Russia. But in the case of all these powers except Austria, whose cultural diversity posed problems which in the long run the dynasty found impossible to solve, it is at least probable that a nation would have developed even without the talents of their monarchs; nations less extensive, perhaps, and less cohesive, but distinct entities none the less, defined by their geography and their culture. The sprawling estates of the Electors of Brandenburg, which had to borrow the name of an extinct Slavic tribe to give them even a semblance of national cohesion, would not have come together as a unit but for the random acquisitions of their reigning princes, and would not have survived as a unit but for the policies of those princes. Elsewhere—especially in England—the State was created by the interaction of dynasty and community. The Prussian State as such, made up as it was of discontinuous possessions sprawling untidily across Central Europe, had no existence except that given to it by the Hohenzollerns, and the Hohenzollerns created it, with all its bureaucratic mechanisms of control, primarily to provide an army to support their power. As has been repeatedly stressed both by her friends and by her enemies, eighteenth-century Prussia was not so much a State which possessed an army as an army which possessed a State. The position of army and dynasty in the old Prussian State was unique. One could conceive—as many did conceive—of a loyalty to 'England' or to 'France' or to 'Spain' independent of allegiance to the Crown. In Prussia before the nineteenth century this was literally inconceivable.

The second peculiarity is equally evident. At a time when in France the monarchy was manoeuvring the landed aristocracy into a position of privileged and decorative impotence, and when in England power was passing from both monarchy and the old aristocracy into the hands of oligarchs who derived their wealth as much from finance and trade as they did from land, the Hohenzollerns effected an alliance which confirmed the land-owning classes in all their social and economic privileges, in return for their supporting royal power. A social structure which was already threatened by the economic developments of the age became the *rocher de bronze* on which the power of the Prussian monarchy was established. By some strange alchemy, an aristocracy as self-willed and ungovernable as their neighbours the Poles were broken in to the royal service, and applied themselves to their duties in army and bureaucracy with a diligence which they exacted in their turn from those bound to serve them on their estates. This ethic of service, rendered and exacted in a precisely defined hierarchy, an ethic strengthened by a Protestantism which here found an expression at least as satisfying as it did in capitalistic accumulation, lay at the centre of what was to become identified as 'Prussianism' (*Preussentum*); an ethic seen by its opponents as one of dominance and oppression, by its defenders as one of subordination and service, but one in any case deeply at variance with the concepts of communal liberties which underlay Anglo-Saxon constitutionalism, and even more with those of a priori individual rights which the leaders of the French and American Revolutions were to derive from the thinkers of the Enlightenment.

At the time however the Great Elector was not believed to be doing anything very peculiar, and neither did he believe that he was, himself. His policy consisted of expedients, ad hoc measures for survival. Nor was the militaristic monomania of Frederick William I considered by his contemporaries as anything other than a personal idiosyncrasy. At the beginning of the eighteenth century the princes of Germany still had much in common with the *condottiere* of an earlier generation, men like Bernard of Saxe-Weimar and Albert Wallenstein, whose armies constituted their fortune. Frederick William building up his army was no more than a miser hoarding the most acceptable form of wealth; and Frederick the Great can be regarded, at least in his early years, as a prodigal heir squandering the fortune accumulated by his ancestors so as to cut a figure on the world's stage. His defenders, of course, think that there was more to him than this, and justify his seizure of Silesia as a calculated risk which, unpredictably expensive as the outcome may have been, paid off handsomely since it transformed Prussia's position in Europe from a petty principality to a major power.

What is important to notice, however, is that this stroke of *Machtpolitik* was not considered by contemporaries to display any peculiarly *Prussian* characteristics. Indeed, it was very much out of character with the prudent, even docile behaviour of Frederick's immediate forbears. As an act it was certainly seen as immoral or at best sharp practice, but it was certainly not regarded as barbaric. Indeed it made Frederick eminently *bundnis fähig*, a good alliance partner, courted first by the French and then by the British; though he may well have wondered in his more desperate moments, when he had been tricked and abandoned with the same ruthlessness as he had displayed in initiating the whole process, whether the game had really been worth it. His contemporaries admired or disliked him as a skilful player on the board of power politics and as a military leader of genius. But no one, in that sceptical and unimaginative age, saw in him the true successor of the Teutonic Knights. Eighteenth-century Prussia was just another power in the Concert of Europe, sharing the same ideology, contributing to the same culture and playing by the same rules.

The French Revolution was to change all that. It unleashed in Europe two developments which only the most skilful of statesmen found themselves able to master. In the first place it proclaimed an ideology which, by asserting that all political power needed to be legitimised by the free consent of the people whose rights and liberties were inherent and in no way derived from the State, undermined the whole foundation of dynastic legitimacy on which the European order was based. Secondly, by harnessing popular national self-consciousness to military power, it created in France a dynamic State far more powerful and threatening than any established under the ancien régime. The question which faced the other powers of Europe was, whether they could survive in the presence of this elemental new force without undergoing a similar transformation.

In Germany the material for such a transformation was certainly there. It was provided not so much by those who accepted the French doctrines of the Rights of Man and wished to imitate the democratic patterns derived from them—patterns which in the immediate aftermath of the Terror did not appear very attractive—as by the movement already well under way of which Herder was to be the prophet, Fichte and Arndt the great apostles; which saw political authority as deriving neither from atomistic individual rights nor from divine authority, but from the historical growth of distinct societies, of 'peoples' who developed their own idiosyncratic ways of life which found expression in the existence of the State and which the State, in its turn, existed to defend.

Such a doctrine, which developed with incomparable richness and diversity in Germany at the turn of the eighteenth and nineteenth centuries, did not threaten the social and political foundations of the Prussian state in the same manner as did the egalitarian and democratic dogmas of the French Revolution. Indeed one finds in the writings of Fichte and Arndt the beginnings of that identification of the genius of the German people with the historical development and mission of Prussia which was to become the leitmotiv of Prussian historiography in the nineteenth century. Nor was it only Prussians who saw Berlin as the natural centre for a specifically *German* resistance to the alien ideas from beyond the Rhine: Gebhard von Scharnhorst, Karl von Stein and August von Gneisenau were only the most eminent of the soldiers, statesmen and scholars from outside Prussia who believed that Germany had to be built and that the Prussian monarchy was the institution best placed to do it.

Yet for the best part of a century the Hohenzollerns themselves were resistant to the idea. From Frederick William III to William I, they regarded any suggestion that their power derived in some sense from the People (*Volk*), even in so generalised and imprecise a sense as the German national movement understood that term, rather than from divine mandate, as an unacceptable derogation of their authority; and the more strongly the winds of democracy blew as the century went on, the more stubbornly did the Hohenzollerns entrench themselves behind the ramparts of Divine Right. In 1848 Frederick William IV refused to "pick up the crown of Germany from the gutter" though it was his for the asking; and William I was grumblingly to refer to his apotheosis as German Emperor in the Hall of Mirrors in Versailles on January 18, 1871, as the most miserable day in his life.

The history of Germany in the first part of the nineteenth century revolves very largely round this tension between the German national movement and the Prussian tradition so jealously guarded by the Hohenzollern dynasty and its supporters; between those who wished to set Prussia at the head of a new united and expanding Germany and those who saw it as the protector of an increasingly threatened ancien régime. The heroic days of the *Erhebungszeit,* the era of Liberation of 1813–15, when the King of Prussia had, however reluctantly, been persuaded to issue a proclamation *an meinem Volk* and when the Prussian armies raised by Scharnhorst and Hermann Boyen and led by Blücher and Gneisenau had played the leading role in the destruction of Napoleon, was a golden era kept alive in the minds of the young by such heroic survivors as Dahlmann, Arndt and Haüsser, as well as by the new generation of ardent nationalists represented by Droysen and Treitschke. For Treitschke, the Saxon, Prussia represented the only hope for German unity, as it had for his countryman Gneisenau, and for the Hanoverian Scharnhorst. Austria, the only other possible focus of political power, stood implacably for the preservation of the old order, that *Kleinstaaterei* from which the nationalists were so desperate to escape. For those who wished to create, or re-create, Germany, only Berlin offered any hope.

But the new generation of German nationalists of the 1850s, influenced by English ideas if not by French, were as reluctant to accept the survival of aristocratic social privilege and royal political authority as were the Hohenzollerns to become constitutional monarchs subordinating their authority, as had Queen Victoria of England and Louis Philippe of France, to some kind of parliamentary democracy. In the 1860s William I and the 'camarilla' that surrounded him saw themselves fighting what was basically an ideological struggle, to preserve the old values of the Prussian monarchy against a Zeitgeist which they deeply distrusted; a Zeitgeist compounded not only of the democratic ideals of the French Revolution, but of the more subtly demoralising principles associated with the new industrial power of England and the economic doctrines of Manchester; doctrines which depicted society as no more than a joint-stock company operating in an international market, and saw the State as a mechanism whose only function was to enable its members to make money.

It was now that the concept of *Preussentum,* of Prussia as the guardian of a system of values distinct from and hostile to those developing in 'the

West', in Britain, France and the United States, began to take shape in the minds of German thinkers. In the 1860s a great synthesis was to be developed, in the realm of ideas as much as that of politics. While Bismarck was resolving the political crisis by harnessing the power of the Prussian monarchy to the cause of German nationalism, thinkers such as Droysen, Sybel, Haüsser and, pre-eminently, the young Heinrich von Treitschke were proclaiming from their university chairs to audiences composed, not only of enthusiastic students (young men who were to reach maturity at the turn of the century) but of townspeople, officials and officers of the armed services, the doctrine that Prussia embodied the true spirit of the German people, that she alone had preserved for a thousand years that essential core of heroism and virtue, undebased by foreign ideas from south of the Alps and west of the Rhine. Prussia, they proclaimed, was the true Germany; the Germans of the south and southwest states had been led astray and subverted by alien influences, and could cleanse themselves only by returning to their original loyalties, and accepting the leadership of Berlin.

The victory over France in 1870 was thus greeted as much for its ideological as for its political implications—and this not in Germany alone. It was seen not only as the humiliation of an arrogant and troublesome neighbour, but as the vindication of a specific value-system; one based on loyalty, obedience, disciplined courage, and religious faith, as against that democratic creed widely regarded as atheistical, materialist, individualistic and morally decadent. With remarkable speed and unanimity the liberals of 1848 abandoned French or English ideas and embraced the "Prussian" model. Conservative opinion throughout Europe, not least in France, saw in the German victory a long-overdue readjustment of a moral and ideological balance, as well as the creation of a new political one. Even in England the emergence on the Continent of a hegemonic power of a kind which she had repeatedly gone to war to suppress was viewed with great equanimity. Bismarck's new Germany was so obviously a force devoted to the preservation of the status quo. 'For US there is no loss, rather a gain', said a leading British conservative statesman, Lord Stanley, 'in the interposition of a solid barrier between the two great aggressive powers of the Continent'.[4] Bismarck's Prussianised Germany appeared as a bulwark even more reliable than Metternich's decrepit Austria against the forces of revolution which still threatened the European system.

But there were others who were less sure about this. Liberal opinion in England had been appalled by Bismarck's defeat of the parliamentary forces in Germany in the 1860s, and the triumph of an archaic system which appeared so explicitly to turn its back on all their own ideals. It was as if their own civil war of the seventeenth century had been fought all over again; but this time parliament had lost. The anachronistic life-style and attitudes of the ruling classes in Berlin, already being termed 'militaristic' by contemporaries, were deeply worrying to some observers from beyond the Channel, and even more to those beyond the Rhine. As a perceptive British diplomat wrote from Berlin in January 1870, '[I]t is not the actual army, it is the Prussian system which is a standing menace to her neighbours'.[5] And 'the Prussian system' was deeply embedded in the new Germany. The dominant position of the army in society; the privileged position of military leaders in, if not indeed above, the government; ministers responsible for their actions only to the Crown; the preservation within Prussia of a weighted system of voting designed to preserve the ascendancy of the landed classes: all this indicated a spirit deeply at variance with the whole pattern of democratic and liberal development which in mid-Victorian Britain and Republican France was assumed to be inevitable and universal.

And indeed it was so at variance. The new Germany was determined to strike out a new pattern for itself instead of accepting those made in Paris or in Manchester—or rather, she was determined to rediscover her old, true culture and recreate it from its historical and literary roots; roots, as the Germans were now being insistently told, stretching back to medieval Prussia. The preservation or revival of the bold black-letter *Schrift* was only the most obvious example, as was the purging from the German language of foreign importations, and their exclusion for the future. German culture was seen (as was increasingly to be the case with all new nations) as a dimension of the power of the German State, and German scholars considered it to be their patriotic duty to expand and enhance it. Their achievements were universally admired. Scientists, historians, classicists, engineers flocked from all over the world to the great German universities and *Technische Hochschulen* to learn their trades. German became the international language of science and scholarship, Germany a throbbing power-house of technology and learning as well as of commerce and industry. But the framework of this power-house was the old Prussian military and social system, presided over by an All-Highest War Lord. The dominant figures within that system viewed the gigantic economic achievements of German industry with mixed feelings. They were magnificent so long as they could be harnessed to the power and security of *Preussentum*, the preservation of its traditional values in an increasingly dangerous world. but did not these very developments pose in themselves a threat to those traditional values?

Treitschke for one believed that they need not. A man of inexhaustible energy and eloquence, he set himself to do for the German nation in its hour of triumph what Fichte had done for it in its hour of tribulation. For twenty years he lectured in Berlin to large and enthusiastic audiences, proclaiming the principles of the Prussian faith; lectures in which the nationalism of Fichte and Arndt were combined with the teleological ide-alism of Hegel and the newly-fashionable Social-Darwinism to create an immensely powerful new dogma.

For Treitschke the essence and purpose of the Prussian State was power (*Macht*), always had been power, and it existed only to increase its power. It was only right therefore that the symbol and instrument of that power, the Army, should be dominant in society. 'The State', he declared, 'is no Academy of Arts, much less a Stock Exchange. It is Power, and so it is in contradiction with its very essence if it neglects its Army'.[6] 'Every moral judgement by historians must take as its starting point that the State is, before anything else, Power, to assert its Will both in domestic and foreign policy; and a man can be given no higher or more noble task than to co-operate with the State in fulfilling this duty'.[7] 'The denial of its own power', he concluded, 'is indeed for the State the sin against the Holy Ghost'.[8]

It was, maintained Treitschke, the true genius of Prussia and her leaders to have always realised this and to have manifested that Will to Power which had alone enabled her to survive and defeat her rivals; and that Will must be continually strengthened if Germany was to survive in her turn. 'Only valiant peoples have a secure existence, a future, a possibility for development. Weak and cowardly peoples go to the wall, and rightly so. In this everlasting contest of different States lies the beauty of History, and to wish to abolish this conflict is sheer nonsense'.[9] Prussia had risen to greatness through war; Germany had been forged by war; now she must be preserved and if the need arose extended by war. War moreover would preserve the quality of the *Volk*. For sickly peoples (*krankende Volker*) it was indeed the only cure. To eliminate heroism from mankind would be a perversion of morality. Without war there would be no progress, no new developments in history. 'It has always been the weary, dispirited and worn-out eras which have toyed with the dream of everlasting peace'.[10] But no matter: '[T]he living God will ensure that war will always recur, as a terrible medicine for mankind'.[11]

This glorification of war, not just as a necessary instrument of policy (*Politik*) in the Clausewitzian sense but as an end in itself, was far removed from the cool pragmatism of the Great Elector and Frederick the Great.

It was quite out of keeping with the true ethos of the Prussian Junker families who, whatever their pride in their martial ancestry and the traditions of the regiments in which they served, were for the most part men of modest life-style, limited ambitions and, often, considerable piety. As for the German people as a whole, it was their very passivity and peacefulness, their traditional acceptance as he saw it, of cultural *inferiority* that Treitschke saw it as his mission to transform by his electrifying addresses. It was for this reason, claims his most recent biographer,[12] that he saw it necessary to glorify German culture and character at the expense of all others; to deride Russian barbarism, French frivolity and cynicism, American materialism, British hypocrisy and, increasingly, the corrupting influence in German society of the Jews. He did not claim, as did the French and the British, that German culture embodied universal principles which, if generally accepted, would create a happier and more peaceful world. On the contrary: the virtue of German culture lay precisely in its Germanness (*Deutschtum*) as against the enervating internationalism of the West. Its superiority was self-evident, but it could not be extended by persuasion and conversion; only by conquest, the Good German Sword.

Treitschke's own academic colleagues increasingly distanced themselves from him as his advocacy became wilder; but his lectures continued to be popular and influential, attended as they were by such military and political leaders as Alfred von Tirpitz and Heinrich Class. There were indeed comparable thinkers in other countries, extreme nationalists like Charles Maurras in France and Professor J. A. Cramb in England, but these were eccentric, peripheral figures, not admired and patronised, as was Treitschke, by the entire political establishment. Treitschke did much to shape the minds of the ruling classes of the Wilhelmine era, and that shape he and others, especially foreigners, regarded as being distinctively 'Prussian'.

Treitschke's ideas were to be given an even wider circulation a quarter of a century later in the work of his disciple General Friedrich von Bernhardi, *Germany and the Next War*. Rightly described by Professor Gerhardt Ritter as 'a giant literary success and a political misfortune',[13] this was written at the height of the Agadir crisis in 1911 in which the German government and the German people, in the view of the author, were failing to show sufficient resolve. Bernhardi was a brilliant but difficult man who had retired early from the army. His views can no more be regarded as typical of the thinking of the General Staff than that of Treitschke was typical of German academics as a whole. But his book was immensely popular, going into seven editions and being translated into every major language, including Japanese. Its publication in England in 1912 made a very considerable impact indeed, confirming as it did all the suspicions that had been gathering there during the past decade about the militarization of German society and the implacably aggressive nature of German foreign policy.

Bernhardi's militarism was open and explicit. War, he wrote, was 'not merely a necessary element in the lives of nations, but an indispensable factor of culture, in which a true civilized nation finds the highest expression of truth and vitality'.[14] 'War', he argued, 'had forged that Prussia, hard as steel, on which the new Germany could grow up as a mighty European State and a World Power of the future'.[15] So far from avoiding wars, statesmen should if necessary seek them out, as had Bismarck and Frederick the Great: '[W]ars which have been deliberately provoked by far-seeing statesmen have had the happiest results'.[16] Old concepts of 'the balance of power' must be denounced, as should the sanctity of treaties (such as that guaranteeing Belgian neutrality) concluded under different conditions. 'We must', proclaimed Bernhardi, 'rouse in our people the unanimous wish for power . . . together with the determination to sacrifice on the altar of patriotism, not only life and property, but also private views and preferences in the interest of the common welfare'.[17] The object must be the full assertion of German power on a global scale, whatever the cost. '*Weltmacht oder Niedergang!* [World power or downfall] must be our rallying cry'.[18]

Both the style and the timing of this publication ensured that its effect would be catastrophic. The German invasion of Belgium within two years and the German Chancellor's unfortunate and widely publicised reference to 'a scrap of paper' served to confirm the belief that Bernhardi had accurately described the nature of German culture and the intentions of the German State; that the Prussian *pickelhaube* and jackboot now ruled in Germany and would rule wherever German military power could extend. The British Prime Minister, Herbert Asquith, was expressing a generally agreed interpretation of the nature of German politics and society when he declared in the House of Commons on February 23, 1915, 'We shall never sheathe the sword, which we have not lightly drawn . . . until *the military domination of Prussia* [emphasis added] is wholly and finally destroyed'.[19]

By the First World War, then, it was firmly established in the minds of the British, the French, and increasingly the Americans, that Prussia was the evil spirit of Germany, and that only when it had been exorcised would Germany cease troubling Europe. The emergence of another and very different 'Prussia' in 1919, after the abolition of the old electoral system had destroyed the hegemony of the landed classes, passed very largely unnoticed outside Germany. It did indeed become evident that there were other evil spirits around in post-war Germany which did not originate in Prussia; the South German roots of the Nazis, for example, were evident for all to see, and Prussians were not prominent in the party's leadership. But the ideology and objectives of Hitler and his associates were all too truly in the tradition of Treitschke and Bernhardi; and the support which Hitler received from von Papen and his associates of the *Herrenklub,* culminating in the ceremony at the Garrison Church at Potsdam on March 21, 1933, when Hindenburg, to all appearances, received Hitler into the inner sanctum of *Preussentum* with a ceremonial 'laying on of hands', makes the arguments of those who would deny any connection between the good old traditions of Prussia and the bad new ones of National Socialism something less than convincing. There were indeed heroic Prussian figures like Moltke and his friends of the Kreisau circle whose inner rectitude drove them to oppose Hitler at the cost of their lives; but there were others, perhaps a majority of the old Prussian governing classes, who saw no conflict of loyalties and who served Hitler to the end of their days; accepting his objectives, as they saw them, even if they disliked his methods. The phrase 'Prusso-Nazism', in such general use among the Allies during the Second World War, was not entirely a contradiction in terms.

Now that the 'evil spirit of Prussianism' has been well and truly exorcised, historians can pass a more dispassionate judgement on the place of Prussia in European History. We can recognise that the Prussian tradition, as was admitted by one of its last and greatest exponents, Friedrich Meinecke, did indeed play a central role in bringing about 'the German catastrophe'. But we must make two reservations. First, although the exalted patriotism, the subordination of the individual to state authority and the glorification of war as a preferred life-style which typified the 'Prussian school' of the late nineteenth century were indeed an intrinsic part of National Socialism, the Nazi creed and Nazi power drew on many other sources not specifically Prussian or even specifically German. Anti-Semitism in particular was a disease that infected the whole of Europe, especially Eastern Europe. Indeed the tradition of religious toleration which was one of the most attractive elements in old Prussia made the acceptance of Jews into German society remarkably rapid after the end of discriminatory legislation in the early nineteenth century.

Second, the old Prussian virtues *were* virtues, and remain so. Industry; piety; frugality; self-discipline; physical courage; a capacity for self-subordination to a common cause: without these no society can survive, whatever its political complexion. Indeed, in the great confrontation of ideologies which today divides the world and so lamentably divides Germany,* it is the side which can cultivate these qualities most successfully which is likely, in the long run, to prevail.

*Written in 1983.

4

Empire, Race and War in pre-1914 Britain

Among all the fiends in the liberal demonology today, Imperialism, Racism and Militarism reign supreme; an evil trinity at whose collective door most of the wrong-doing in the world can conveniently be laid. Yet little more than three generations ago, within the memory of people still alive, these words and the ideas associated with them evoked, even among professed Liberal thinkers, a very different response. Empire, Race and War: these were seen as facts of life to be accepted if not indeed welcomed; certainly ones that presented challenges to be met and problems to be solved if disaster was not to ensue. It was generally assumed in Britain at the turn of the century that the white races were inherently superior to the brown and the black and so had the right, indeed the duty, to govern them. It was assumed by all save a small dissident minority that the British Empire was the greatest force for good that the world had seen since the disintegration of the Roman Empire, and by bringing the benefits of peace, prosperity and civilisation to so vast an area of the world's surface was even more worthy of respect. And it was taken for granted—by all save a slightly larger minority—that the Empire, having been built up by war, might be legitimately extended by war, and would probably have one day to be defended by war. The military virtues were thus considered part of the essence of an Imperial Race.

For the inhabitants of these islands at the beginning of this century the British Empire was for better or worse what Lord Curzon described as 'a great historical and political and sociological fact which is one of the guiding factors in the history of mankind'.[1] Most of them (at least outside Ireland) seem to have thought it to be for the better. It was, in a term which came into very general use at this period, a 'Heritage', built up by the heroism and labour of past generations, to be handed on, intact or increased. Rudyard Kipling used the word as the title for the poem which he wrote to introduce a sumptuous volume which appeared in 1905 called *The Empire and the Century*:[2]

> Dear-bought and clear, a thousand year
> Our fathers' title runs,
> Make we likewise our sacrifice,
> Defrauding not our sons.

One can perhaps trace in the consciousness of inherited responsibility so frequently reiterated in this period the beginnings of that loss of confidence which historians of a later generation were to discern among the late Victorians and Edwardians. But we must set these people in the context of their times. They had grown up at a time when Britain was at her apogee. Born at mid-century, they would in childhood have heard the talk of men and women who remembered the Napoleonic Wars. They would have been brought up in the nursery on the patriotic verse of Robert Southey and Thomas Campbell. At school their minds would have been moulded by men with the robust and simple-minded patriotism of Charles Kingsley and of William Johnson Cory, that vehement enthusiast who taught so many future members of the ruling class at Eton, not least among them Lord Rosebery and Lord Esher. From schools where they came under the influence of such teachers, this generation passed to universities where they came in contact with professors like John Ruskin: Ruskin, who told the audience at his Inaugural Lecture as Slade Professor of Fine Art at Oxford in 1870 that it must be the task of the Englishmen 'still undegenerate in race; a race mingled of the best northern blood', to 'found colonies as fast and as far as she is able, formed of her most energetic and worthiest men;—seizing every piece of fruitful waste ground she can set her foot on, and there teaching these her colonists that their chief virtue is to be fidelity to their country, and that their first aim is to be to advance the power of England by land and sea'.[3] If they were historians, they would be introduced to the works of Carlyle and Froude, who spread the same message: the need for the British, who were so clearly marked out by their history and their culture as a master race, to extend their habitations and their principles throughout the world (this, be it noted, a good twenty years before the *economic* arguments for Empire became fashionable). They would have read Charles Dilke's *Greater Britain* which, published in 1867, had urged the British to people the empty spaces of the world with their stock and to raise up and educate the inferior races they found there.

And in the 1880s, when this generation was entering early middle age, all these vague aspirations towards settlement and extension of authority and enlargement of prestige and power would have come together in the concept of Empire; a concept first crystallised in the work *The Expansion of England,* which Professor J. R. Seeley of the University of Cambridge published in 1883.

For Seeley the Empire did not consist, as had previous Empires, of the rule of a metropolis over alien peoples abroad. For him the Empire was the British nation itself, which had grown slowly but inexorably according to its own laws and was now spread all over the world; and which needed a new self-consciousness in order to realise the full potential of its greatness. The world, he discerned, as had de Tocqueville before him, was moving from the age of European powers into that of global, or as we would today call them, Superpowers. 'Russia and the United States', he prophesied, 'will surpass in power the states now called great as much as the great country-states of the sixteenth century surpassed Florence'. But the links which were building up the great continental states by land had in the case of the British to be created and maintained by sea. It was, and must be, an oceanic power. Its destiny lay beyond the seas, and there need be no limit to its natural growth.

So began, in Britain, the age of Imperialism. From being a sentiment, Imperialism became a programme, and one supported by politicians of all parties. In 1884 there was founded an Imperial Federation League, very largely in direct response to the challenge posed by Seeley. More effective than most such organisations, it convened an Imperial Exhibition in London in 1886, for which Lord Tennyson and Arthur Sullivan combined to write an anthem. It established a bricks-and-mortar shrine of Imperialism in the Imperial Institute at South Kensington, the tower of which remains, splendidly flamboyant among the utilitarian clutter of the (still) Imperial College of Science and Technology; and it convened in 1887 a Colonial Conference in London in the hope that this would lead to the creation of a great, unified Imperial Federation on the model of the United States. It did nothing of the kind, largely because the colonies of Australia, New Zealand, Canada and South Africa, having escaped from the tutelage of London, showed no enthusiasm to submit to it again. But the age of High Imperialism was ushered in by these celebrations, an age which found its Laureate in the facile talent of the young Rudyard Kipling. Ten years later the age reached its apogee with the Diamond Jubilee celebrations; an apogee from which, as a slightly more mature Rudyard Kipling pointed out in his *Recessional*, decline was, if not inevitable, at least all too likely.

Such a decline did not, however, lie within the horizon of that archpriest of Empire, Cecil Rhodes; and it is worth recalling the original terms of the will which Rhodes drew up in 1877, at the age of twenty-four, since, fantastic as they seem today, there is little evidence that he ever seriously changed his mind about his ultimate objectives. His intention was to set up a trust

> To and for the establishment, promotion and development of a Secret Society, the true aim and object whereof shall be the extension of British rule throughout the world, the perfecting of a system of emigration from the United Kingdom, and of colonisation by British subjects of all lands where the means of livelihood are attainable by energy, labour and enterprise, and especially the occupation by British settlers of the entire Continent of Africa, the Holy Land, the Valley of the Euphrates, the Isles of Cyprus and Candia, the whole of South America, the Islands of the Pacific not heretofore possessed by Great Britain, the whole of the Malay Archipelago, the seaboard of China and Japan, the ultimate recovery of the United States of America as an integral part of the British Empire, the inauguration of a system of colonial representation in the Imperial Parliament which may tend to weld together the disjointed members of the Empire, and finally the foundation of so great a power as hereafter to render wars impossible and promote the best interests of humanity.[4]

Few of Rhodes's contemporaries would have dared to spell out their secret hopes quite so explicitly, but those hopes were not untypical. Lord Rosebery, the President of the Imperial Federation League, stated in 1893 that it 'was part of our responsibility and our heritage to take care that the world, as far as it can be moulded by us, shall receive an Anglo-Saxon and not another character'.[5] A man of a slightly younger generation, Leopold Amery, who was born in 1873 in time to be influenced as a precocious schoolboy by the writings of Seeley and Froude, was to write in his memoirs that '[i]f the feeble control of the Manchu dynasty should break down entirely, as that of the dynasty had broken down in India, then presumably we might have to take on greater responsibilities. . . . No one was clamouring to see Queen Victoria Empress of China as well as Empress of India. But none, at the time of her Diamond Jubilee would have dismissed the idea as inconceivable'.[6]

Nor must we forget that it was to be Amery's generation which, in the aftermath of the First World War, actually did extend the frontiers of Empire to embrace, however briefly, the Holy Land and the valley of the Euphrates; and did not conceal its desire to extend them into regions of central Asia which not even Rhodes had thought about.

The Empire might thus have continued to grow, whether to create favourable conditions for British trade, as it did in West Africa and might have done in China; or to gain strategic security, as it did in Mesopotamia and might have done in Persia; or to obtain more land for white settlement, as it did in Southern Africa and conceivably might have done in South America; as well as from the general sense, which historians must neither underrate nor mock, that it was its destiny to continue to grow, and that Englishmen had the duty and responsibility to ensure its growth. It was this accumulated national and imperial dynamic which was to be concentrated on South Africa at the turn of the century, where Kruger and the Boers were seen as irritating and anachronistic obstructions in the path of a historical process as inevitable as it was necessary.

Necessary, certainly; for what would happen in the almost inconceivable eventuality of the British people betraying their trust and *not* showing themselves worthy of their destiny? There was the general feeling that what did not expand must shrink; what did not grow must decline. Seeley had prophesied the advent of the age of the Superpowers in the 1880s, and Halford Mackinder was to buttress his prophetic vision with geo-political analysis a quarter of a century later. The former Great Powers of Europe were dwindling, in historical perspective, to the scale of the Italian city-states. Big was now beautiful, in political as in economic organisation, where the great industrial cartels were forming, and with them the big unions. As one imperial publicist put it in 1905, 'The day of the individual and the small nation has gone for England with the advent of rivals. In any era of competition, Providence is on the side of the big battalions'.[7] The examples admired and applauded, by Liberals and Conservatives alike, were those provided on the Continent by Bismarck and Cavour, who had so clearly led their nations towards their manifest destinies; and as they had forged the small particles of their communities into great nation-states, so must the British create their own yet greater world-state. The idea, if not the phrase, which was to become current in Germany, *Weltmacht oder Niedergang*, was no less prevalent in England; we must become a power on a global scale, or we shall go under.

This was the fear expressed by Joseph Chamberlain, the spokesman for those economic interests in the Midlands which were beginning to feel the blast of international competition. Chamberlain's Imperialism was frankly economic. 'Is there', he demanded in 1888, 'any man in his senses who believes that the crowded population of these islands could exist for a single day if we were to cut adrift from us the great dependencies which now look to us for protection and assistance and which are the natural markets for our trade'?[8] The example of the German *Zollverein* was infectious, both as providing a solution in itself to Britain's economic problems and, as in Germany, as a step towards political unification of the Empire.

There might be disagreement about the details of the solution— whether the Empire should become an economically autarkic entity, or be sustained as it had been hitherto by the great and uninterrupted currents of free trade—but there was very general agreement about the nature of the problem. It was defined in a rough and ready way by Rhodes himself. 'I never lose an opportunity of pointing out to the people', he said in 1892, 'that in view of the fact that these islands can only support six out of their thirty-six millions, and in view also of the action of the world in trying to exclude our goods, we cannot afford to part with one inch of the world's surface which affords a free and open market to the manufacture of our countrymen'.[9] There must be great new spaces in which to settle. For an increasingly explosive social situation at home, the Empire seemed to provide a simple and obvious answer. Instead of a restive proletariat remaining bottled up in the stinking cities of late-Victorian England, the industries in which they worked increasingly vulnerable to foreign competition, with unemployment and social squalor driving them to drink or, worse, to revolution, let there be massive emigration to the new lands of white settlement, where the emigrants could rediscover the good life, establish healthy pastoral communities, and provide secure markets for their brethren who remained at home.

Lord Rosebery declared in 1893 that '[a]n Empire such as ours requires as its first condition an imperial race—a race vigorous and industrious and intrepid. In the rookeries and slums which still survive, an imperial race cannot be reared'. 'A drink-sodden population', he said a few years later, 'is not the true basis of a prosperous Empire'.[10] It had to be admitted that the urban population of Britain in the first decade of the new century did not *look* very much like empire-builders; and writers educated in the

classics, as so many of the university-trained population still were, began
to discern alarming similarities with the later development of Imperial
Rome. A classical scholar writing on the eve of the Great War found the
analogies with Roman decline all too apparent. There was, it seemed,

> the same decay of agriculture; the same predominance of town over
> country life; the same deterioration of physique and general health;
> the same growth of luxury and desire for bodily comfort; the same
> increasing distaste for the burdens of married life; the same decline
> in the birth rate; the same excessive taxation, the same decadence in
> public morals; the same reaction towards morbid and monstrous
> superstitions; the same substitution of State gratuities for parental
> duties; the same love of display in social life; the same lust for gla-
> diatorial exhibitions of athletic skills; the same decreasing sense of
> national responsibility and self-sacrificing patriotism.[11]

Much the same thought occurred to Lord Cromer, one of the greatest
proconsuls of the High Imperialist era, when he reviewed Thomas Hodgkin's study *Italy and Her Invaders* in 1908. 'Are we so far deceived', he
asked, 'and are we so incapable of peering into the future as to be unable
to see that many of the steps which now appear calculated to enhance and
to stereotype Anglo-Saxon domination are but the precursors of national
decay and sterility'?[12]

The Edwardian era was thus one of growing doubts about the validity
even of the imperial solution to the problems which were beginning to
dominate Metropolitan Britain. Were the British really, as Joseph Chamberlain had termed them in 1895, 'the greatest Imperial Race the world
has ever seen'?

At the time Chamberlain had made this claim there were few who
doubted it. The books and newspapers of the period are full of references
to the Imperial Race, the Island Race, the Island Breed, British stock, and
so on, without a shadow of apology or even of self-consciousness. This
was the way it was. The white man *was* superior to the dark-skinned man;
a position which gave him privileges and responsibilities, rights and duties.
He *was* more civilised, and had to uphold and extend the standards of that
civilisation. It was a burden which weighed on all white men alike (though
people were never quite sure about the Russians) but upon the Anglo-
Saxon races most of all. When at the end of the century the Americans at
last plunged into colonial adventure and took over, with the best possible
of intentions, the governance of the Philippines from the palsied hands of

Spain, the general reaction in the British Press was well summed up in Kipling's poem *The White Man's Burden*: about time too.

The term 'Race' was used at the time very loosely; not that we can claim that it is employed with any great precision today. Usually when people used the term they meant what today we would term 'cultures', and certainly any writer who allowed himself to be cross-examined about the actual composition of the so-called Anglo-Saxon Race would have found himself in difficulties. But all recent ages have used jargon derived from a skimpy knowledge of one or more of the sciences. As we tend to think in ill-digested concepts drawn from economics, or sociology, or cybernetics, or, most fashionable of all, ecology, so at the end of the last century publicists of all kinds thought in terms of the anthropological and biological sciences, especially as popularized by Charles Darwin. Probably as few people had actually read Darwin as have, in more recent times, read Max Weber, or Maynard Keynes, or Lévi-Strauss; but all literate Europeans and Americans reckoned that they knew what he had said. Life had evolved, in popular Darwinian theory, by a process of adaptations of species to their surroundings; an adaptation which inevitably involved conflict. Those species which proved themselves best able to exploit and dominate their environment, including competition from rival species, were those which survived. Those which could not so adapt and prevail in the struggle for life disappeared.

Into this framework there fitted very easily the work of early anthropologists on the development and distinctions between the various races of mankind, which naturally became of absorbing interest as the nineteenth century made global travel possible for more than a small number of traders, soldiers and adventurers. Further, such travel brought the West for the first time into continuous contact with a wider range of societies than the familiar high cultures of the East, Arab, Indian, Chinese, with whom the West had trafficked for centuries without any feeling of superiority other than the normal xenophobia of the ignorant. Even with those societies, where Europeans had until the eighteenth century interacted on a basis of cultural equality, the scientific and technical transformations of the early nineteenth century had now put the white man on a new footing of effective superiority. Their steamships, their railways, their manufacturing machinery, and not least their weapons, turned them from privileged traders exercising a loose political suzerainty into dominators and rulers, firmly imposing new cultural patterns. As for the black-skinned peoples with whom the Europeans only began to come into close and continuous contact when they began to open up the hinterland of Africa during the second half of the nineteenth century, the cultural difference was from the beginning so vast, so apparently unbridgeable that the concept of 'equality', except in the purely theological sense, seemed irrelevant and inapplicable. Marjorie Perham expressed the situation well in her Reith Lectures in 1961 dealing primarily with West Africa: 'the suddenness and strength of this penetration [which] meant taking over tribal Africa just as it was, almost intact, and then confronting it with twentieth-century Europe . . . [was] a cruel trick which history played on [the Africans] and . . . upon us Europeans'.[13]

This kind of cultural confrontation was probably far more influential in shaping British attitudes about what they loosely called 'race' than any of the notorious works of Joseph-Arthur Gobineau or Houston Stewart Chamberlain, which were probably read, if at all, only by a small number of cranks. We do know, however, that an enormous number of people did read Benjamin Kidd. His book *Social Evolution*, first published in 1893, sold so many copies and ran into so many editions that he was able to retire from the civil service and subsist for the remaining twenty-three years of his life as a freelance writer.

It is still worth reading *Social Evolution* to see how Social-Darwinism ideas were disseminated among a popular audience. The criterion of survival, wrote Kidd, was 'social efficiency', and survival had to be fought for in a highly competitive environment. 'Societies, like the individuals comprising them, are to be regarded as the product of the circumstances in which they exist,—the survival of the fittest in the rivalry which is constantly in progress . . . the resources of the individual are drawn upon to the fullest extent to keep the rivalry (of societies) to the highest pitch; the winning societies gradually extinguish their competitors, the weaker peoples disappear before the stronger, and the subordination or exclusion of the least efficient is still the prevailing feature of advancing humanity'.

According to Kidd, 'The wide interval between the people who have attained the highest social development and the lowest races is not mainly the result of a difference in intellectual, but of a difference in ethical development. . . . Members of the inferior races . . . scarcely ever possess those qualities of intense application and of prolonged persevering effort, without which it is absolutely impossible to obtain high proficiency in any branch of learning. . . . The lacking qualities are not intellectual qualities at all; they are precisely those which contribute in so high a degree to social efficiency and racial ascendancy and they are consequently, as might be expected, the invariable inheritance of those races which have reached a state of high social development and of those races only'. It was, said

Kidd, 'the Teutonic peoples [who] possess . . . qualities, not in themselves
intellectual, which contribute to a higher degree to social efficiency'; and
this accounted for 'the . . . triumphant and overwhelming expansion of
the peoples of Teutonic stock'.[14]

The Teutonic races, and the British race in particular, thus owed their
pre-eminence to having developed, over the centuries, the correct blend
of social and individual qualities which best enabled them to survive and
defeat their rivals in a highly competitive environment. One need look no
further for their right to rule.

That right was seen as carrying with it the positive duty of exercising
authority in regions, such as India and Egypt, where conquest or trade
had brought the British into contact with 'inferior' races; for their authority, in the words of Alfred Lord Milner, 'is the only one capable, under
present circumstances, of ensuring to the peoples of these countries the
primary blessings of order and justice'.[15] It never occurred to Milner and
his contemporaries to doubt that 'order and justice', as the British understood it, was what these peoples needed, and when one considers the
administrative confusion in which they found Egypt in the 1880s, and
the situation which they confronted in West Africa a decade later, it would
have been surprising if it had. The cultural relativism of the anthropologist
did not come naturally to them. They felt they had duties, responsibilities.
They moved into these areas with the tight-lipped determination of san-
itary squads cleansing infected buildings, making them fit for human hab-
itation.

Nowhere can one see this more clearly than in Egypt, where Milner
first cut his imperial teeth. Milner's study, *England in Egypt,* became one
of the text-books of Imperialism at the turn of the century. The British
went into Egypt, according to Milner, simply to restore order, but this
meant reforming the Egyptian administration root and branch. And they
intended to stay there until the Egyptians could run their own affairs
properly. There was nothing in it, economically, for Britain. Egypt's trade
in the eighties and nineties was overwhelmingly with countries other than
the British. But they had to stay until the Egyptians showed themselves
capable of doing a decent job. Milner described an imaginary conversation
between an Englishman and an Egyptian, with the former saying, 'We do
not want to stay in your country for ever. We don't despair of your learning
to manage decently your own affairs. . . . You need to be shown what to
do, but you also need to practise doing it. You need energy, initiative, self-
reliance'.[16] Thus might the head of a house at a British public school exhort
a rather unsatisfactory junior rugger team.

This consciousness of racial superiority, and of the responsibilities that went with it, inspired all the great British proconsuls. Frederick Lugard in West Africa described how, 'as Roman imperialism laid the foundations of modern civilisation and led the wild barbarians of these islands along the path of progress, so in Africa today we are repaying the debt, and bringing to the dark places of the earth, the abode of barbarism and cruelty, the torch of culture and progress, while ministering to the needs of our own civilisation'; and declared firmly, 'We hold these countries because it is the genius of our race to colonise, to trade, and to govern'.[17]

And in a very revealing article on 'The Government of Subject Races', originally printed in *The Edinburgh Review* for January 1908, Lord Cromer set out the views of what he called 'a sound but reasonable Imperialist'.[18] It was of course necessary, he wrote, to govern in the interests of the subject peoples. But he added,

> We need not always enquire too closely what these peoples, who are after all *in statu pupillari,* themselves think best in their own interests, although that is a point which deserves serious consideration. But it is essential that each special issue should be decided mainly with reference to what, by the light of Western knowledge and experience tempered by local considerations, we conscientiously think is best for the subject race, without any real or supposed advantage which may accrue to England as a nation or—as is more frequently the case—to the special interests represented by some one or more in-fluential class of Englishman.

If the English pursued such a just and disinterested policy they might hope to gain, not the love of their subjects, but some sort of cosmopolitan allegiance grounded 'on the respect always accorded to superior talents and unselfish conduct, and on the gratitude derived both from favours conferred and from those to come'.

What Cromer and his contemporaries preached in fact was enlightened despotism; always the most precarious and the shortest-lived of regimes. 'Do not let us for a moment believe', Cromer warned,

> that the fatally simple idea of despotic rule will readily give way to the far more complex conception of ordered liberty. The transfor-mation, if it takes place at all, will probably be the work, not of generations, but of centuries. . . . Our primary duty is, not to intro-duce a system which under the specious cloak of free institutions, will enable a small minority of natives to misgovern their country-

men, but to establish one which will enable the mass of the population to be governed according to the code of Christian morality. . . . Before Orientals can attain anything approaching to the British ideal of self-government, they will have to undergo very numerous transmigrations of political thought.[19]

It can be said that although the British governed the Egyptians for two generations on the whole very honourably and very justly, they did not begin to understand them; and though the Egyptians learned to respect certain qualities in their British rulers, they did not begin to like them. It was not a good formula for an enduring regime, and it was Milner himself who first recognised, after the war of 1914–18, that it had broken down, and that the Egyptians, whatever their lack of qualifications for the task, must be left to govern themselves. The capacity of the British race to govern the Egyptians better than they could themselves was still undoubted. What was in question was their continuing will to do so.

What, finally, of war? Compared with previous empires, the military element in the growth and maintenance of British rule was not large. The main impulse in British expansion had been one of trade and settlement, and the principal task of naval and military forces had been to eliminate Britain's European rivals from the scene. But in the second half of the nineteenth century the emphasis began to change. In India, the Mutiny transformed what had been basically a trading Empire into an explicitly military one, with an army of occupation whose primary duties were to assist the civil power in maintaining British rule. Simultaneously the advance of Russian power towards the Oxus gave Britain what she had not had in her history since the Act of Union with Scotland; a land frontier with another and potentially hostile State. The British Army for the first time had a permanent raison d'être, comparable to those of its great continental rivals, and began to emerge as a comparable factor in administration, if not in politics. It was of India that the British primarily thought when the Army was mentioned, and the work of Kipling did much to fix the stereotype in the popular mind. But most of the actual fighting occurred in Africa; against the Egyptians, against the Boers, against the Zulus, against the Ashantis, and finally against the Boers again. The generation of High Imperialists were very conscious of the military basis of British expansion during their lifetime, and they saw that their children were as well. The works of G. A. Henty and of Rider Haggard were staple reading for boys in the Edwardian era, and there can have been few school libraries or schoolrooms which did not contain a lavishly illustrated edition of *Deeds that Won the Empire*.

At the level of what we might term High Culture, this emphasis on military matters was no less intense. From Darwin, on the one hand, and Hegel, on the other, the belief in the inevitability of, and the social necessity for, armed conflict in the development of mankind was deeply rooted in the minds of the late Victorians and the Edwardians; though the matter was discussed with much greater enthusiasm before rather than after the Boer War. Writing in *The Nineteenth Century* in 1899, Sidney Low pointed out that '[t]here is scarcely a nation in the world—certainly not in our high-strung, masterful, Caucasian world—that does not value itself chiefly for its martial achievements. . . . A righteous and necessary war is no more brutal than a surgical operation. Better give the patient some pain, and make your own fingers unpleasantly red, than allow the disease to grow upon him until he becomes an offence to himself and the world and dies in lingering agony'.[20] That the war which broke out in South Africa a few months later was 'righteous and necessary' seemed to Low and most of his colleagues quite self-evident. Professor Cramb of London University welcomed it ecstatically. 'War', he declared, 'is the supreme act in the life of the State, and it is the motives which impel, the ideal which is pursued, that determine the greatness or insignificance of that act. . . . The War in South Africa . . . is the first event or series of events upon a great scale; the genesis lies in this force named Imperialism. It is the first conspicuous expression of this ideal in the world of action— of heroic action, which now as always implies heroic suffering'.[21] For the Social Darwinians it was part of the process by which the British people had to show themselves fit to survive. War, Karl Pearson warned his countrymen in 1900, involved 'suffering, intense suffering' but without wars progress would be impossible. 'The dependence of progress on the survival of the fitter race, terribly black as it may seem to some of you, gives the struggle for existence its redeeming features; it is the fiery crucible out of which comes the finest metal'. A nation, he said, had to be 'kept up to a high pitch of efficiency by contest, chiefly by war with inferior races, by the struggle for trade routes and for the sources of raw material and of food supply'.[22]

It was as Benjamin Kidd had written in *Social Evolution* in 1896: 'The law of life has always been the same from the beginning,—ceaseless and inevitable struggle and competition, ceaseless and inevitable progress'.[23] And what was so worrying about the Boer War was that the confusion and incompetence of its conduct made people wonder whether the British

really were 'fit to survive'. It was something that worried the Fabians no
less than it did the Imperialists of the Right Wing. In his pamphlet *Fabianism and the Empire* George Bernard Shaw demanded, as part of 'the
effective social organisation of the whole Empire, and its rescue from the
strife of classes and private interest', the transformation of the army into
a citizen body based on national service for all, involving 'a combination
of physical exercises, technical education, education in civil citizenship . . .
and field training in the use of modern weapons'.[24] It led Kipling to his
philippic against the established orders in *The Islanders,* with their 'flan-
nelled fools at the wicket or the muddied oafs at the goal'; the indifferent
landed gentry, the greedy and short-sighted commercial classes, the self-
absorbed workers, the frivolous intellectuals; and to his vision, published
in 1904, of *The Army of a Dream,* an elaborate fantasy in which compulsory
military service dissolved all the class conflicts of the time and made England Merrie again.[25]

Writing in 1909 to a master at Eton, Lord Esher told him that his boys
'cannot begin too early to train to defend their country and Empire. It is
not only physical training that is required, but they should acquire early
the habit of thinking over the problems of National Defence. . . . If our
country is to maintain the place which our forefathers won for us, physical
training is a vital part of the Englishman's equipment, and rational thinking men who watch the trend of events, not only in Europe but all over
the world, begin to see that the use of arms is also an essential part of a
sound educational curriculum'. In order to survive in the new, harsher
world of the twentieth century, the young manhood of Britain, like its
contemporaries on the Continent, had to be carefully and scientifically
trained and indoctrinated for war. 'It is', Esher added, 'most necessary that
their minds as well as their bodies should be trained on military lines
when they are young. It is just as important to be taught early to think
correctly upon matters affecting the defence of our country and the Empire
as to be taught the truths of history and science'.[26] It was also a consideration not far from the minds of the authorities of the University of
Oxford when in 1909 they established a Chair in the History of War.[27]

What seemed particularly disturbing was the probability, increasingly
accepted during the first decade of the new century, that in the very near
future the British fitness to survive would be put to the test by an adversary
even stronger and better armed than the Boers; and if the British military
capacity could be stretched to breaking point by the Boers, how could it
cope with the Germans—a nation among whom the teachings of Hegel
and Darwin were taken even more seriously than they were in Britain? For

those Edwardians who concerned themselves with such matters, the need to create a military organisation, and to evoke a military spirit to inspire it, became a matter of increasing concern; no longer to defend the frontiers of Empire, and to maintain order within them, but to save Britain herself from a national humiliation far worse than Jena or Waterloo.

Confronted by a bombardment of German militaristic writings between 1904 and 1914, British writers showed themselves less inclined than were their Teutonic cousins to glorify war as the supreme act of the State, and adopted a more pragmatic and defensive approach to the military problems which confronted them. Not all did, however. In 1907 Colonel F. N. Maude brought out a book entitled *War and the World's Life*; probably in connection with the new edition of Clausewitz *On War* to which he contributed a foreword. Much of the work was a direct transcription of Benjamin Kidd; but whereas Kidd had evoked the ethical principle of character, hard work, and self-abnegation which subordinates the individual to the group as a feature of social life in general, for Colonel Maude it was applicable solely to war. 'Two Races', he warned, 'may be equal in physical capacity, in intelligence and directing ability, but if the standard of self-sacrifice in the one is lower than in the other, the balance will infallibly turn against it in the final arbitrament on the field of Battle'. 'Races have survived in precise proportion to the purity of the conception of self-sacrifice embodied in their respective creeds', he wrote. 'We are governed by the spirits of our dead; and I submit that this inherited instinct of self-sacrifice is so deeply ingrained in the race that the intellectual disturbances of the moment, whatever they may be from time to time, no more ruffle its foundation than the waves of a storm trouble the bed of the ocean'.

The British people he believed to be sound at heart; and '[i]f we succeed in imparting to the youth of the Nation the elementary concepts of religion and morality, together with a respect for the deeds of their forefathers, and a knowledge of all they have bequeathed to us, then I think that the training for the final act of battle can be well attained in the time available'. His final conclusion was inspiring or macabre, depending on the way one looks at it. 'Given a Leader who, conscious of the power latent in the Race and the means by which to develop it, applies all the means which science has now rendered available to the definite end of teaching men "to know how to die"—not how to avoid dying—and we shall soon find men as ready as ever were their ancestors to clamour for the right of rushing to what will appear to them to be certain death, when they know that thereby they will attain a great end'.[28]

One can by selective quotation from a narrow range of writers present an alarming picture of pre-1914 Britain as a proto-Fascist society, but in fact it was nothing of the kind. The ideas expressed by such writers as Maude existed generally in very mild solution. The pride in Empire, the belief in the superiority of Anglo-Saxon culture, the consciousness of military achievement in the past and the determination if necessary to parallel it in the future, all this was there, but without rancour or fanaticism; still underpinned by a strong Christian ethic and leavened by the values of Victorian liberalism. What could have happened if Britain had lost the war; whether these sentiments would have turned sour and fanatical and acquired the sinister power that they did elsewhere in Europe is, fortunately, no part of the historian's task to assess; but it would be realistic to assume that we would not have been immune to the disease.

As it was, although Edwardian Britain was conscious of the need for the martial virtues and spasmodic efforts were made to inculcate them, it cannot be called a militaristic society; indeed the lack of active interest in military matters and the low prestige enjoyed by the Army among the bulk of the population was a matter of repeated complaint. The flood of 'next war' literature which reached a climax with the 'Dreadnought Scare' of 1909 had as its almost constant theme the total unpreparedness of Britain to deal with the probable eventuality of a German invasion. The repeated official inquiries into the dangers posed by such an invasion all took as their starting point the assumption that it would have to be dealt with by the Navy and the Army in the context of an indifferent, certainly an un-mobilised, population. The agitation for the introduction of National Service, though it mustered such impressive leaders as Lord Milner and Field Marshal Lord Roberts, never became a matter for serious discussion within the government. The Territorial Army was created as a second-line reserve, and found little difficulty in recruiting the enthusiastic amateurs who previously had founded the volunteer regiments in the towns or officered the Militia and Yeomanry in the country, but this was very far from being a People in Arms. H. G. Wells complained, in *Mr. Britling Sees it Through*, of this remoteness of the Armed Forces from the rest of the nation.

> The army had been a thing aloof, for a special end. It had developed all the characteristics of a caste. It had very high standards along the lines of its specialisation, but it was inadaptable and conservative. Its exclusiveness was not so much a deliberate culture as a consequence of its detached function. . . . Directly one grasped how apart the army lived from the ordinary life of the community, from industri-

alism or from economic necessities, directly one understood how the great mass of Englishmen were simply 'outsiders' to the War Office mind, one began to realise the complete unfitness of either government or War Office for the conduct of so great a national effort as was now needed.[29]

The creation of a nation in arms thus remained no more than an aspiration of largely maverick politicians and publicists until the outbreak of war in 1914 took matters out of their hands.

The trouble was that the whole traditional apparatus of Empire, and the patterns of thought associated with it, could only with difficulty be adjusted to dealing with the type of continental threat offered by Germany. None of the stock responses, naval, military or civilian, were appropriate to it. Almost as a matter of habit publicists like Lord Esher and Spenser Wilkinson, in campaigning for the National Service League, continued to talk about 'the Defence of the Empire', but the defence of the Empire was no longer the principal problem. By 1909 Britain had made peace with her main imperial rivals, France and Russia. No one was now going to attack India or Egypt, let alone Canada, Australia or South Africa. Germany could not get at them. But Germany could get at Britain herself, if she defeated France on land and the Royal Navy at sea; and when Esher declared, as he did in a speech to the Imperial Press Conference in 1909, that '[t]he basis of Imperial defence was the unity of the Empire under one flag', and that 'if we were to hold our own among the Imperial races of the world, the wealth and population of the Empire should be organised in peace with a view to the demands which would inevitably be made on them in war',[30] he was not really talking about the defence of the Empire as such. He was talking about the mobilising of imperial resources under British control for the defence of the United Kingdom, which was a different matter; as such statesmen as Deakin of Australia and Laurier of Canada realised very well.

Moreover the essence of Imperial Defence, as was generally recognised, was naval, not military. If Britain lost 'command of the sea' she would lose both her Empire and her own immunity from invasion. And command of the sea had to be fought for, not in the North Atlantic or the Indian Ocean, but in the North Sea, and it was there that the Admiralty wished to see the Imperial Fleet concentrated. Similarly the General Staff wished to see the military organisation and armament of the Empire standardised on the British model and integrated with the British staff organisation— to make it look better it was renamed the Imperial General Staff—to enable contingents from the Empire to take their place alongside British troops on the battlefields where the war would finally be decided; and the overwhelming probability was that this would be in Europe. As it happened, the entry of the Ottoman Empire into the war on the side of the Central Powers was to provide Imperial troops—Indian, Australian and New Zealanders—with imperial battlefields of their own, the Dardanelles, Palestine and Mesopotamia; but basically the Empire had to be defended in France and Flanders in a struggle the grimness and prolonged nature of which came as no surprise to a generation which had been brought up from boyhood to expect just such a test of the Nation's 'fitness to survive'.

Eventually the war was won, and the Imperial contribution was handsomely acknowledged. Cenotaphs everywhere commemorated the dead of the British Empire. An Imperial War Museum was established to record the struggle, an Imperial Defence College to study its lessons. But already the mood had changed. Within the Colonial Office the concept of Imperial Rule was increasingly seen as one of 'trusteeship'. How could it be otherwise, after a war allegedly fought in the name of democracy and self-determination? The work of Lugard and his colleagues had introduced ideas of cultural relativism that eroded the serene assumption of racial superiority. The diffusion of European ideas of self-government among indigenous elites could be contained only by violent repression of a kind that the newly-enlarged domestic electorate was unwilling to support. As for the defence of the Empire, this was beginning to present problems on so massive a scale that Britain's military leaders were foremost among those who, in the 1930s, wished to avoid or at least postpone war at almost any cost. The Empire was still a 'fact', but increasingly seen (except by Lord Beaverbrook) as an embarrassing one. It was still certainly a Heritage, but one which, like so many estates inherited within Britain itself during this period, was too large to be kept up by a new and impoverished generation. The consciousness of being an 'Imperial Race' was not widespread among the British after 1918. After 1945 it disappeared altogether. The way was clear for a new, but no less moralistic, generation to castigate their forebears for ever having entertained such illusions.

5

The

Edwardian

Arms

Race

The moral is obvious; it is that great armaments lead inevitably to war. . . . The increase of armaments that is intended for each nation to produce consciousness of strength, and a sense of security, does not produce these effects. On the contrary, it produces a consciousness of the strength of other nations and a sense of fear. . . . The enormous growth of armaments in Europe, the sense of insecurity and fear caused by them—it was these that made war inevitable.[1]

In this much-quoted passage of his memoirs Lord Grey of Falloden reflected with understandable bitterness on the failure of his life's work. It is indeed one of the great ironies of British history that a parliament that could with some reason claim to be the first fully to represent the new mass electorate, and a government that, far more even than those of Mr. Gladstone, embodied all the irenical aspirations of Richard Cobden and John Bright, should not only have taken Britain into the most terrible war in its history but have presided over the greatest peace-time increase on armaments expenditure that the country had ever witnessed.

In his eve-of-poll speech in the Albert Hall on December 21, 1905, the incoming Prime Minister, Sir Henry Campbell-Bannerman, pledged himself to control arms expenditure. 'A policy of huge armaments keeps alive and stimulates and feeds the belief that force is the best if not the only solution of international differences'. Such a programme, he pointed out, swallowed up resources needed for the policy of radical social reform to which his party had pledged itself. So 'what nobler role,' demanded

Campbell-Bannerman in words to be enthusiastically welcomed by the radical press, 'could this great country assume than at the fitting moment to place itself at the head of a League of Peace through whose instrumentality the great work of peaceful arbitration is to be effected?'[2]

A few weeks later the electorate returned a House of Commons whose support for such proposals was overwhelming. Four hundred and fifty Liberal and Labour members crowded the government benches. Unionists (as the Conservatives were then called) and Irish Nationalists mustered only 240 votes between them. Nothing had been seen like it since the landslide of 1833, though something very comparable was to happen again in 1945. Two-thirds of the total membership, and half the Liberal representation, had never sat in the Commons before; 'young men', in Elie Halévy's words, 'intellectuals, journalists, university professors, champions of all those eccentric causes which arouse the enthusiasm of British philanthropy. They had stood for election or allowed themselves to be put up simply in order that as far as possible the Liberal vote might be taken in every constituency. Now they found themselves returned, often to their utter amazement'.[3] Such a body of forward-thinking idealists, consciously rejecting the prejudices of the previous century and controlling the legislature of the most powerful nation in the world, might have been expected, if anyone could, to bring the arms race under control and introduce a new era of international relations in which states would peacefully settle their differences by arbitration. As it was, after reducing expenditure on the armed forces from £66 million in 1905–6 to £59.2 million two years later, they were then to increase it progressively until on the eve of the First World War they voted the sum, unprecedented in peacetime, of £77 million to the armed services.[4]

Whatever went wrong? For some, the explanation was to be found in the machinations of the armaments manufacturers, those 'merchants of death', whose undeniable success in exploiting the situation to the profit of their shareholders was to be documented by two generations of radical writers.[5] For others it was the activity of the Admiralty or of the newly created Army General Staff. Explanations such as these tend to overrate the persuasiveness of the pressure-groups concerned and the naivety of political decision-makers; who had, after all, to defend their policies before both their electorates and their implacably inquisitorial back-benchers. As Lloyd George, the Chancellor of the Exchequer, warned Asquith in February 1909,

I will not dwell upon the emphatic pledges given by all of us before and at the last election to reduce the gigantic expenditure on armaments built up by the recklessness of our predecessors. Scores of our most loyal supporters in the House of Commons take these pledges seriously and even a £3 million increase will chill their zeal for the Government and an assured increase of £5–6 million for next year will stagger them. . . . [They] will hardly think it worth while to keep in office a Liberal Ministry.[6]

The argument was rammed home by repeated petitions and motions by Liberal and Labour members for the reduction of military expenditures. There would have been no lack of public and parliamentary support for Ministers if they had decided to make a stand against the 'militarists' and the merchants of death.

The failure of the Liberal Cabinet to do anything of the kind, and their acquiescence in the increasing demands made on the taxpayer by their military and still more by their naval advisers, can not be explained by any such weakness or simplemindedness. They participated in 'the arms race' because they had, slowly and with the greatest reluctance, come to certain conclusions about the international situation; conclusions whose validity seemed confirmed with every year that passed and with which few historians would quarrel today. Basically it appeared to them that the dominant elements inside Germany, a nation with which British liberals were anxious to preserve traditional links of friendship, were increasingly dissatisfied with what they saw as a disparity between the potential and the actual power of their country; increasingly alarmed by internal tensions that they felt could be relieved only by external expansion; and increasingly inclined to view Britain, and specifically British naval supremacy, as the principal obstacle to that transformation of the status quo which would alone make possible the fulfilment of their large if misty aspirations towards *Weltmacht*.[7]

The maintenance of peace always depends on general agreement as to the acceptability of the existing status quo, and it was by no means evident in the first decade of the twentieth century that any such agreement existed. It was in fact the sad destiny of the new Liberal Administration to take office at the precise moment that the century-old pattern of international relations on which British security depended was being transformed. Traditional rivalries over imperial possessions with the traditional adversaries, France and Russia, were ceasing to have any but marginal significance. Russia's impotence after her defeat at the hands of the Japanese was being exploited by the Germans to force a confrontation with France over Morocco; and another military defeat of France à la 1870 would leave the way clear for a Germany whose naval building programme, and the political agitation associated with it, suggested that her ruling classes were only awaiting a favourable opportunity to confront and humiliate England herself.

Such was the situation in Europe, at least as perceived from the Foreign Office, when the Campbell-Bannerman Administration took office at the end of 1905; full of honourable goodwill, anxious to transcend the evils of the old 'balance of power' system and aspiring to take the lead among the Great Powers in reducing great armaments and establishing a new League of Peace.

In spite of the sombre international outlook, an appropriate opportunity for taking such an initiative presented itself almost at once. In April 1906 the Russian government invited the Powers to meet again the following year at The Hague, to continue the task of building institutions for peace and establishing restraints on war begun at the first Hague Conference in 1899. Although arms limitation was not on the suggested agenda, the Liberal Administration, under strong pressure from its supporters both inside and outside the House of Commons, thought that this would be a good forum in which to raise the question, and Campbell-Bannerman made public his intention to do so in an article published by the new radical journal, *The Nation,* in March 1907.[8] At the time of the first Hague Conference, he pointed out,

> it was already perceived that the endless multiplication of the engines of war was futile and self-defeating; and the years that have passed have only served to strengthen and intensify that impression. . . . It would surprise me to hear it alleged that the interests of the Powers in any respect impose on them a divergence of standpoint so absolute and irreconcilable that the mere discussion of the limitation of armaments would be fraught with danger.

He concluded with the yet more sanguine expectation, that reduction of armaments would not affect British command of the seas:

> The sea power of this country implies no challenge to any single State or group of States. I am persuaded that throughout the world that power is recognised as non-aggressive, and innocent of designs against the independence, the commercial freedom and the legitimate development of other States, and that it is, therefore, a mistake to imagine that the naval Powers will be disposed to regard our

position on the sea as a bar to any proposal for the arrest of armaments. . . . Our known adhesion to those two dominant principles—
the independence of nationalities and the freedom of trade—entitles
us of itself to claim that, if our fleets be invulnerable, they carry with
them no menace across the waters of the world, but a message of
the most cordial good will.

Alas: Campbell-Bannerman was not the last British Prime Minister to
assume that his values and perceptions were universally shared by his continental neighbours. Like most members of the 'Peace Lobby' at the time
and since, he identified 'peace' with the maintenance of the status quo;
and since the status quo rested upon British command of the seas, even
the Radicals took British maritime supremacy for granted and had done
so ever since the days of Cobden and Bright.

Foreigners, unfortunately, saw things differently. Germany was not the
only country where the British proposal was seen as an attempt to freeze
the arms balance while it was still favourable to the United Kingdom. 'This
quaint manifesto', as Halévy drily described it, 'which began with a pacifist
act of faith to conclude by subscription to the creed of [Alfred Thayer]
Mahan created a bad impression in every Continental country'.[9] The German government flatly refused to discuss the question at all. The British
government then fell back on the suggestion that the Powers might at least
communicate their proposed naval construction programmes to each
other, to avoid misperception and misunderstanding. This fell equally flat:
the German and Austrian governments threatened to walk out if it was so
much as discussed. The only fruit of Campbell-Bannerman's brave initiative was an anodyne conference resolution to which not even the Germans
could object, confirming a resolution of the previous Conference with
regard to the limitation of military burdens and declaring it 'highly desirable to see governments resume the serious study of the question'.[10]

The governments principally concerned, needless to say, did nothing of
the kind, and the following January (1908) Grey warned his constituents
at Alnwick that no reduction in naval expenditure could be expected.
Britain, he told them, had no right to complain of the measures taken by
other States to protect their national interests, but upon the British fleet
depended not only the trade, but the very life and security of the country.
The Admiralty was therefore justified in maintaining a safe margin of
security, and this could not be done for nothing.[11]

It was of course on naval expenditure that public attention focussed.
Expenditure on the Army had been effectively cut back since the end of

the war in South Africa and remained thereafter at a tolerable figure. Richard Haldane's work in modernising the Army awoke little interest; partly because of his success in obscuring what he was doing by some of the most tedious and unintelligible speeches ever delivered to the House of Commons; and partly because, as *The Nation* loftily declared in June 1907, 'Army reorganisation, if safely and fitly pursued . . . may be well enough in its way, but it is no special problem of Liberalism, whose mastering ideas are intellectual and moral, which has to survey the whole field of democracy'.[12]

More to the point, Haldane reduced the Army estimates to £27.75 million in 1907 and did not permit them to rise above £28 million for the rest of the decade. The naval estimates however, which in 1907 stood little above those of the Army at £31.4 million, were within two years to rise to over £35 million and in the spring of 1914 were approaching the £50 million mark. These were the 'great armaments' that worried the Liberals so much, and had done ever since the naval arms race had got under way with the Naval Defence Act of 1889.

Four factors combined to make the naval race particularly acute. The first was the general perception, emphasised naturally by navalist propaganda but seriously denied by no one, that British security and indeed survival rested upon her naval strength. The danger that caused most concern to her naval experts was blockade, which in those civilized days was foreseen in terms of an interruption of trade sufficient to cause economic chaos rather than the outright starvation of the civilian population. The popular fear, however, and one played on by scores of cheap novels, was of foreign invasion consequent on the loss of command of the sea; an invasion almost always carried out, after Erskine Childers had set the fashion with *The Riddle of the Sands* in 1903, by Germans. In fictional literature the invasion was usually thwarted by the initiative and ingenuity of two or three adolescent males ranging in age from twelve to twenty-two; but none the less the newly constituted Committee of Imperial Defence had to spend many weary hours discussing whether an invasion was really possible and if so what should be done about it.

The Navy never wavered in its belief that neither invasion nor blockade was feasible so long as Britain maintained command of the sea, and command of the sea, it was believed, depended on the possession of a superior battle fleet. The theories of Alfred Thayer Mahan set forth in his historical writings in the early 1890s had by now become rigid dogmas shared by naval thinkers throughout the 'civilised' world. Command of the seas enabled the nation that possessed it both to thwart the enemy's attempts at blockade or invasion and to mount its own. Further, it preserved communications with those overseas possessions that industrial nations needed (so the theory ran) to maintain secure access to essential sources of raw materials and provide outlet for potentially disruptive urban populations at home. Command of the seas, it followed, went to the Nation whose strength enabled it to eliminate the enemy's battlefleet and then go on to deal with his commerce-raiders and troop transports. That strength could be precisely measured, therefore, by the number and the fighting capacity of its battleships. The battleship, with its only slightly less formidable adjunct the battle-cruiser, thus became the unit in which naval power came to be measured; and since such power alone made possible a great overseas Empire, it became also the measure, not of security alone but also of national 'greatness'. The battleship was thus a symbol of enormous emotive power, whether it symbolised national prestige or, as it did for so many British Radicals, stability, prosperity and peace.[13]

This then was the second factor accelerating the naval competition; it could be reduced to simple terms that every reader of the *Daily Mail* could be expected to understand. Nor was it at the time an oversimplification. The ocean-going submarine, which was to upset all calculations, had yet to be developed. Mines and torpedo-boats presented complex tactical problems but did not fundamentally change the balance. As a unit of power the battleship with its speed, its armour and above all its heavy guns was not only symbolic but actual, as Admiral Togo proved in the Russo-Japanese War.

Given this general assumption, was it really conceivable that the German Empire, with its industrial strength, the highly militaristic attitude of its ruling élites, and its growing aspirations after world power, would *not* join in the naval race? The politics and pressure-groups behind Tirpitz's successive naval laws have been exhaustively analysed by a succession of historians during the past twenty years.[14] They have delineated for us the motives and interests—political, industrial and social—which led to the initial decision in 1898 to lay down a battlefleet that would constitute a significant factor in any calculations of international power, and which fuelled the subsequent programme of expansion. But even if these specific forces had not been at work, is it likely that a Germany which was now challenging or surpassing British primacy in so many fields would, whatever its political and social structure, have been content indefinitely to carry on its overseas trade and colonial policy by permission of the Royal Navy? For that was the position in which it found itself. As Mahan himself pointed out in 1902, 'The dilemma of Great Britain is that she cannot help commanding the approaches to Germany by the mere possession of the very means essential to her own existence as a state of the first order'.[15] The security of the British Isles, in fact, depended on the maritime subordination of everyone else.

This was the dilemma: a battlefleet large enough to provide Germany with security against England, let alone one that effectively embodied Germany's concept of her own 'greatness', would by its very existence imperil the security not just of the British Empire but of the British Isles themselves. The structure of the situation was bad enough, but it was made a great deal worse by the popular emotions to which it gave rise. It is now fairly clear not only that anti-British feeling in Germany was deliberately provoked and exploited by interests behind the *Flottenpolitik*, but that this feeling had by 1908 reached an intensity beyond the power of the German government to control. Of this the British government was fully and anxiously aware. On March 29 of that year Grey admitted to the House of Commons how difficult it was to ask 'the German Government to expose itself before its own public opinion to a charge of having co-operated to make the attainment of our views [on arms limitation] easier'; while the following August the Kaiser brusquely informed Sir Charles Hardinge that '[n]o discussion with a Foreign Government [about German naval strength] could be tolerated; such a proposal would be contrary to the national dignity, and would give rise to internal troubles if the Government were to accept it'.[16] On the British side there was no lack of chauvinistic response to the German challenge, but as the German Ambassador in London, Count Metternich, constantly stressed, British hostility to Germany was not caused by resentment at her colonial ambitions or envy for her booming industry and trade. It was focussed entirely upon the growth of the German Navy; and so long as that Navy continued to grow, good relations between the two countries would be very hard to maintain. To which the Kaiser commented, unhelpfully if understandably, 'The British must get used to the German fleet', and he scornfully rejected 'the shameless suggestion that English friendship depends upon a curtailment of German sea power'.[17]

The third factor accelerating the naval race was thus the intensity of the fears and ambitions—British fears, German ambitions—to which it gave expression. The last was an almost fortuitous technological contribution; the decision taken by the Royal Navy in 1904 to take the lead in initiating a new type of battleship, the *Dreadnought*, which took naval developments over the past hundred years to their logical conclusion by recognising that warships were now simply floating gun-platforms, and that their effective-

ness could therefore be precisely measured in terms of their speed and of
the power and range of their guns; a conclusion that seemed confirmed
by the outcome of the Battle of Tsushima a few months later. With its
main battery of $10 \times 12''$ guns and its turbine engines producing speed
of up to twenty-two knots the *Dreadnought* could outshoot and outsteam
any battleship afloat. It was launched on February 10, 1906; only three
days before the new House of Commons, pledged to the reduction of
great armaments, assembled at Westminster.

This bold innovation caused as much concern to conservatives, both
inside and outside the Royal Navy, as it did to Radicals inside and outside
the House of Commons. Once foreign navies followed suit, as they un-
doubtedly would, the whole battleship strength of the Royal Navy would
be rendered obsolete, and the Two Power Standard on which British security had rested ever since 1889 would have to be calculated in Dreadnoughts alone. To this the First Sea Lord, Admiral Sir John Fisher, had
two answers. The first was that technological innovation in arms was inevitable and that if the British did not take the lead someone else would.
His second argument was more questionable: it was that, although the
Royal Navy would now have to start from scratch in maintaining its naval
ascendancy, the undoubted capacity of the British shipbuilding industry
to build faster than its competitors would always keep it comfortably in
the lead. As the outgoing Conservative First Lord, the Earl of Cawdor,
expressed it in his valedictory memorandum of December 1905,

> However formidable foreign shipbuilding programmes may appear
> on paper, we can always overtake them in consequence of our re-
> sources and our power of rapid construction. . . . While [we] antic-
> ipate at present that the output of four large ships a year should
> suffice to meet our requirements, there will be no difficulty whatever
> in increasing this output to whatever may be necessary in conse-
> quence of any increase of naval power abroad.[18]

These and other reassurances were generally accepted, and there is no
doubt that the introduction of the Dreadnought programme seriously
embarrassed the Germans. Their Naval Law of 1900 had made provision
for the construction of battleships over a twenty-year programme. The
additional expenditure called for by a Dreadnought programme now made
necessary a new Supplementary Law, while the increased size of the vessels
necessitated, at great cost, the widening of the Kiel Canal. Fisher himself
had no qualms whatever, and raised no objections when the incoming
Liberal Administration reduced the current building programme from

four ships to three, with a promise of a further reduction to two if the
Hague Conference could produce agreement on arms limitation. Britain
could at that time look forward to possessing seven Dreadnoughts and
heavy battle-cruisers (*Invincibles*) by 1909, by which date Germany would
still have none. The existing margin of supremacy over Germany was so
great, wrote Fisher in September 1906, 'as to render it absurd to talk of
anything endangering our naval supremacy, *even if we stopped all shipbuilding altogether!*'[19]

Given these circumstances it is not surprising that the German government showed no interest in British proposals for freezing the status quo.
But the German naval building programme was in any case determined by
internal forces more complex than any simple assessment of the Dreadnought balance, and by 1906 Tirpitz was already under pressure from the
Right Wing to increase the building of battleships to a rate far beyond
anything that he considered necessary or even safe. Already expenditure
both on the German Army and on social services was suffering in consequence of expenditure on the navy, and any increase could be met only by
heavier taxes on either property or consumption, with all the divisive social
consequences that would follow. Neither could he quite shake off the fear
that, if the German battlefleet grew too obviously and too fast, the British
would destroy it (as the Japanese had destroyed the Russian fleet at Port
Arthur) in a pre-emptive strike.[20] But some increase in the building tempo
was necessary if he was to catch up on the British lead. In 1907 Tirpitz
prepared the Supplementary Law, or *Novelle*, which the Reichstag passed
in February 1908. This increased the building rate (*Bautempo*) to four
ships a year between 1908 and 1911, so as to produce fourteen capital
ships by 1912 and fifty-eight (instead of the thirty-eight originally visualised) by 1920.[21]

The failure of the Hague Conference, the new *Novelle* of 1908 and the
brusque rejections of all offers of limitation disheartened all but the stal-
warts among the British peace lobby. Nevertheless the demands which the
Admiralty published in February 1908 for their building programme for
1908–9 created consternation among the Government's supporters. Those
for the following year brought them to the verge of revolt. The 1908
estimates showed an increase over the previous year of just under a million
pounds and had it not been for the efforts of Lloyd George they would
greatly have exceeded that figure. On the other hand, the Conservatives
and the Naval Lobby saw it as a totally inadequate response to the *Novelle*,
pointing out that with only a slight increase in their building tempo the
Germans might actually gain a lead in Dreadnoughts by 1912. This the

Government strongly denied. But Asquith none the less had to promise that if there was by 1909 any indication that the Germans were likely to attain such an advance, the Cabinet would take the necessary steps to prevent it—something that the superior speed of British shipbuilding would always render possible. The well-meant efforts of the Kaiser to defuse the situation with his letter to Lord Tweedmouth in February and his *Daily Telegraph* interview the following October of course made matters very much worse.

By the end of 1908 indeed both governments were being blown almost out of control by the winds of chauvinistic public opinion in their respective countries. Reports from Germany, not only from diplomats but from journalists, were increasingly alarming. 'At the bottom of every German heart today', the British naval attaché reported in July, 'is rising a faint and wildly exhilarating hope that a glorious day is approaching when by a brave breaking through of the lines which he feels are encircling him, he might even wrest the command of the seas from England and thus become a member of the greatest power by land or sea that the world has ever seen'.[22] He exaggerated of course, but he was summarising very fairly the message of such influential bodies as the *Flotteverein* and the *Alldeutsche Verband*. In England a new breed of super-hawks appeared for whom even the Navy League was too moderate and who founded their own Imperial Maritime League to agitate for greater naval strength. Invasion literature began to proliferate. The scene was set for the Great Panic of 1909.

The story of that Panic has been often and fully told; by Sir Llewellyn Woodward, by Professor Arthur Marder, not least by one of the most eminent of contemporary witnesses, Sir Winston Churchill. It arose out of two distinct if complementary perceptions by the Admiralty of what was going on in Germany. The first was that the Germans were secretly increasing their rate of construction, their *Bautempo*, so that by 1912 they would have, not thirteen Dreadnoughts to the anticipated British eighteen, but at least seventeen and very possibly twenty-one. The second was that this programme was made possible by a huge expansion in the German construction industries in general and Krupps works in particular, which destroyed the basis on which all British calculations of superiority had hitherto been made: that in case of need the British shipyards could always build faster than anyone else.

This alarming information led Reginald McKenna, the First Lord of the Admiralty and once the most rigorous of Gladstonian economists, to recommend in December 1908 that the Royal Navy should lay down six Dreadnoughts in the building programme of 1908–9—a proposal resisted

within the Cabinet both by Lloyd George at the Exchequer and by Winston Churchill at the Board of Trade. They saw the whole thing as an
Admiral's ramp. 'Frankly I believe the Admirals are procuring false information to frighten us', Lloyd George told Churchill on January 3, 1909;
'I do not believe the Germans are at all anxious to hurry up their building
programme, quite the reverse'.[23] But the rumours were coming not only
through official but, even more prolifically, through unofficial channels,
fed naturally enough by the British arms lobby. The unfortunate German
ambassador, Count Metternich, to whom Tirpitz was reluctant to provide
any information whatever, found himself in the impossible position of
having to prove a negative. The storm began to rise on the opposition
benches and in the popular press. McKenna's six Dreadnoughts, which
Churchill and Lloyd George fought to reduce to four, appeared inadequate
to the conservatives and their navalist supporters who clamoured for a
minimum of eight. The 'Peace Lobby', on the other hand, were cowed.
The sombre figures quoted by Government Ministers silenced all but the
most persistent of their Radical critics. The problem, as Grey explained,
was one of German capabilities, not of their intentions. 'The German
intention not to accelerate their programme we perfectly accept, but in all
good faith, without any breach of undertaking . . . they could accumulate
the power to accelerate, supposing the European situation changed and
with it their intention'.[24]

In face of such logic 'our men', as one Radical put it, 'scattered like
sheep'.[25] Only seventy-nine members could be found to vote against the
Government. Asquith deftly defused the issue by fixing the number of
Dreadnoughts to be built immediately at four, with four more to follow
if the case for them could be proved. The building programmes of Germany's allies, Austria-Hungary and Italy, provided the justification that was
to tip the balance in favour of eight.

In the event the alarmists proved wrong. By 1912 the German Navy
had, not twenty-one Dreadnoughts, not seventeen, not even thirteen, but
only nine, with the British riding high with a comfortable total of fifteen.

The Radicals had every reason to be exultant. The 1909 Panic has been
cited in arms race literature ever since as a classic example of misperceptions, stoked by rumour, propaganda and false information, distorting
government policy and feeding an escalating and ultimately disastrous
competition. On some young men at the time—Philip Noel Baker, aged
nineteen, was still at Cambridge, Fenner Brockway, aged twenty, was on
the staff of the radical *Examiner*—it made a life-long impression, and they
were to campaign passionately for disarmament till the last quarter of the

twentieth century. But Winston Churchill, over whose protests the naval programme had gone forward, was more equivocal. In *The World Crisis* he later admitted that 'so far as the facts and figures were concerned we were strictly right. The gloomy Admiralty anticipations were in no respect fulfilled for the year 1912 . . . but although the Chancellor of the Exchequer and I were right in the narrow sense, we were absolutely wrong in relation to the deep tides of destiny'.[26]

To put this in less dramatic terms, although the perception of German intentions—at least in the short term—was incorrect, the perception of their capabilities was not. They could now build as fast as, if not faster than, the British. And it was this that struck home with such a chill shock—a shock comparable to that felt fifty years later in the United States when, in 1958, the launching of *Sputnik* by the Soviet Union revealed that the Americans were no longer world leaders in missile technology. There might not be, as was then believed, an immediate 'missile gap' any more than there had been a 'Dreadnought gap'. But the Americans, like the British before them, had now to live with the knowledge that their safety would in future rest on far more insecure foundations than it had ever done in the past.

It had taken only three years to disperse the euphoric hopes of 1906, and though the Radicals in parliament and the Press continued to rail against the quickening arms race, attributing it increasingly to the machinations of the armaments manufacturers, 'the merchants of death', they found little support in a country where the conviction was now widespread that Germany had thrown down a challenge that sooner or later would have to be accepted; a conviction reflected in the comfortable majorities supporting the Government's growing naval appropriations, which after 1911 were presented with persuasive eloquence by the renegade Churchill. It was generally and not wrongly believed that responsibility for the arms race lay squarely on the shoulders, not of Vickers Armstrong and their agents but of Admiral von Tirpitz and his supporters in the German Reich. And this was a view shared in Germany itself, not least by the new Chancellor, Theobald von Bethmann-Hollweg, by the Finance Minister, Adolf Wermuth, and by the General Staff of the Army; all of whom had excellent reasons for opposing Tirpitz's plans.

For the British decision to take up the German challenge and maintain her naval superiority at whatever cost rapidly began to impose strains on the German political system that gave rise to alarm. Both Bülow and Bethmann-Hollweg, who as Chancellors were responsible for the general conduct of foreign policy, correctly discerned that it was fear of the growing German High Seas Fleet and not simple commercial rivalry that was impelling the British to align themselves increasingly closely with Germany's continental enemies. For Wermuth, who had to find the money, the choice appeared to lie between increasing taxes on consumption, thus further alienating the working classes and strengthening the socialist opposition in the Reichstag, and imposing taxes on landed property (the British solution) and so splitting the precarious coalition between the industrial and the agrarian ruling classes that held the Government together. In August 1909, after the new British programme had been announced, Wermuth warned Tirpitz that 'the internal structure of the Reich, its defense capabilities and its external prestige demand not merely a standstill but the energetic reduction of expenditure'.[27] As for the Army, its appropriations had barely increased since the beginning of the century, and the Agadir crisis in 1911, combined with its alarmed perceptions of the rapid recovery of the Russian Army after their defeat in 1905, led it to press for a massive increase in strength that could hardly be paid for if Tirpitz's programme was to continue unchecked.

It would be wrong therefore to suggest, as so much of the 'arms-race literature' has done, that the British response to the German challenge merely 'escalated' the competition, provoking an inevitable riposte from the Germans. It in fact awoke within Germany a powerful body of resistance to Tirpitz, and set him on a collision course with the Chancellor. When in 1911 Tirpitz brought forward his proposals for countering the British programme by speeding up his rate of construction, he provoked a major political crisis that led ultimately to Wermuth resigning and Bethmann attempting to do so. It was a programme that destroyed all Bethmann's sincere attempts, just as sincerely reciprocated by the British Government through Lord Haldane and others, to reach an accommodation with England.

But the price Bethmann set on any accommodation was in any case impossibly high. 'I must ask you,' he told his Ambassador in London in March 1912, 'to leave no doubt . . . in Sir E. Grey's mind that I must be absolutely certain of an agreement guaranteeing the neutrality of England and approximating to a defensive alliance with us before I can advise His Majesty to surrender important sections of the . . . supplementary naval law'.[28] It was fair enough. If Germany was to abandon command of the seas to Britain, she had the right to demand reasonable guarantees that Britain would not align herself with Germany's continental adversaries. But if Britain stood by and did nothing while Germany overwhelmed those adversaries, for how long thereafter would she retain command of the seas?

It was an impasse that could not be resolved even by men inspired by such good will as were Edward Grey and Bethmann-Hollweg. But Grey's goodwill was not reciprocated and Bethmann's was not representative. On March 13, 1911, Grey made a speech in the House of Commons deploring the growing burden of arms expenditure that 'must in the long run break civilisation down', expressing the fear that the burden was becoming intolerable and might 'lead to war precisely because it is becoming intolerable'. He ended with a moving plea voicing all the aspirations of the Peace Movement, that the world should turn towards the rule of law and away from the rule of force, that international disputes should be settled by arbitration, and that armed forces should be drastically reduced to a size where they would no longer present threats to one another but could act as the police of the world.[29] Rapturously applauded by the English Radicals, to the German Government it appeared to signify simply a failure of nerve. 'Grey's surrender (sic) is due to the Navy Law alone', reported the hawkish German naval attaché in London, Captain Widenmann, 'and the unshakeable resolution of the German nation not to allow any diminution of this important instrument'.[30] The official German response which Bethmann delivered in the Reichstag a few days later not only made the quite valid point that in the ideal world visualised by Grey the British would still insist on naval superiority, but denied the whole ideological validity of his argument:

> The condition of peaceableness is strength. The old saying still holds good that the weak will be the prey of the strong. When a people will not or cannot continue to spend enough on its armaments to be able to make its way in the world, then it falls back into the second rank, and sinks down to the rôle of a 'super' on the world's stage. There will always be another and a stronger there who is ready to take the place in the world which it has vacated.[31]

But this was largely rhetoric. It appears probable that by 1912 Tirpitz had shot his bolt and that the opposition to him inside Germany was now so strong that no amount of propaganda would produce any more money for the Navy. Like the French at the end of the seventeenth century, the Second Reich was finding that the strain of maintaining effective military superiority by land and simultaneously challenging Britain for command of the seas was more than her economy could stand.

The view expressed by Bethmann was certainly widespread in Britain as well as in Germany, and by considering war as acceptable it also made it more likely. But to argue further that the arms race—or at least the naval race—itself caused the war, or as Grey put it 'led inevitably to war' is to go beyond the evidence. The naval race was the result of a rivalry that eventually culminated in war, but it was the rivalry itself that caused the war rather than the weapons that expressed it. It was not the German fleet itself that alarmed the British but the intentions that lay behind it. Both the rivalry and the race might have ended peacefully if the Germans really had abandoned their challenge, as the French had abandoned theirs on several previous occasions. They might also have ended if the British had been prepared to share primacy of place with Germany, as they consented to share it with the United States a decade or so later. But so long as Germany was not prepared to accept British naval supremacy and Britain was not prepared to yield it, the competition was bound to go on until economic exhaustion compelled one side to desist. 'The arms race' preceded the war and was the result of a rivalry that powerfully contributed to the war. But it did not of itself cause it.

6

Men against Fire: The Doctrine of the Offensive in 1914

In 1898 there was published in Paris a six-volume work entitled *La guerre future; aux points de vue technique, economique et politique*. This was a translation of a series of articles which had been appearing in Russia, the fruit of collective research but masterminded and written by one of the leading figures in the world of Russian finance and industry, Ivan (or Jean de) Bloch (1836–1902). Sometimes described as 'a Polish banker', Bloch was in fact an entrepreneur almost on the scale of the Rothschilds in Western Europe or Carnegie in the United States. He had made his money in railroad promotion, and then turned to investment on a large scale, promoting and sharing in the great boom in the Russian economy of the 1890s. He had written prolifically about the economic problems of the Russian Empire, and was increasingly alarmed by the degree to which they were complicated, then as now, by the military need to keep abreast, in an age of rapidly developing technology, with the wealthier and more advanced states of the West. Having been responsible for organizing the railway supply for the Russian armies in their war with the Ottoman Empire in 1877–78, Bloch had an unusual grasp of military logistics. And he brought to the study of war an entirely new sort of mind, one in which the analytical skills of the engineer, the economist, and the sociologist were all combined. His book was in fact the first work of modern operational analysis, and nothing written since has equalled it for its combination of rigor and scope.

Only the last of the six volumes was translated into English, under the title *Is War Now Impossible?*[1] This volume conveniently summarizes the argument of the entire work, and it was itself summarized by the author in an interview with the English journalist W. T. Stead which is printed as an introduction to the book. Bloch began by stating his conclusions: war between great states is now impossible—or, rather, suicidal. 'The dimensions of modern armaments and the organisation of society have rendered its prosecution an economic impossibility'.[2] This could be almost mathematically demonstrated. The range, accuracy, and rate of fire of modern firearms—rifles lethal at 2,000 meters, artillery at 6,000—made the 'decisive battles' which had hitherto determined the outcome of wars now impossible. Neither the infantry could charge with the bayonet nor cavalry with the saber. To protect themselves against the lethal storm of fire which would be unleashed on the modern battlefield, armies would have to dig themselves in: '[T]he spade will be as indispensable to the soldier as his rifle. . . . That is one reason why it will be impossible for the battle of the future to be fought out rapidly. . . . Battles will last for days, and at the end it is very doubtful whether any decisive victory can be gained'.[3]

Thus far Bloch was not breaking new ground. He was only setting out a problem which intelligent officers in all European armies had been studying ever since the experiences of the Franco-Prussian War in 1870 and the Russo-Turkish War in 1877–78 had shown (quite as clearly as, and rather more immediately than, those of the American Civil War) the effect of modern firearms on the battlefield. The introduction of 'smokeless powder' in the 1880s, increasing the range and accuracy of all firearms and making possible the near invisibility of their users, would, it was generally agreed, complicate the difficulties of the attack yet further. But even these, it was widely assumed, would not change the fundamental nature of the problem.

The answer, it was believed, lay in the development of the firepower of the assailant, especially of his artillery. The assaulting infantry had to approach closely enough, making all use of cover, to be able to deploy a hail of rifle fire on the defenders' positions. Artillery must cooperate closely, keeping the defenders' heads down with shrapnel and digging them out of their trenches with high explosives. As for machine-guns, these, with their mobility and concentrated firepower, were seen as likely to enhance the power of the attack rather than the defense. 'Fire is the supreme argument', declared Colonel Ferdinand Foch in his lectures at the École de Guerre in 1900.[4] 'The superiority of fire . . . becomes the most important element of an infantry's fighting value'. But the moment would always come when the advance could get no further: 'Before it is a zone almost impassable; there remain no covered approaches; a hail of lead beats the ground . . . to flee or to charge is all that remains'. Foch, and the majority of French thinkers of his time, believed that the charge was still possible and could succeed by sheer dint of numbers: 'To charge, but to charge in numbers, therein lies safety. . . . With more guns we can reduce his to silence, and the same is true of rifles and bayonets, if we know how to make use of them all'.[5] Others were less sure. The Germans, who still after thirty years had vivid memories of the slaughter of their infantry at Gravelotte, preferred if possible to pin the enemy down by fire from the front but attack from a flank. Nobody was under any illusion, even in 1900, that frontal attack would be anything but very difficult and that success could be purchased with anything short of very heavy casualties. There would probably indeed have been a wide measure of agreement with Bloch's calculation, that a superiority at the assaulting point of 8 to 1 would be necessary to ensure success.[6]

It was in the further conclusions which Bloch deduced from his study of the modern battlefield that he outpaced his contemporaries—not so much because they disagreed with him, but because they had given the problems which he examined virtually no thought at all.

What, asked Bloch, would be the eventual result of the operational deadlock that was likely to develop on the battlefield? 'At first there will be increased slaughter—increased slaughter on so terrible a scale as to render it impossible to push the battle to a decisive issue. . . . Then, instead of a war fought out to the bitter end in a series of decisive battles, we shall have to substitute a long period of continually increasing strain upon the resources of the combattants'. This would involve 'entire dislocation of all industry and severing of all the sources of supply by which alone the community is enabled to bear the crushing burden. . . . That is the future of war—not fighting, but famine, not the slaying of men but the bankruptcy of nations and the break-up of the whole social organisation'.[7] In these circumstances the decisive factors would be 'the quality of toughness and capacity for endurance, of patience under privation, of stubbornness under reverse or disappointment. That element in the civil population will be, more than anything else, the deciding factor in modern war. . . . Your soldiers', concluded Bloch grimly, 'may fight as they please; the ultimate decision is in the hands of *famine*'.[8] And famine would strike first at those proletarian elements which, in advanced industrial societies, were most prone to revolution.

It is important to recognize that Bloch got a great deal wrong. He assumed that the prolonged feeding and administration of the vast armies which rail transport made possible would be far beyond the capacity of the military authorities, and that armies in the field would quickly degenerate into starving and mutinous mobs. He predicted that the care of the sick and wounded would also assume unmanageable proportions, and that on the battlefield the dead and dying would have to be heaped up into macabre barriers to protect the living from enemy fire. As did many professional soldiers, Bloch doubted the capacity of reservists fresh from civil life to stand up to the strain of the battlefield: '[I]t is impossible to rely upon modern armies submitting to sacrifice and deprivation to such an extent as is desired by military theorists who lose sight of the tendencies which obtain in Western society'.[9] In fact the efficiency with which armies numbering millions were to be maintained in the field, the success with which the medical services were, with certain grisly exceptions, to rise to the enormous task that confronted them and the stoical endurance displayed by the troops of all belligerent powers in face of hardships worse than Bloch could ever have conceived were perhaps the most remarkable and admirable aspects of the First World War. Bloch, like so many pessimistic prophets (including those of air power a generation later), underestimated the capacity of human societies to adjust themselves to adverse circumstances.

But Bloch also had astonishing insights. The scale of military losses, he pointed out, would depend on the skill of the commanders, and 'it must not be forgotten that a considerable number of the higher officers in modern armies have never been under fire'; while among junior officers the rate of casualties would, if they did their job as leaders, be inordinately high. Finally, there was the problem of managing the wartime economy; what were the long-term effects of that likely to be? 'If we suppose,' Bloch surmised, 'that governments will be forced to interfere in the regulation of prices and to support the population, will it be easy after the war to abandon this practise and re-establish the old order?'[10] Win or lose, therefore, if war came 'the old order' was doomed—by transformation from above if not by revolution from below.

This remarkably accurate blueprint for the war which was to break out in Europe in 1914, last for four and a half years, and end only with the social disintegration of the defeated belligerents and the economic exhaustion of all was the result, not of second-sight, but of meticulous analysis of weapons capabilities, of military organisation and doctrine, and of financial and economic data—five fat volumes which still provide a superb source book for any student of the military, technological, and economic condition of Europe at the end of the nineteenth century. Nobody took Bloch's economic arguments and attempted to disprove them. They were just ignored. Why, it may be asked, was so little account taken of them by statesmen and military leaders? Why did they continue on a course which led ineluctably to the destruction of the old order which Bloch so unerringly predicted? The question is one uncomfortably relevant to our own times.

The answer is of course that societies, and the pattern of international relationships, cannot be transformed overnight on the basis of a single prophetic insight, however persuasively it may be argued. Bloch's thinking and influence were indeed two elements in persuading Czar Nicholas II to convoke the first International Peace Conference which met at The Hague in May 1899, and were even more significant in mobilizing public support throughout Europe for that conference's objectives. But the conference was no more than a ripple in the current of international politics. A more immediate problem, as Bloch himself repeatedly pointed out, was that there existed nowhere in Europe bodies charged with the task of thinking about the problems of warfare in any kind of comprehensive fashion, rather than about the narrowly professional questions that concerned the military. As for the military specialists, they were not likely to admit that the problems which faced them were insoluble, and that they would be incapable in the future of conducting wars so effectively and decisively as they had in the past.

The force of Bloch's arguments, however, was powerfully driven home when, within a few months of the publication of *La guerre future,* there broke out in South Africa a war in which for the first time both sides were fully equipped with the new technology—magazine-loading small-bore rifles, quick-firing artillery, machine-guns—and things turned out on the battlefield exactly as he had predicted. The British army, moving in close formations and firing by volleys, were unable to get anywhere near an enemy whom they could not even see. At Spion Kop, at Colenso, at the Modder Rover, and at Magersfontein, their frontal attacks were driven back by the Boers with horrifying losses. As the leading British military theorist, Colonel G. F. R. Henderson, who accompanied the army in South Africa, wrote shortly afterwards,

> There was a constant endeavor to make battle conform to the parade ground . . . to depend for success on courage and subordination and to relegate intelligence and individuality to the background . . . the fallacy that a thick firing line in open country can

protect itself, outside decisive range, by its own fire, had not yet been exposed. It was not yet realised that the defender, occupying ingeniously constructed trenches and using smokeless powder, is practically invulnerable to both gun and rifle.[11]

Unsympathetic continental observers tended to play down the significance of the South African experience on the grounds that the British army and its commanders were unsuitably trained for confronting a 'civilized' adversary, having been spoiled by the easy victories in Egypt and the Sudan. Further, they suggested that the differences in terrain made the lessons to be learned from that war, as they had made those from the American Civil War, irrelevant in the European theatre. The British themselves, while unable to deny the unsuitability of their traditional tactics and training to the transformed conditions of warfare, could none the less point out that, once they had mastered the necessary techniques, they had been able successfully to go over to the offensive, and had then rapidly won the war. This they had done by pinning down the Boers in their positions by firepower and maneuvering round their flanks with cavalry—cavalry used not in its traditional role for shock on the battlefield, but to develop the kind of strategic mobility which was essential if the problems created by the new power of the defensive were to be overcome. When in 1901 Bloch described to an audience at the British Royal United Services Institution how the experience of the British Army in South Africa, repeated as it would be in Europe on an enormous scale, precisely illustrated his arguments, his audience was able to point out that in fact Lord Roberts had shown how to combine the tactical advantages of firepower with the strategic advantages of horse-borne mobility to secure precisely those decisive results which Bloch had maintained would, in future, be impossible.[12]

A study of the voluminous military literature of the period shows that between 1900 and 1905 a consensus developed among European strategic thinkers over two points. The first was the strategic importance of cavalry as mobile firepower. If the firepower of the defence made it now impossible for cavalry to assault unshaken infantry—a view which had been reluctantly accepted ever since the disasters of the Franco-Prussian War of 1870—cavalry would now develop their own firepower, enhanced by mobile, quick-firing artillery and machine-guns, and exploit opportunities on a scale undreamed of since the days of the American Civil War. The South African experience indeed sent back intelligent cavalrymen, especially in England, to studying the Civil War, often for the first time.[13] In the British

Army, it was laid down that the carbine or rifle would henceforth be 'the principal weapon' for cavalry. But for most cavalrymen this was going altogether too far. In no country in Europe was this proudest, most exclusive, most anachronistic of arms prepared to be, as they saw it, downgraded to the role of mounted infantry. That kind of thing could be left to colonial roughriders. Writing as late as 1912, the German general Friedrich von Bernhardi bitterly observed that '[t]he cavalry looks now . . . upon a charge in battle as its paramount duty; it has almost deliberately closed its eyes against the far-reaching changes in warfare. By this it has *itself* barred the way that leads to greater successes'.[14] Within the cavalry in every European army therefore a controversy raged which was settled only by the kind of compromise expressed by the British Cavalry Manual of 1907: 'The essence of the cavalry spirit lies in holding the balance correctly between fire power and shock action . . . it must be accepted as a principle that the rifle, effective as it is, cannot replace the effect produced by the speed of the horse, the magnetism of the charge, and the terror of cold steel'.[15]

The mood of the cavalryman on the eve of the First World War is perhaps best captured in an analysis of British military doctrine published in 1914:

> Technically the great decisive cavalry charge on the main battlefield is a thing of the past, yet training in shock tactics is claimed by all cavalry authorities to be still essential to the strategic use of the arm, and even on the battlefield shock tactics may, under special conditions, conceivably still be possible, while brilliant opportunities will almost certainly be offered for the employment in perhaps a decisive manner of the power conferred by the combination of mobility with fire action. . . . For whatever tactics are adopted, the desire to take the offensive will always remain the breath of life for cavalry, and where shock action is impossible, the cavalryman must be prepared to expend, rifle in hand, the last man in an advance on foot, if the victory can thus only be achieved.[16]

So training in shock action continued; for even the reformers had to admit that cavalry would have to meet and defeat the enemy's cavalry, presumably in a gigantic mêlée, before it could fulfil its strategic task. 'The opening of future wars,' wrote Bernhardi in 1912, 'will, therefore, in all likelihood be characterised by great cavalry combats'.[17]

So the cavalry continued to practise sword drill; and the infantry continued, for the same reason, to practise bayonet drill. The German writer

Wilhelm Balck saw no reason to alter, in the 1911 edition of his huge study *Tactics,* the doctrine preached in the first edition of 1896:

> The soldier should be taught not to shrink from the bayonet attack, but to seek it. If the infantry is deprived of the arme blanche, if the impossibility of bayonet fighting is preached . . . an infantry will be developed which is unsuitable for attack and which moreover lacks a most essential quality, viz. the moral power to reach the enemy's position. . . . [And he went on to quote from the Russian General M. I. Dragomirov, a well-known fanatic on the subject:] 'The bayonet cannot be abolished for the reason, if for no other, that it is the sole and exclusive embodiment of that will-power which alone, both in war and in everyday life attains its object, whereas reason only facilitates the achievement of the object'.[18]

The British General Staff manuals expressed the same idea slightly differently: 'The moral effect of the bayonet is out of all proportion to its material effect, and not the least important of virtues claimed for it is that the desire to use it draws the attacking side on". To deprive the infantry of their bayonets would be like depriving the cavalry of their swords; it 'would be to some extent to take away their desire to close'.[19]

That brings us to the second point over which a rather more troubled consensus developed among European military thinkers as a consequence of the South African War: the unprecedented difficulty of carrying through frontal attacks, even with substantial artillery support, would now make necessary more extended formations in the attack. On this point also there had been a continuing controversy ever since 1870. The normal formation for the infantry attack, inherited from the Napoleonic era, consisted of three lines. First came the skirmishers in open formation, making maximum use of cover so as to reach positions from which they could bring a concentrated fire on the enemy in order, in cooperation with the artillery, to 'win the fire fight'. Behind them came the main assault line, normally in close formation under the immediate control of their officers, to assault with the bayonet. Finally came the supports, the immediate tactical reserve.

The German army, remembering the massacres of their infantry in the assault at the battles of Wörth and St. Privat in August 1870, had always inclined to the view that once the attacking infantry came under fire, close formations in the old style would be impossible. The main assault line would itself now have to scatter and edge its way forward to thicken up the skirmishers or extend their line, feeling for an exposed flank. Effectively it was now the skirmishers who bore the brunt of the attack, and success could be achieved only by the dominance of their fire. The bayonet, if used at all, would only gather up the harvest already reaped by the rifle and the gun.[20]

This was the doctrine against which Dragomirov and his disciples everywhere set their faces. It must be admitted that it did present real problems. Once the assaulting troops were scattered and left to themselves, out of range of the officers whose task it was to inspire them and the non-coms whose job it was to frighten them, what incentive would there be for them to go forward in face of enemy fire? Once they went to ground behind cover, would they ever get up again? There were several notorious instances in 1870 when substantial proportions of German assaulting formations had unaccountably 'got lost'. Colonel Charles Ardent du Picq, who had been killed in that war and whose posthumously published *Études sur le combat* contains some of the shrewdest observations on troop morale that have ever been written, had described the terrifying isolation of the soldier on a modern battlefield (even before the days of smokeless powder) once he was deprived of the solid support of comrades on either side which had enabled men to face death ever since the days of the Roman legions. 'The soldier is unknown even to his comrades; he loses them in the disorienting confusion of battle, where he fights as a lonely individual; solidarity is no longer guaranteed by mutual surveillance'.[21] All now depended on the morale and reliability of the smallest units; 'by force of circumstances all battles nowadays tend more than ever to become soldiers' battles'.[22] How could these lonely, frightened men, deprived of the intoxication of drums and trumpets, the support of their comrades, the inspiration of their leaders, find within themselves the courage to die?

The French army, its traditions of martial leadership and close formations for the attack antedating even the Napoleonic era, was particularly reluctant to accept the logic of the new firepower. For a decade after 1870 its leaders had attempted to impose the open tactical formations on their units, but they never really succeeded. By 1884 regulations were again prescribing 'the principle of the decisive attack, head held high, unconcerned about casualties'. The notorious regulations of 1894 laid it down that attacking units should advance elbow to elbow, not breaking formation to take advantage of cover, but assaulting en masse 'to the sound of bugles and drums'.[23] Stirring stuff, and the French were not alone in preferring it that way. So did the Russians, in spite of their chastening experiences before Plevna in 1877; and so did the British. They also, after a decade of uncertainty inspired by the events of 1870, returned to their old traditions. In the regulations of 1888, wrote Colonel Henderson:

> The bayonet has once more reasserted itself. To the second line, relying on cold steel only, as in the days of the Peninsula, is entrusted the duty of bringing the battle to a speedy conclusion. . . . The confusion of the Prussian battles was in a large degree due to their neglect of the immutable principles of tactics and . . . they are a bad model for us to follow. The sagacity of our own people is a surer guide and if, after 1870, we wanted a model, the tactics of the last great war waged by English-speaking soldiers would have served us better.

The Americans on both sides had always launched frontal attacks in close formations, having found that 'to prevent the battle degenerating into a protracted struggle between two strongly entrenched armies, and to attain a speedy and decisive result, mere development of fire was insufficient'. The lesson was clear: 'close order whenever it is possible, extended order only when it is unavoidable'.[24]

By 1900 Henderson was a sadder and a wiser man. Events in South Africa had once again shown the world that under fire close order was *not* possible; and the argument that it was good for morale was seen to be ludicrous. 'When the preponderant mass suffers enormous losses; when they feel, as others will feel, that other and less costly means of achieving the same end might have been adopted, what will become of their morale? . . . The most brilliant offensive victories', went on Henderson, 'are not those which were mere "bludgeon work" and cost the most blood, but those which were won by surprise, by adroit manoeuvre, by mystifying and misleading the enemy, by turning the ground to the best account, and where the butchers' bill was small'.[25] A generation later Henderson's countryman Liddell Hart was to elaborate this insight into an entire philosophy of war, but long before 1914 the British army was to discard this subversive suggestion that discretion might be the better part of valor.

Over the matter of close *versus* open formations for the attack, however, the South African experience was generally seen to be decisive. Even the French high command, while attributing the catastrophes which had overtaken the British entirely to Anglo-Saxon ineptitude, rewrote its regulations in 1904, abandoning the *coude à coude* formations of 1894 and prescribing advance by small groups covering each other by fire—the kind of infantry tactics that were to become general in the Second World War.[26]

It is doubtful however whether these eminently sensible guidelines made any impression on an army which had been thrown, in the aftermath of the Dreyfus case, into a state of administrative confusion verging on anarchy.[27] Certainly the performance of the French infantry in 1914 shows no evidence of it. In any case, such tactics demanded of the ordinary soldier a degree of skill and self-reliance such as neither the French nor any other European army (with the possible exception of the Germans) had hitherto expected, or done anything to inculcate, either in their junior officers or in their other ranks.

And there remained unsolved the nagging, fundamental problem of *morale*—a problem all the greater since a large part of all armies would now be made up of reservists whose moral fiber, it was feared, would have been sapped by the enervating influences of civil life. Concern about the morale of the army was thus generalized, among European military thinkers, into concern about the morale of their nations as a whole; not so much whether they would stand up to the economic attrition which Bloch was almost unique in foreseeing, but whether they could inculcate in their young men that stoical contempt for death which alone would enable them to face, and overcome, the horrors of the assault.[28]

It was while this concern was at its height that war broke out between Japan and Russia in the Far East. In February 1904 the Japanese navy launched a surprise attack on the Russian fleet at Port Arthur and, with local command of the sea thus secured, effected amphibious landings on the Korean and Manchurian coasts. It took the Japanese army a year to establish themselves in the disputed province of Manchuria, capturing Port Arthur by land assault and fighting its way north along the railway to capture the main Russian forward base at Mukden in a two-week battle involving altogether over half a million men. It was a war fought on both sides with the latest products of modern technology: not only magazine rifles and quick-firing field artillery but mobile heavy guns, machine-guns, mines, barbed wire, searchlights, telephonic communications and, above all, *trenches*. The Russo-Japanese War proved beyond any doubt that the infantryman's most useful weapon, second only to his rifle, was a spade. Though the war inevitably had unique characteristics—both sides fought at the end of long supply lines, in sparsely inhabited country, which sharply limited the scale of force they could employ—it could not be dismissed, as so many conservative thinkers on the Continent dismissed the Boer War, as a colonial irrelevance. The Russian army was one of the greatest— certainly one of the largest—in Europe. The Japanese had had their armed forces equipped and trained by Europeans, mainly Germans, to the finest European standards. European—and American—military and naval observers with the fighting forces sent back expert reports on the operations, which were digested and mulled over by their general staffs. The British, the French, and the German armies all thought it worth their while to produce multi-volume histories of the Russo-Japanese War, and for the next ten years, until interest was eclipsed by events nearer home, its lessons were analysed in the most precise detail by pundits writing in military periodicals. It was neither the Boer War nor the American Civil War nor even the Franco-Prussian War that European military specialists had in mind when their armies deployed in 1914: it was the fighting in Manchuria of 1904–5.

As usual, the experts tended to read into the experiences of the war very much what they wanted to find. Conservative cavalrymen observed the failure of the Russian cavalry, trained as it was to the use of the rifle, to achieve anything very much either on the battlefield or off it; absence of 'the offensive spirit' making both its raids and its reconnaissance remarkably ineffectual. Reformers noted, on the contrary, how effectively the Japanese had deployed their cavalry in the role of mobile firepower, and the important part it had played at the battle of Mukden. Everyone agreed that artillery, with its accuracy, range, and rate of fire, was now of supreme importance; that it must almost always employ indirect fire; that shrapnel rather than high explosive was its most effective projectile; and that the consumption of ammunition would be enormous. Valuable lessons were learned about supply and communication problems and the need for inconspicuous uniforms; every European army quickly reclothed its armies in various shades of brown or grey, and it was political rather than military conservatism that fatally delayed this reform on the part of the French. But most important of all was the general consensus that infantry assaults with the bayonet, in spite of the South African experience, were still not only possible but necessary. The Japanese had carried them out time and again, and usually with ultimate success.

The Japanese bayonet assaults came, it was true, only at the end of a long and careful advance. They approached whenever possible by night, digging in before dawn, lying up by day, and repeating the process until they could get no further. Then, breaking completely with the European tradition of advancing in extended lines, they dashed forward in small groups of one or two dozen men, each with its own objective, moving rapidly from cover to cover until they were sufficiently close to assault. A French observer described one such scene:

The whole Japanese line is now lit up with the glitter of steel flashing from the scabbard. . . . Once again the officers quit shelter with ringing shouts of 'Banzai!' wildly echoed by all the rank and file. Slowly, but not to be denied, they make headway, in spite of the barbed wire, mines and pitfalls, and the merciless hail of bullets. Whole units are destroyed—others take their places; the advancing wave pauses for a moment, but sweeps ever onward. Already they are within a few yards of the trenches. Then, on the Russian side, the long grey line of Siberian Fusiliers forms up in turn, and delivers one last volley before scurrying down the far side of the hill at the double.[29]

The Japanese losses in these assaults were heavy, but they succeeded; and, so argued the European theorists, such tactics would succeed again. 'The Manchurian experience,' as one British military writer put it, 'showed over and over again that the bayonet was in no sense an obsolete weapon. . . . The assault is even of more importance than the attainment of fire mastery which antecedes it. It is the supreme moment of the fight. . . . Upon it the final issue depends. . . . From these glorious examples it may be deduced that no duty, however difficult, should be regarded as impossible by well-trained infantry of good morale and discipline'.[30]

It was this 'morale and discipline' of the Japanese armed forces that all observers stressed, and they were equally unanimous in stressing that these qualities characterized not only the armed forces but the entire Japanese nation. General A. N. Kuropatkin, the commander of the Russian forces, noted ruefully in his memoirs, 'In the late war . . . our moral strength was less than that of the Japanese; and it was this inferiority, rather than mistakes in generalship, that caused our defeats. . . . The lack of martial spirit, of moral exaltation, and of heroic impulse, affected particularly our stubbornness in battle. In many cases we did not have sufficient resolution to conquer such antagonists as the Japanese'.[31]

The same quality gave a representative of Japan's British ally, General Sir Ian Hamilton, almost equal concern:

It is not so much the idea that we have put our money on the wrong horse that now troubles me. . . . But it should cause European statesmen some anxiety when their people seem to forget that there are millions outside the charmed circle of Western Civilisation who are ready to pluck the sceptre from nerveless hands so soon as the old spirit is allowed to degenerate. . . . Providentially Japan is our ally. . . . England has time, therefore—time to put her military affairs

in order; time to implant and cherish the military ideal in the hearts
of her children; time to prepare for a disturbed and an anxious
twentieth century. . . . From the nursery and its toys to the Sunday
school and its cadet company, every influence of affection, loyalty,
tradition and education should be brought to bear on the next generation of British boys and girls, so as deeply to impress upon their
young minds a feeling of reverence and admiration for the patriotic
spirit of their ancestors.[32]

Such expressions of admiration for the creed of Bushido are to be found
widely scattered in the military and militarist literature of the day. Particularly important for our purposes, however, was the general recognition
that the Japanese performance had proved, up to the hilt, the moral and
military superiority of *the offensive*. The passive immobility of the Russians,
in spite of all the advantages they should have enjoyed from the defence,
had in the long run ensured their defeat. It was a conclusion which the
military everywhere, after the miasmic doubts engendered by the Boer
War, embraced with heartfelt relief. 'The defensive is never an acceptable
role to the Briton, and he makes little or no study of it', wrote Major
General Sir W. G. Knox flatly in 1914.[33] 'It was not by dwelling on the
idea of passive defense', wrote the Secretary of State for War R. B. Haldane
in 1911, 'that our forefathers made our country what it is today'.[34] In
Germany General Alfred von Schlieffen, on retiring as Chief of the General
Staff in 1905, held up to his successors the model of the German armies
in 1870: 'Attacks, and more attacks, ruthless attacks brought it unparalleled losses but also victory and, it is probably true to say, the decision of
the campaign'.[35] And his successor, the younger Helmuth von Moltke,
acknowledged the heritage: 'We have learned the object that you seek to
achieve: not to obtain limited successes but to strike great, destructive
blows. . . . Your object is the annihilation of the enemy, and all efforts
must be directed towards this end'.[36]

Nowhere was the lesson more gratefully received, however, than in
France. Marshal J. J. Joffre, whose offensive operations from 1914 through
1916 are now generally considered to have been a succession of unmiti-
gated disasters, described the French reaction to the Russo-Japanese War
in his memoirs with quite unrepentant frankness. After the Boer War, he
wrote, 'a whole series of false doctrines . . . began to undermine even such
feeble offensive sentiment as had made its appearance in our war doctrines
. . . an incomplete study of the events of a single war had led the intellectual

elite of our Army to believe that the improvement in firearms and the power of fire action had so increased the strength of the defensive that an offensive opposed to it had lost all virtue'. After the Russo-Japanese War, however, 'our young intellectual elite finally shook off the malady of this phraseology which had upset the military world and returned to a more healthy conception of the general conditions prevailing in war'.[37]

Joffre admitted that the new passion for the offensive did take on a 'somewhat unreasoning character,' citing Colonel Louis de Grandmaison's famous lectures of 1911 as an example. 'Unreasoning' is the right word. One must always, declared Grandmaison to his audience, 'succeed in combat in doing things which would be *impossible* in cold blood. For instance . . . advancing under fire. . . . We must prepare ourselves for it, and prepare others by cultivating, passionately, everything which bears the mark of the offensive spirit. To take this to excess would probably still not be far enough'.[38]

There was nothing in this to indicate the careful use of ground and of mutual fire support which had characterized the actual Japanese tactics— tactics in fact remarkably close to those prescribed in the despised French infantry regulation of 1904. But Grandmaison was not so much setting out a military doctrine as echoing a national mood—a generalized sense of chauvinistic assertiveness which dominated the French 'establishment', civil and military alike, in 1911–12.[39] It was a mood which did much to restore the morale of an army battered and confused after the excesses of the Dreyfus affair, but it could not of itself create the battlefield skills which had also characterized the Japanese army, and without which 'the spirit of the offensive' was not so much an assertion of national morale as a generalized death wish. It was in this mood that French officers led the attacks in August–September 1914 which within six weeks produced 385,000 casualties, of which 100,000 were dead.[40]

Bloch died in 1902, but he could have taken much comfort from the experiences of the Russo-Japanese War. Its battles were prolonged, costly, and indecisive. Victory came through attrition; and defeat, for Russia, brought revolution. But Bloch's critics could equally well argue that his major thesis had been disproved. War had been shown to be neither impossible, nor suicidal. It was still a highly effective instrument of policy for a nation which had the courage to face its dangers and the endurance to bear its costs—especially its inevitable and predictable costs in human lives. Those nations which were not prepared to put their destinies to this test, they urged, could expect no mercy in the grim battle for survival which had always characterized human history and which seemed likely, in the coming century, to be waged with ever greater ferocity. It was in this mood, and with these hopes, that the nations of Europe went to war in 1914.

7

Europe
on the
Eve of
the First
World
War

In a place of honour in the Oxford Examination Schools there hangs a portrait of the Emperor William II of Germany, wearing the robes of the Honorary Doctorate of Civil Law which was bestowed on him by the University of Oxford in November 1907. Seven years after the Kaiser received his degree, out of a total of seven Oxford honorands in June 1914, five were German. The Duke of Saxe-Coburg-Gotha, Professor Ludwig Mitteis of the University of Leipzig, and the composer Richard Strauss all received their degrees at the Encaenia on June 25. Special sessions of Convocation were held to bestow honorary doctorates on the King of Württemberg and the German Ambassador, Prince Lichnowsky. At a banquet in the latter's honour the Professor of German reminded his audience that the Kaiser's great-grandfather, King Frederick William III of Prussia, had also received an honorary DCL exactly 100 years before. He welcomed the presence of so many German students in Oxford (fifty-eight German Rhodes Scholars had matriculated over the previous ten years) and expressed the hope that thereby the two nations would be 'drawn nearer to one another', quoting the belief of Cecil Rhodes 'that the whole of humanity' would be best served if the Teutonic peoples were brought nearer together and would join hands for the purpose of spreading their civilization to distant regions'.

Three days after this Encaenia the Archduke Franz Ferdinand was assassinated at Sarajevo. When the University reconvened three months later in October 1914 many of the young Germans and Englishmen who had rubbed shoulders at those celebrations had enlisted in their respective armies and were now doing their best to kill one another. The Examination Schools had been turned into a hospital. The number of undergraduates in residence had dwindled by over half, from 3,097 to 1,387. (By 1918 it was to be down to 369.) In the vacation over a thousand of them had been recommended for commissions by a committee established under the vice-chancellor, and were already serving with the army. As yet only 12 had been killed; the slaughter of the first Battle of Ypres was still a few weeks away. Several colleges had been taken over to house troops. Organized games had virtually ceased, while the Officer Training Corps (OTC), to which all able-bodied undergraduates now belonged, trained for five mornings and two afternoons a week. As if this were not enough, the Chichele Professor of Military History, Spenser Wilkinson, advertised a course of lectures 'for those who are preparing themselves to fight England's battles' which was to begin with a description of 'the nature and properties of the weapons in use—the bullet, the shell, the bayonet, the sword and the lance'.[1]

In one way it can therefore be said that the war came out of a clear sky. But the events I have described do not indicate a profoundly pacific community taken totally by surprise and adjusting itself only with difficulty to astonishing and terrible new conditions. Everyone seems to have known exactly what to do, and to have done it with great efficiency. Arrangements to take over the Examination Schools and colleges had been made by the War Office two years earlier. The OTC was already flourishing: one undergraduate in three belonged to it, and 500 were in summer camp at Aldershot when the news of the assassination came through. And, in so far as such iconographical evidence can be legitimately adduced, the group photographs of Oxford colleges and clubs show how the lolling dandies of the turn of the century, with their canes, blazers, and dogs, had given way soon after the Boer War to a new generation of muscular young men—fit, serious, short-haired, level-eyed—whose civilian clothes already seemed to sit uneasily upon them. This generation may not have expected war to break out in the summer of 1914, but it was psychologically and physically ready for it when it came. The challenge was expected, and the response full of zest.

In this respect Oxford was a microcosm, not only of Britain, but of Europe as a whole. Europe was taken by surprise by the occasion for the war—so many other, comparable crises had been successfully surmounted during the past five years—but not by the fact of it. All over the Continent long-matured plans were put into action. With a really remarkable absence of confusion, millions of men reported for duty, were converted or, rather, reconverted into soldiers, and loaded into the trains which were to take them to the greatest battlefields in the history of mankind. It cannot be said that during the summer weeks of 1914, while the crisis was ripening towards its bloody solution, the peoples in Europe in general were exercising any pressure on their governments to go to war, but neither did they try to restrain them. When war did come, it was accepted almost without question; in some quarters indeed with wild demonstrations of relief.

The historian is faced with two distinct questions. Why did war come? And when it did come, why was it so prolonged and destructive? In the background there is a further, unanswerable question: If the political and military leaders of Europe had been able to foresee that prolongation and that destruction, would the war have occurred at all? Everyone, naturally, went to war in the expectation of victory, but might they have felt that at such a cost even victory was not worth while? That is the kind of hypothetical question which laymen put and historians cannot answer. But we can ask another and less impossible question: What did the governments of Europe think would happen to them if they did *not* go to war? Why did war, with all its terrible uncertainties, appear to them as a preferable alternative to remaining at peace?

Clausewitz described war as being compounded of a paradoxical trinity: the governments for which it was an instrument of policy; the military for whom it was the exercise of a skill; and the people as a whole, the extent of whose involvement determined the intensity with which the war would be waged.[2] This functional distinction is of course an oversimplification. In all the major states of Europe military and political leaders shared a common attitude and cultural background, which shaped their perceptions and guided their judgements. The same emotions which inspired peoples were likely also to affect their political and military leaders; and those emotions could be shaped by propaganda, by education, and by the socialization process to which so much of the male population of continental Europe had been subject through four decades of at least two years' compulsory military service at a highly impressionable age (though it must be noted that the British, who were not subjected to the same treatment, reacted no differently from their continental neighbours to the onset and continuation of the war). Still, the triad of government, military, and public opinion provides a useful framework for analysis, and one that I shall use for the remainder of this chapter.

First, the governments. Although none of them could foresee the full extent of the ordeal which lay before them, no responsible statesman, even in Germany, believed that they were in for 'a fresh, jolly little war'. It was perhaps only when they had taken their irrevocable decisions that the real magnitude of the risks which they were running came fully home to them, but that is a very common human experience. Bethmann-Hollweg in particular saw the political dangers with gloomy clarity: a world war, he warned the Bavarian minister, 'would topple many a throne'.[3] There had indeed been a certain amount of wild writing and speaking over the past ten years, especially in Germany, about the value of war as a panacea for social ills; and the remarkable way in which social and political differences did disappear the moment war was declared has tempted some historians to assume that this effect was foreseen and therefore intended: that the opportunity was deliberately seized by the Asquith Cabinet, for example, to distract attention from the intractable Irish problem to continental adventures, or that the German imperial government saw it as a chance to settle the hash of the Social Democrats for good.[4] One can say only that minute scrutiny of the material by, now, several generations of historians has failed to produce any serious evidence to support this view.

Rather, the opposite was the case: governments were far from certain how their populations would react to the coming of war, and how they would stand up to its rigours. A whole generation of English publicists had been stressing the social consequences of even a temporary blockade of the British Isles: soaring insurance rates, unemployment, bread-riots, revolution.[5] The French army, for ten years past the butt of left-wing agitation, was gloomy about the prospects of anything like an enthusiastic response from conscripts recalled to the colours, and the French security services stood by to arrest left-wing leaders at the slightest sign of trouble.[6] It was only with the greatest reluctance that the German army enforced military service on the supposedly unreliable population of the industrial regions. The Russian government had within the past ten years seen one war end in revolution, and for at least some of its members this seemed good reason to keep out of another.[7] It was one thing to enhance the prestige of the government and undermine support for its domestic enemies by conducting a strong forward policy, whether in Morocco or in the Balkans. It was another to subject the fragile consensus and dubious loyalties of societies so torn by class and national conflict as were the states of Europe in 1914 to the terrible strain of a great war. Governments did so only on the assumption, spoken or unspoken, that that war, however terrible, would at least be comparatively short; no longer, probably, than the six months which had seen out the last great war in Europe in 1870. How could it be otherwise? A prolonged war of attrition, as Count Alfred von Schlieffen had pointed out in a famous article in 1909, could not be conducted when it required the expenditure of milliards to sustain armies numbered in millions.[8] The only person in any position of responsibility who appears to have thought differently was Herbert Lord Kitchener: a British imperial soldier who had served outside Europe throughout his career and who had never, so far as we know, seriously studied the question at all.

But whether the war was short or long, it was for all governments a leap into a terrible dark, and the penalties for defeat were likely to be far greater than the traditional ones of financial indemnities and territorial loss. So we come back to the question: What appeared to be the alternatives? And in the event of victory, what appeared the probable gains? Why, in the last resort, did the governments of Europe prefer the terrifying uncertainties of war to the prospect of no war?

Let us begin where the war itself effectively began, in Vienna. Was not the prospect which lay before the statesmen of Vienna, even if this crisis were successfully 'managed', one of continuous frustration abroad and disintegration at home? Of a Serbia, doubled in size after the Balkan Wars, ever more boldly backing the claims of the Bosnian irredentists, while the South Slavs agitated with ever greater confidence for an autonomy that the Magyars would never permit them to exercise? What serious prospect was there of the Empire hanging together once the old Emperor had gone? A final settling of accounts with Serbia while Germany held the Russians in check must have appeared the only chance of saving the Monarchy, whatever Berlin might say; and with a blank cheque from Berlin, Vienna could surely face the future with a greater confidence than had been felt there for very many years. No wonder the Foreign Minister, Count Leopold von Berchtold, and his colleagues took their time in drafting their ultimatum: they must have found the process highly enjoyable. A successful war would put the Monarchy back in business again, and keep it there for many years to come.

What about the government in Berlin? Was this the moment it had been waiting for ever since the famous Council of War in December 1912?[9] This controversy has consumed many tons of paper and gallons of ink. But if one again asks the questions, what the imperial German government had to lose by peace and gain by war, the answers seem very clear. One of the things it had to lose by peace was its Austrian ally, which would become an increasingly useless makeweight as it grew ever less capable of solving its internal problems or protecting its own (and German) interests in the Balkans against the encroachments of Russia and Russia's protégés. Another was Germany's capacity to hold her own against a Dual Alliance in which French capital was building up a Russian army whose future size and mobility appeared far beyond the capacity of any German force to contain. It would not be too anachronistic to suggest that the shadow of Russia's future status as a superpower was already rendering out of date all calculations based on the traditional concept of a European balance. If war was to come at all—and few people in the imperial government doubted that it would—then it was self-evidently better to have it now, while there was still a fair chance of victory. By 1917, when the Russians had completed the Great Programme of rearmament and railway building which they had begun, with French funding, in 1912, it might be too late.

And, for Germany, there was a lot to be gained by war. The domination of the Balkans and perhaps the Middle East; the final reduction of France to a position from which she could never again, even with allies, pose a military threat to German power; the establishment of a position on the Continent that would enable her to compete on equal terms with England and attain the grandiose if ill-defined status of a world power: all this, in July 1914, must have appeared perfectly feasible. In September, when the Programme of her war aims was drafted, it looked as if it had almost been achieved. Even in a less bellicose and more self-confident society than Wilhelmine Germany, the opportunity might have appeared too good to miss.[10]

In Vienna and Berlin, then, there seemed much to be lost by peace and gained by war. In St. Petersburg, the ambitions for Balkan expansion and the 'recovery' of Constantinople, checked in 1878 and 1885, were far from dead, but they can hardly be counted a major element in Russian political calculations in July 1914. More serious were the costs of remaining at peace: abandoning Serbia and all the gains of the past five years; facing the wrath of the pan-Slavs in the Duma and their French allies; and watching the Central Powers establish and consolidate an unchallengeable dominance in south-east Europe. Even so, these costs were hardly irredeemable. Russia had been humiliated before in the Balkans and been able to restore her authority. She had no vital interests there which, once lost, could never be recovered. Above all, she had nothing to lose, in terms of military power, by waiting, and a great deal to gain. Of all the major powers, Russia's entry into the war can be categorized as the least calculated, the most unwise, and ultimately of course the most disastrous.[11]

As for Paris and London, a successful war would certainly remove—as it ultimately did—a major threat to their security. But the advantages to be gained by a war did not enter into their calculations, whereas the perils of remaining at peace quite evidently did. The French government took little comfort from the long-term advantages to be gained from the growth of Russian military power and the consequent advisability of postponing the issue until 1917. It was more conscious of its immediate weakness confronted by the growing numbers of the German army. In 1914, after the increase of the past two years, the German peacetime strength had reached 800,000 men, the wartime strength 3.8 million. Thanks to their new and controversial Three-Year Law, the French could match this with 700,000 men in peace, 3.5 million in war. But with a population only 60 per cent of the German, that was almost literally their final throw. Completion of the Russian reforms was three long years away. In the long run Russian strength might redress the balance, but in the long run a large number of Frenchmen could be dead and their nation reduced to the status of Italy or Spain. So the French government saw no reason to urge caution on St. Petersburg, and even less reason to refrain from supporting its ally when Germany declared war on her on August 1.[12]

For the British government, composed as it was very largely (though by no means entirely) of men to whom the whole idea of war was antipathetic and who were responsible to a parliamentary party deeply suspicious of militarism and of continental involvement, there appeared nothing to be gained by war, and perhaps more than any of its continental equivalents it was conscious of the possible costs. But it was equally conscious of the cost of remaining at peace. Britain would not be the *tertius gaudens* in a continental war. She had no demands to make on any of the belligerents, no territorial aspirations, no expectation of economic gain. So far as the British government was concerned, Norman Angell's famous book *The Great Illusion* was preaching to the converted. But if the Dual Alliance defeated Germany unaided Britain would be, for the two victors, an object of hostility and contempt. All the perils of imperial rivalry temporarily dispersed by the Entente with France of 1904 and the accords with Russia of 1907 would reappear. If, on the other hand, Germany won and established a continental hegemony, Britain would face a threat to her security unknown since the days of Napoleon. Leaving any consideration of honour, sentiment, or respect for treaties on one side—and let us remember that that generation of Englishmen did *not* leave them on one side but regarded them as quite central—every consideration of realpolitik dictated that Britain, having done her best to avert the war, should enter it on the side of France and Russia once it began.[13]

When the statesmen of Europe declared war in 1914, they all shared one common assumption: that they had a better-than-even chance of winning it. In making this assumption they relied on their military advisers; so it is now time to look at the second element in our triad: the soldiers.

The first thing to note about the soldiers, certainly those of Western Europe, is that they were professionals; most of them professionals of a very high order. Those of them who were well-born or aspired to that status certainly shared all the feudal value-system so excoriated by Arno Mayer in his work *The Persistence of the Old Regime*. Those who were not probably had more than their fair share of the prevalent philosophy of Social-Darwinism and regarded war, not as an unpleasant necessity, but as a test of manhood and of national fitness for survival. In all armies, then as now, there were incompetents who through good luck or good connections reached unsuitably high rank; but a study of the military literature of the period strongly indicates that the military, especially those responsible for the armament, training, organization, and deployment of armies, were no fools, worked hard and took their professions very seriously indeed. And they also shared certain common assumptions.

The first was that war was inevitable. The now much-quoted statement made by General Helmuth von Moltke at the so-called Council of War in December 1912, 'I hold war to be inevitable, and the sooner the better',[14] can be paralleled with comparable expressions by responsible figures in every army in Europe. They may have differed over the second part of the sentence—whether it was better to get it over with quickly or wait for a more favourable moment—but from 1911 onward it is hard to find any military leader suggesting that war could or should any longer be avoided. The change of mood in the summer of that year, provoked by the Agadir crisis, was very marked. In France a new political leadership appointed new military chiefs, who belatedly and desperately began to prepare their ramshackle army for the test of war. The Dual Alliance was reactivated, Russian mobilization schedules were speeded up, and the Great Programme of Russian military modernization was set on foot. In Germany the agitation began which contributed so powerfully to the massive increase in the military strength of the German army. In Britain the Government gave its blessing to the army's plans for sending the British

Expeditionary Force to France, and Winston Churchill was sent to the Admiralty to bring the navy into line. The extent to which war was generally regarded as inevitable or desirable by the public as a whole is still difficult to gauge—though if the 'distant drummer' penetrated into the summer idylls of A. E. Housman it is reasonable to suppose that less remote figures found the sound pretty deafening. But certainly for the military the evidence is overwhelming that the question in their mind was not 'whether' but 'when'. They saw their job as being, not to deter war, but to fight it.

The second assumption, which they shared with the statesmen they served, was that the war would be short. It required quite exceptional perspicacity to visualize anything else. Ivan Bloch in his work *La guerre future,* published in 1898, had forecast with amazing accuracy how the power of modern weapons would produce deadlock on the battlefield and how the resulting attrition would destroy the fabric of the belligerent societies.[15] Bloch's thesis was widely known and much discussed in military periodicals. But since he was in effect saying that the military were now faced with a problem which they could not solve, it was not to be expected that many soldiers would agree with him. As for his conclusion, that war in future would be, if not impossible, then certainly suicidal, it had already been shown not to be true.

In 1904–5 Russia and Japan had fought a war with all the weapons whose lethal effects were so gruesomely described by Bloch, and Japan had won a clear-cut victory which established her in the ranks of the major powers. The effect on Russia had been much as Bloch had described, but revolution and defeat always stalked hand in hand. The war had indeed lasted for well over a year, but it had been fought by both belligerents at the end of long and difficult supply lines. In Europe, where communications were plentiful and short, and armies at hair-trigger readiness, the pattern of the German wars of unification seemed much more relevant: rapid mobilization and deployment of all available forces, a few gigantic battles—battles, indeed, which might be prolonged for days if not weeks as the protagonists probed for a flank or a weak point in the enemy defences—and a decision within a matter of months. Because that decision would be reached so quickly, it was important that all forces should be committed to action. There was no point in bringing up reserves after the battle had been lost. There was even less point—if indeed it occurred to anyone to do so—to prepare an industrial base to sustain a war of *matériel* which might last for years. The idea was that any national economy could endure such an ordeal was self-evidently absurd.

This shared assumption—that the war would inevitably be short—led on to another: that the best chances of victory lay in immediately taking the offensive. With the wisdom of hindsight it is easy for subsequent generations to condemn the suicidal unreality of this idea, but in the circumstances of the time it appeared reasonable enough. An offensive gave the best hope of disrupting or pre-empting the mobilization of the opponent and bringing him to battle under favourable conditions. As in a wrestling-match which had to be settled in a matter of minutes, to yield the initiative was to court defeat. The French had stood on the defensive in 1870 and been defeated. The Russians had stood on the defensive in 1904–5 and been defeated. Those who had studied the history of the American Civil War, who included all students of the British Army Staff College at Camberley, knew that the only hope of a Confederate victory had lain in a successful offensive, and that once Lee passed over to the defensive after the Battle of Gettysburg his defeat was only a matter of time. The lessons of history seemed to reinforce the strategic imperatives of 1914.

And let us not forget what those strategic imperatives were. The Germans had to destroy the French power of resistance before the full force of Russian strength could be developed. The Russians had to attack sufficiently early, and in sufficient strength, to take the weight off the French. The Austrians had to attack the Russians in order to take the weight off the Germans. For the French alone a defensive strategy was in theory feasible, but the precedent of 1870 made it understandably unpopular, and the national mood made it inconceivable. The doctrine of the offensive was certainly carried, in the pre-1914 French army, to quite unreasonable lengths, but that does not in itself mean that a posture of defence would necessarily have been any more effective in checking the German advance in 1914 than it was in 1940.

Finally we must remember that the stalemate on the western front did not develop for six months, and that on the eastern front it never developed at all. The open warfare of manoeuvre for which the armies of Europe had prepared was precisely what, in the autumn of 1914, they got. It resulted in Eastern Europe in a succession of spectacular German victories, and given bolder and more flexible leadership it might very well have done the same in the West. The terrible losses suffered by the French in Alsace in August and by the British and Germans in Flanders in November came in encounter battles, not in set-piece assaults against prepared defensive positions; and they were losses which, to the military leadership at least, came as no great surprise.

For this was the final assumption shared by soldiers throughout Europe: in any future war, armies would have to endure very heavy losses indeed. The German army, for one, had never forgotten the price it paid for its victories in 1870, when the French had been armed with breech-loading rifles which in comparison with the weapons now available were primitive. Since then the effects of every new weapon had been studied with meticulous care, and no professional soldier was under any illusions about the damage that would be caused; not simply by machine-guns (which were in fact seen as ideal weapons of a mobile offensive), but by magazine-loading rifles and by quick-firing artillery firing shrapnel at infantry in the open and high explosives against trenches. Their effects had been studied not only through controlled experiment, but in action, in the South African and Russo-Japanese wars. The conclusion generally drawn was that in future infantry would be able to advance only in open formations, making use of all available cover, under the protection of concentrated artillery fire.

But whatever precautions they took, sooner or later troops would have to assault across open ground with the bayonet, and they must then be prepared to take very heavy losses. This had happened in Manchuria, where the Japanese were generally seen as having owed their success not simply to their professional skills, but to their contempt for death. European Social Darwinians gravely propounded the terrible paradox, that a nation's fitness to survive depended on the readiness of its individual members to die. Avoidance of casualties was seen as no part of the general's trade, and willingness to accept them was regarded as a necessity for commander and commanded alike. Into the literature of pre-war Europe there crept the word which was to become the terrible leitmotiv of the coming conflict: 'sacrifice'; more particularly, 'the supreme sacrifice'.

That may have been all very well for professional soldiers whose job it is, after all, to die for their country if they cannot arrange matters any less wastefully. But the people who were going to die in the next war were not going to be just the professional soldiers. They would be the People: men recalled to the colours from civilian life or, in the case of England, volunteering to 'do their bit'. Would these young men, enervated by urban living, rotted by socialist propaganda, show the same Bushido spirit as the Japanese? This question was constantly propounded in military and right-wing literature during the ten years before the war. Kipling for one, surveying the civilians of Edwardian England in the aftermath of the Boer War, very much doubted it, and taunted his fellow countrymen in a series of scornful philippics:

Fenced by your careful fathers, ringed by your leaden seas,
Long did ye wake in quiet and long lie down at ease;
Till ye said of Strife, 'What is it?' of the Sword,
                                        'it is far from our ken';
Till ye made a sport of your shrunken hosts and a toy
                                        of your armèd men.[16]

In Germany Heinrich Class and Friedrich von Bernhardi, in France Charles
Maurras and Charles Péguy expressed the same doubts about the capacity
of their peoples to rise to the level of the forthcoming test. But the astonishing thing was that, when the time came, they did so rise. Why?

This brings us belatedly to the third element in the triad, the People.
Without the support, or at least the acquiescence of the peoples of Europe,
there would have been no war. This is the most interesting and most
complex area for historians to investigate. We know a lot—almost to excess—about the mood of the intellectuals and the élites in 1914,[17] but
what about the rest? There are now some excellent studies of local and
popular reactions in Britain, largely based on the superb sources at the
Imperial War Museum. Jean-Jacques Becker had done path-breaking work
for France in his study *1914: Comment les Français sont entrés dans la guerre*
(Paris, 1977) but elsewhere there remains much research to be done or,
where done, brought together. My own ignorance forces me to treat this
vast subject briefly and impressionistically, and I hope that others will be
able to correct some of my misconceptions and fill some of the yawning
gaps.

What does appear self-evident is that the doubts which European leaders felt about the morale of their peoples proved in 1914 to be ill-founded.
Those who welcomed war with enthusiasm may have been a minority
concentrated in the big cities, but those who opposed it were probably a
smaller minority still. The vast majority were willing to do what their
governments expected of them. Nationalistically oriented public education; military service which, however unwelcome and tedious, bred a sense
of cohesion and national identity; continuing habits of social deference:
all this helps explain, at a deeper level than does the strident propaganda
of the popular press, why the populations of Europe responded so readily
to the call when it came. For the 'city-bred populations' so mistrusted by
right-wing politicians the war came as an adventure, an escape from hum-
drum or intolerable lives into a world of adventure and comradeship.
Among the peasants of France, as M. Becker has shown us, there was little

enthusiasm, but rather glum acceptance of yet another unavoidable hard-ship in lives which were and always had been unavoidably hard; but the hardship fell as much on those who were left behind as on those who went away. The same can no doubt be said of the peasants of Central and Eastern Europe as well.

There was probably only a tiny minority, also, which considered the idea of war in itself repellent. Few military historians, and no popular historians, had ever depicted the realities of the battlefield in their full horror, and only a few alarmist prophets could begin to conceive what the realities of future battlefields would be like. Their nations, so the peoples of Europe had learned at school, had achieved their present greatness through successful wars—the centenaries of the battles of Trafalgar and of Leipzig had recently been celebrated with great enthusiasm in Britain and Germany—and there was no reason to think that they would not one day have to fight again. Military leaders were everywhere respected and pop-ular figures (Kitchener and Roberts more so, probably, than Arthur Bal-four and Herbert Asquith); military music was an intrinsic part of popular culture. In the popular mind, as in the military mind, wars were seen not as terrible evils to be deterred, but as necessary struggles to be fought and won.

I have touched on the Social-Darwinism of the period: the view, so widespread among intellectuals and publicists as well as among soldiers, that struggle was a natural process of development in the social as in the natural order of the world, and war a necessary procedure for ensuring survival of the fittest, among nations as among species. It is hard to know how seriously to take this. Its manifestations catch the eye of a contem-porary historian if only because they are, to our generation, so very shock-ing. But how widely were such views really held, and how far were people like F. N. Maude, Sidney Low, or Benjamin Kidd generally regarded as cranks? The same applies to the much-touted influence of Nietzsche and of Bergson among intellectuals—the creed of liberation from old social norms, of heroic egotism, of action as a value transcending all others. How widespread was their influence? Did it make the idea of war more generally acceptable than it otherwise would have been? Intellectuals, I am afraid, tend to overrate the importance of other intellectuals, or at best attribute to them an influence which becomes important only among later gener-ations. Webern and Schoenberg may have been composing in pre-war Vienna, but the tunes which rang in the ears of the 1914 generation were those of Franz Lehár and Richard Strauss.

And if there was a 'War Movement', there was also, far more evident and purposeful, a Peace Movement, derived from older liberal-rationalist roots. It was stronger in some countries than in others; then as now, it flourished more successfully in Protestant than in Catholic cultures, at its strongest in Scandinavia, the Netherlands, and Britain (not to mention the United States), weakest in Italy and Spain.[18] It was indeed the apparent strength and influence of the Peace Movement, especially at the time of The Hague Conferences, that provoked so much of the polemical writings of the Social Darwinians and caused so much concern to nationalistic politicians. In imperial Germany the Peace Movement had an uphill struggle; but if Heinrich Class and the Pan-German League were thundering out the dogmas of the War Movement, the far larger and more important Social Democratic Party rejected them[19]—as did the overwhelmingly dominant Liberal-Labour coalition in England and the left wing led by Jean Jaurès which triumphed at the polls in France in the spring of 1914. Social-Darwinism may have been not so much the prevailing Zeitgeist as a sharp minority reaction against a much stronger and deeply rooted liberal, rational and progressive creed whose growing influence seemed to some to be undermining the continuing capacity of nations to defend themselves.

But the events of 1914 showed these right-wing fears to be misplaced. Everywhere the leaders of the Peace Movement found themselves isolated: small and increasingly unpopular minorities of idealists, intellectuals and religious zealots. Events made it clear that, whatever their influence among intellectuals and élites, both the Peace and the War movements were marginal to the attitudes of the peoples of Europe. Those peoples did *not* reject war. Nor did they regard it as the highest good, the fulfilment of human destiny. They accepted it as a fact of life. They trusted their rulers and marched when they were told. Many did so with real enthusiasm; perhaps the more highly educated they were, the greater the enthusiasm they felt. None knew what they were marching towards, and any romantic notions they had about war shredded to pieces the moment they came under artillery fire. But they adjusted to the ordeal with astonishing speed and stoicism. It was indeed because they adjusted so well that the ordeal lasted for as long as it did.

8

1945–
End
of an
Era?

The Second World War finished in 1945, and this year we have been celebrating the fortieth anniversary of the end of a nightmare.* For every country in Europe the nightmare was slightly different. It was at its most terrible in the Soviet Union, whose land and people were subjected to a war of extermination which recalls the worst times of the Dark Ages. For the British these were mainly long years of tedium and deprivation, though we had our share of air bombardment as well. For Germany, nemesis came only in the last years of the war as Allied bombers destroyed her cities one by one. Her Italian ally experienced the torment of, in Winston Churchill's phrase, 'the hot rake of war' being drawn slowly up the length of the country. The occupied lands of Europe suffered helplessly as their Nazi conquerors plundered their economic resources, led off their populations to forced labour and ferretted out their hapless Jews. In 1945 Europe was almost too hungry and exhausted to celebrate. All the more reason why we should catch up forty years later.

At the time we were only conscious of, and grateful for, the fact that the Second World War—'Hitler's War'—was over. We dared not speculate more boldly what more, if anything, the Allied victories might imply. Those who were not alive at the time may find it difficult to appreciate the extent to which European politics in the post-war years were governed by the fear of a German revival and directed to making sure that this never happened again. The Third Reich had displayed such diabolical strength and her armies had fought with such skill and courage that it seemed

*This lecture was delivered in the University of Leiden in December 1985.

wildly optimistic to suppose that Germany would not once more trouble the peace of the world; that there would not be yet a Third German War. Perhaps that is a fear which has not been totally extinguished in the minds of some of the older generation, especially in Eastern Europe. But most of us would now agree that 1945 meant the end not only of the war which had begun in 1939, but of that German attempt to expand and establish herself as a hegemonial power which has been so well described by Fritz Fischer as Germany's *Griff nach der Weltmacht*. It was the end of half a century of German wars, and of the Germany which had provoked them.

This one can now say with a fair amount of certainty. Whatever conclusion we may reach about German responsibility for the events which led to the outbreak of war in 1914, no one can deny the ambitions nurtured by dominant elements in the German ruling classes before the war. These ambitions and the war aims announced shortly after the outbreak of war aimed quite explicitly at a hegemony of Europe which should itself provide a basis for World Power, or as we would now put it, 'Super-Power' status: a status enjoyed in 1914 by Germany's rival England, whose defeat had been the ambition of many Germans before the war and which became the main objective of German official policy once the war began. *Weltmacht oder Niedergang!* Germany must become a superpower or disappear. This was the self-fulfiling prophecy enunciated by the German Right Wing in 1914.

Twenty-five years later, Hitler resumed this quest for World Power, but preferred a different route. Rather than directly challenging British power, which he had learned to respect, and destroy her Empire, which he had come to admire, he preferred to establish German hegemony on the basis of East European conquests. He would destroy the Soviet Union and establish an unshakable power-base by controlling the Eurasian 'World Island': an empire which might well last the promised thousand years, and in comparison with which all other actors on the global scene would dwindle into insignificance. To a German brought up in pre-war Vienna who saw the old German-Slavic rivalry as the basic struggle of the twentieth century, this orientation came more naturally than did the westward-looking aspirations of the era of Tirpitz and Kaiser Wilhelm II. Hitler saw Germany's natural colonies as lying to the east. The task of eastward expansion and subjugation, suspended for five hundred years, must therefore be resumed. By consolidating German domination in this heartland of the world, the Slavs would be reduced to the subordinate status for which nature had intended them; the menace of Bolshevism, which threatened to destroy Western civilization from within, would be banished for ever;

and the Third Reich would be invulnerable against the only other world powers that might threaten her: Great Britain and the United States.

Whichever route the German leaders chose to World Power however, whether by building on the ruins of the British Empire or on those of the Soviet Union, the path lay through the establishment of a hegemony over Europe as complete as that enjoyed by Napoleon. The old balance of sovereign states reciprocally limiting one another's power had to be destroyed and an Empire, be it formal or informal, established over Germany's neighbours. Such would have been the consequence of German victory in the First World War, as it was briefly during the second. It is sometimes asked why during the First World War the British and French peoples endured the horrors of trench warfare for as long as they did. Why they did not do the sensible thing and make peace? The answer is that the price of such a peace appeared to involve the acceptance of German hegemony in Europe; a prospect which that generation found intolerable so long as they had the capacity to prevent it.

So 1945 did indeed see the end of the era of the German *Griff nach der Weltmacht* which spanned the first half of the twentieth century. Most of the generation which experienced that era felt that they need look no further and no deeper for an explanation of its events than the phenomenon of Germany itself. Dozens of books have been written since the war in an attempt to explain this phenomenon, seeking the explanation in German philosophy, or culture, or institutions, or the pattern of her historical development. Yet Germany was not the first State to seek hegemony in Europe.

I have already mentioned Napoleon. But the expansion of Napoleonic France was mostly seen at the time as being no more than a renewal of French hegemonial ambitions which had reached an earlier peak under Louis XIV. Nor has the memory of an earlier *Griff nach der Weltmacht,* that of Philip II of Spain, ever been entirely effaced. Is twentieth century Germany to be seen, therefore, simply as the successor, the inheritor of an aggressive impulse which has possessed each great European state in turn as each has attempted to consolidate its power? Was the 'German phenomenon' no more than the manifestation of a process inherent in the development of the European state-system as each State, having consolidated its authority at home and repelled attacks on its borders, sought greater security by extending its territory, until compelled by the power of its adversaries to accept the best frontiers it could get and settle down peacefully within them? And if that *is* so, was 1945 really the 'end of an era' at all; with 'the German problem' perhaps being settled, as was the French problem in 1815 and the Spanish problem in 1648, only to give place to another, and yet more troubling: the Soviet problem? Would Hitler's grasp after World Power simply be succeeded by that of Stalin? That was the way it appeared to many people within a few years—within a few months, indeed—of the Second World War.

Before attempting to answer this last question, which understandably concerns us so much today, let us examine a little further this historical process, of the rise and fall of hegemonial states. Was Hitler really no more than the twentieth-century equivalent of Philip of Spain and Louis XIV of France? Would a German hegemony of Europe have been simply one more chapter in a history book which already chronicled the Spanish hegemony of the sixteenth century, the French in the seventeenth and the English in the nineteenth?

I do not believe that this was the case; not because Germany was inherently different from other European nations, or the Germans different from other European peoples, nor even because of the technology which in the twentieth century transformed the capacity of governments to control their own peoples and make war on others; but because of the seismic upheaval of the French Revolution, whose after-effects continue to rumble even today in the remotest regions of the world. Wars of princes became wars of nations; more difficult to control, far more difficult to arrest.

This is not to underrate the importance of nationalism in earlier wars. The English, after four hundred years of warfare with the French from the fourteenth to the eighteenth centuries, had become deeply aware and proud of their own identity; and however much the Revolt of the Netherlands may have originated in the determination of local grandees to maintain their privileges against the encroachments of a centralising Spanish monarchy, eighty years of conflict forged a very self-conscious and self-confident Dutch nation. But the nationalism of the nineteenth century was something different. It was not simply historic; it was ideological and teleological. It was not just self-conscious: it involved a sense of mission, a concern for the dissemination of a system of values which, although rooted in one's own nation, were believed to be of universal validity and which it was therefore one's duty to spread as widely as possible. The impulse which propelled the armies of Revolutionary France throughout Europe was not simply devotion to the historic idea of France—an idea embodied, indeed, in the Monarchy which had just been destroyed. It was the idea that France was herself the instrument of a universal ideal; that ideal of liberty and equality and fraternity which arose from the philosophy of the Enlightenment, which had inspired American revolutionaries and English radicals as much as it did Frenchmen, and whose symbol, the tricolour, was seen—initially at least—as a liberating force wherever it was planted. The leaders of Revolutionary France saw themselves as the chosen instruments of history to break the chains of a corrupt old order which held all Europe in thrall. Having liberated themselves, they saw it as their duty to liberate others. Theirs was the first of those 'wars for national liberation' which in the nineteenth century were to spread to Italy and the Balkans and, in the twentieth, to the rest of the inhabited world.

Nevertheless, although the French armies believed that they carried liberty on the points of their bayonets, they were still *French* armies, and a bayonet is always a bayonet, whatever the cause in which it is wielded. 'Liberation' is sometimes indistinguishable from conquest, or so it seemed in most of the countries liberated by the French Revolutionary armies. With all its faults 'the old order' stood for traditional and indigenous values in a way that foreign forces of liberation did not. The peoples conquered by France began in self-defence to explore the roots of their own nationality. The Germans in particular began to discover themselves as 'a nation', and one deriving its identity from very different roots than the French. For German thinkers, France had discredited the liberal ideology—rather as, in our own day, the Soviet Union has discredited the ideology, once so attractive, of Communism. For German liberals the very terms 'liberty' and 'equality' had a foreign ring: *Einheit und Recht und Freiheit,* unity and law and freedom, did not. And it was on such distinctively *German* qualities, respect for the authority of the State, respect for law, respect for the power of the sword, that Germany was to be built: qualities which they believed to derive not from any universal moral imperatives but from the very nature of the German *Volk*.

So by the end of the nineteenth century national rivalries had become more than traditional power-struggles between States. They had become almost wars of religion, conflicts between competing 'ways of life'. In Western Europe new States came into existence—Germany and Italy— which both embodied and cultivated the new nationalistic ideals. In Eastern Europe, from the Baltic to the Balkans, the conflict took the form of increasingly bitter confrontation between Germans (or Hungarians) and Slavs. Imperial rivalries overseas were fuelled as much by the spirit of competing nationalism as they were by the quest for economic gain. It became a matter of national honour that as much of the world as possible should receive a French, or an English, or a German stamp; not simply to increase and enhance the power of the State, but in fulfilment of a civilizing mission, the dissemination of a value-system of which that nation felt itself to be the true guardian. For the generation of Cecil Rhodes in England it was seen as a cowardly betrayal to leave the dark places unenlightened, and it was, if anything, even worse to see them fall into the hands of the French.

This was the frame of mind of the generation which was to fight the First World War, and that conflict seemed, to all its participants, to be one for national fulfilment or survival. The Germans, whether in the Second Reich or in the Habsburg Empire, fought against what they saw as the encroaching Slav tide from the East. The French and the Italians fought their hereditary foes, the Germans, for the redemption of their national territory. The British Empire—and let us remember that Australians, Canadians and New Zealanders volunteered by the thousands to fight, to say nothing of Indians, who had less choice in the matter—fought against the German rival, who aimed so explicitly to supplant her as the World Power of the twentieth century.

Further, this was a war which seemed to many if not most, of those who fought in it to be natural, inevitable and almost desirable. The ideas of Charles Darwin had been crudely translated into political terms. It was widely held that progress came about, in international as in biological terms, through the survival of the fittest, and war was nature's way of eliminating the nations unfit to carry into the future the torch of civilization. In the political as in the natural world, it was necessary that the individual should die so that the species should survive. Throughout Western Europe, especially in Germany and Britain, there was a nagging doubt as to whether the street-bred populations of their increasingly urbanised societies would have the moral and physical stamina to meet the test when it came, would show the necessary readiness to die for their country. Events proved that they did have that readiness, to a quite amazing degree. The nation had become the object of a quasi-religious cult, and young men flocked to its banners as to a crusade. The generation of 1914 did not slither into the war by accident; they marched into it with shouts of joy.

This readiness for war was very general throughout Europe before 1914, but it existed in Germany in particularly strong concentration. The military traditions of the old Prussian ruling class had been deepened and extended by the triumph of 1870, which was attributed, with some reason, to the excellence of Prussian military institutions. The dynamic ambitions of the new bourgeoisie led them to align themselves with, rather than oppose, those traditions. The result was a mood of aggressive militarism which gave a new meaning to the concept of *Preussentum,* and which appalled foreign visitors to pre-war Germany. The mood of Berlin in 1914 was notably different from that in London or Paris or Vienna: the emissary of the President of the United States, Colonel Edward M. House, described it as 'militarism run stark mad'.

The terrible experiences of the First World War were enough to extinguish such militarism where it existed west of the Rhine, and it is remarkable that it should have survived even in Germany. But it did; reinforced by the bitterness of a defeat which seemed all the more intolerable after an almost unbroken series of victories by the German armies on every front, and of a dictated peace which, in its settlement of Germany's eastern frontiers, deprived her of what many saw as the heartland of her nation. Certainly, the old class basis of Prussian militarism, focussed as it had been on a Monarchy, a court and a privileged officer-corps, had been destroyed; but it was replaced by National Socialism, a populist movement giving unbounded scope to ambition and prejudice wherever it existed. In the creed of Nazism, it was as if the old national spirit which, taken in moderation, could prove a healthy tonic, was concentrated into a horribly lethal poison. The old and entirely justifiable pride in German culture was perverted into a spurious biological doctrine of racial supremacy. The old readiness to fight for one's country, a readiness without which, in the last resort, no State can achieve or maintain its independence, was perverted into a worship of war as a life-style, a warrior ethic which saw in war not just a necessary instrument of national policy but an end in itself. Nazism was both the culmination and the betrayal of European nationalism, and the flagging national spirit of other European States had to be revived in order to defeat it.

German hubris was followed by nemesis: not only was German nationalism destroyed, but so was the German State which it had created. But it was not simply the German bid for hegemony that was ended in 1945: it was the entire era of European nationalist conflict which had opened with the French Revolutionary Wars at the end of the eighteenth century. Naturally national feeling in Europe survives and under certain circumstances may revive, but we can prophecy with a fair degree of confidence that the nations of Europe, as nations, will not go to war with each other again.

But 1945 saw the end of another and yet more significant era in world history—that of the centrality, and ultimately the dominance, of Europe itself. That era had spanned half a millennium; opening at the end of the fifteenth century with the first emergence of the great European powers and their gradual, tentative exploration of the wider world and culminating in that sudden expansion, almost explosion of European power, made possible by scientific and technological advances, which by the end of the nineteenth century had extended European dominance to almost every corner of the inhabited world. Perhaps the most significant event of 1945 was not the suicide of Hitler in his bunker, or even the explosion of the atomic bombs over Hiroshima and Nagasaki. It was the meeting of Soviet and American troops at Torgau on the Elbe, shaking hands over the ruins of an old Europe that would never dominate the world again.

It was the Frenchman Alexis de Tocqueville, writing almost a century earlier, who had first had the prophetic vision of a world dominated by these two continental powers, the United States and Russia, whose potential strength, once they were able to exploit it, would dwarf that of the European nations as completely as the European powers had dwarfed the Italian city-states of the Renaissance, or as the Greek city-states had been dwarfed by the power of Rome. By the end of the nineteenth century this was clear to a far wider circle of European thinkers. The prospect does much to explain the frenetic efforts of the British to turn their sprawling global possessions into an Empire which would be a Greater Britain, and of the continental powers to acquire imperial possessions at all, in order to retain their status in what was now going to be not just a European but a global power system.

The defeat of Germany in two world wars was to signify more than the elimination of one of these European competitors for world power. The effort involved in defeating her so exhausted her European rivals that they were themselves unable to sustain that share of world domination which they already possessed. Britain's effort to maintain a world role was doomed after her decision to grant independence to the Indian sub-continent (a decision made inevitable by the events of the Second World War) though it was not until the Suez debacle in 1956 that the full hopelessness of that effort became clear. France fought more bitterly to retain her possessions in Africa and Asia. The Netherlands and Portugal, the oldest imperial powers of all, relinquished theirs with varying degrees of regret.

Only one thing could have prolonged the existence of the European Empires—the continuing approval and support of the United States. It was the denial of that support that spelled the end of the old European Empires. The citizens of the United States had not joined in the Second World War to prop up a system of imperial domination against which they had been the first people to revolt. And it has been with genuine bewilderment that they find themselves today so generally reviled as its inheritors.

It might seem that the present Soviet–American rivalry is a continuation, on a larger scale, of the old European national antagonism; but this would be a very superficial judgement. In the first place, neither the Soviet Union nor the United States is inspired by the kind of nationalism which found its apogee in the creed of Nazi Germany and was not uncommon in imperialist Britain a generation earlier; the belief that there was something intrinsic about their own people which uniquely qualified them to rule. The very multi-ethnicity of those two vast Unions would make any such belief self-evidently untenable, and both have been singularly unsuccessful in producing an imperial ruling class. Rather, their nationalism is, like that of Revolutionary France at the end of the eighteenth century, based on the belief that their political system embodies certain moral absolutes which are of universal applicability; whether it be the concept of human rights elaborated by the Founding Fathers of the United States but rooted in French, British, and Dutch political ideas of the seventeenth and eighteenth centuries; or that, held by the Soviet leadership, of the evolution of a just and equal society through the class struggle, which, though it may have received its final formulation at the hands of Lenin, was developed by German thinkers in exile in nineteenth-century England and inspired powerful political parties in every European nation long before it started to make political headway in Russia. The United States and the Soviet Union are both in their ways the inheritors of the universalist ideas of the Enlightenment against which European, and especially German nationalism was very largely a reaction. The Star-Spangled Banner and the Red Flag, each stands, as the French tricolour once stood, not so much for a nation as for the idea which had given birth to that nation, and which would or should act as midwife to others. Both expect to find sympathisers among enlightened men and women throughout the world, and are puzzled that they do not find more.

This does not mean that I subscribe to the idea of the 'moral equivalence' of the Super Powers which is fashionable in some circles in Western Europe. But it does mean that the capacity of the Super Powers to extend, and certainly to maintain their influence depends far more on their continuing ability to preserve their image as the focus of a shared system of values than it does on their ability to deploy military, or even economic power. The nations of Western Europe freely associate themselves with the United States because they stand for a political and social system based upon values which we broadly share and which we do not regard as being specifically 'American'. But we must not forget that after the war there were still many Europeans, West as well as East, who saw the value-system focussed on Moscow as holding out a better promise of a just society and who were prepared to collaborate with their Russian comrades in bringing it about.

We must not fall into the error of assuming that the Second World War was like the first, simply a War of Nations. It was an ideological conflict in which many of the participants were themselves deeply divided. It was Hitler's achievement to unite against him the forces in Europe which till his advent had themselves been in a state of internecine conflict since 1918: communists and their sympathisers for whom the Soviet Union, with all its imperfections, represented the wave of the future, and liberals who still believed that a market economy and parliamentary democracy, in spite of their manifold failings, still provided the best prospects for human happiness.

Not until 1941 was that tension relieved. The Nazi-Soviet Pact of 1939 ensured that for two years communists throughout Europe, on instructions from Moscow, opposed and impeded what was depicted as an imperialist war. Only when Hitler invaded the Soviet Union did the opposing streams unite in an anti-Fascist Front. But the defeat of Germany left them again in stark confrontation. The prestige and power of the victorious Soviet Union brought communist parties throughout Europe to a position of such commanding influence that for a few months it looked as if they might really take over power.

It was this threat, rather than that of Soviet invasion as such, that so alarmed West European democrats in the aftermath of the Second World War; and it was as much the loss of confidence in Communism as it was the vestigial American military presence, that prevented the liberating soviet banners from sweeping westward to the Atlantic. Once the Soviet banners were seen as being not liberating but oppressive, representing not a universally valid ideology but an alien Empire intent on maintaining and extending its power—as Revolutionary France had come to be seen at the beginning of the nineteenth century—then they lost all their universalist moral authority. In Western Europe today communism survives only where it can be seen to grow from truly indigenous roots, and association with the Soviet Union is an embarrassment to its leaders. In Eastern Europe, Soviet control will remain precarious unless the peoples of those territories come to regard Moscow with a greater degree of respect and affection than they show any sign of doing at present. As with Revolutionary France, the glorious promise held out to mankind by the Soviet Union has shrunk to a narrow and defensive nationalism which has provoked counter-nationalism wherever it has ventured beyond its borders. Bayonets, as I said earlier, are always bayonets, and unless tipped with a substantial cushion of moral acceptance they provide very uncomfortable seats.

Is American idealism subject to the same hazards? I think that only the most paranoid of politicians, on the extreme left or the extreme right of the political spectrum, would allege that American influence in Western Europe is dependent on their military presence. Rather the opposite: their military presence is only possible because of an influence they have established as a result of genuinely shared values, a common belief that pluralist democracy and a market-oriented economy is, in spite of its evident and appalling inadequacies, a more effective means of creating and distributing wealth and ensuring human freedom than is totalitarianism and state control. Yet even for West Europeans the United States remains a foreign country. Its armed forces remain foreign forces, however friendly; and the less sympathetic one is to American ideology, the more foreign will those forces appear. That anti-American feeling should have developed in Europe after a generation, whether because of nostalgia for former greatness, or hostility to the capitalist system, or simply discontent with the dangers and imperfections of an international order underwritten by American nuclear power—all this is entirely understandable. What is perhaps surprising is that there should not be more.

But whatever the acceptability of the American presence in Western Europe, we must not blind ourselves to the unpopularity of the United States throughout so much of what is misleadingly termed 'the Third World'; an unpopularity evidenced by vote after vote in the United Nations General Assembly, and which the most generous and massive economic aid does nothing whatever to assuage. This is certainly not a reaction to the presence of American bayonets. Indeed it is precisely in those few countries where United States armed forces are deployed overseas—Western Europe, South Korea, Japan—that the Americans are most popular. Rather, it is a reaction to American wealth and power on the part of newly-developing nations which see little if any prospect of ever graduating into the same league and whose cultural orientation makes Western value-systems often appear profoundly alien. Indeed, in the same way as European reaction against liberal universalism in the nineteenth century set historians and lexicographers and poets re-creating and sometimes re-inventing old and often forgotten national cultures—German, Bohemian, Irish, Flemish, Croatian—so the impact of a disturbing and alien Western universalism on the Third World has created élites who defiantly proclaim their ethnic independence by emphasising religious practices, habits of dress and cultural patterns to distance themselves from developments which seem likely to destroy their independent identities—or to prevent such identities from emerging at all. In this respect the Americans are the whipping-boys for the West as a whole.

To suggest that the end of the European era simply means the division of the world between two global ideological empires, the one focussed on Washington and the other on Moscow, is thus misleading. The process of national expansion and reaction initiated by the French Revolution may have burned itself out in Europe, but it has now spread to the entire world. As in the history of Europe, the greater the power, the greater the nationalist reaction is likely to be. Neither Soviet military power nor American economic power can give lasting dominance to those who wield it. At best they can provide opportunities for the values of their respective societies to be sympathetically considered and possibly absorbed. But if those values are absorbed, it will be in a manner compatible with indigenous culture and not one overtly owing allegiance to any foreign creed. There are likely therefore to be as many varieties of Marxism as there are of Christianity; regimes expressing fidelity to democratic ideals will have their own peculiar interpretation of the doctrine of human rights; and many, like the Islamic fundamentalists, will eschew both ideologies and chart their own path in the light of cultural traditions exhumed or manufactured for the purpose.

So though the European era may be ended, the European bequest of diversity and conflict will continue to trouble the world. And to be quite frank, in spite of all the dangers and difficulties which this will involve, it is something that I cannot find it in me to regret. The world is still too young for it to sink into placid and monotonous uniformity, and the womb of history too fecund for us to believe that there are not still many new societies and cultures waiting to see the light of day.

9

Ideology and

International

Relations

A distinctive feature of the evolution of the modern international system has been the emergence of ideologies so universalist in their assumptions that they have ignored, or worse, denied the cultural and political diversities of mankind—diversities which constitute the ineluctable framework of international politics and which make the conduct of foreign affairs such a complex and difficult craft. One major obstacle, however, to understanding the problems which this development poses for the theory and practice of international relations is the fact that the correct usage of the term 'ideology' is very much broader than that which is generally accepted today.

The word is commonly used to describe a particularly rigorous, comprehensive and dogmatic set of interrelated values, based on a systematic philosophy which claims to provide coherent and unchallengeable answers to all the problems of mankind, whether individual or social: a philosophy codified, preserved and expounded as a doctrine above question or challenge. Such a philosophy was that of Thomist Christianity. It is in that sense that we speak today of 'Marxist–Leninist ideology'. It was a term also applied, if in less rigorous form, to the racist values which inspired the Nazi party in Germany and their imitators elsewhere. And it can be applied to one continuing strain of thought in the complex culture of the United States, that of dogmatic Jeffersonian democracy, which has received considerable emphasis over the past decade. When we speak of an *idéologue*, in short, we know what we mean: a priest of a secular religion.

But the true meaning of the word is that given by John Plamenatz in his book *Ideology*: 'a set of closely-related beliefs or ideas, or even attitudes, characteristic of a group or community'.[1] This implies something much broader, looser, and less codifiable: a value-system, a 'mind-set' as the

139

Americans might call it, a Weltanschauung as the Germans *do* call it, or, in the French expression before which my colleagues in the historical profession prostrate themselves in such awe, a *mentalité*. It suggests that richly confused mixture of partly inherited, partly acquired assumptions, very little if at all subjected to deliberate introspection, which most of us accept quite unconsciously as the framework of our lives and which most of us would find it difficult, perhaps impossible, and certainly very embarrassing to codify and defend.

In fact the correct usage of the term 'ideology' bears as much relation to that normally employed as does the *mentalité* of a professing member of the Church of England to the Thirty-nine Articles, or the Athanasian Creed, or any of the other documents where the fundamentals of Christian belief are set out with embarrassing clarity. But to those standing outside our culture, this confused accumulation of inherited or acquired beliefs, attitudes and values, which lose all their essence if we try to codify and define them, may appear more systematic, more logically interconnected, more finite and definable, than we ourselves realize. We are all *idéologues* in spite of ourselves.

The earlier thinkers to whom the term *idéologue* was applied were indeed ideologists in the sense that we understand the term today. These were the French rationalists of the eighteenth century, especially the group who in 1750 launched the *Encyclopédie* as a kind of manifesto: men such as Diderot, d'Alembert, Helvetius, d'Holbach, and their later disciple Condorcet. These people had a clear and systematic philosophy, based on their perception of Man as a rational and reasoning being, capable through his reason of understanding the laws governing both nature and human society and with an inherent right both to exercise that reason and to create an environment enabling him to do so.

Thinkers equipped with such clear and irrefutable insights could thus cut through and reject the muddle of superstition, injustice and prescriptive privilege on which society had hitherto been based—the ideology, in fact, of the ancien régime—and substitute a new, coherent, systematic ideology of their own; one which would define the nature of justice and so make possible the creation of the just society. Truth, Order, and Justice would reign hand in hand. As in *The Magic Flute,* the forces of the Queen of the Night would be put to flight and Sarastro, the High Priest of Reason, would rule supreme. Sarastro, it may be noted, had a very summary way of dealing with his adversaries, but then they were by definition reactionary and disruptive. When a regime embodies justice, freedom and human rights, anyone opposed to it is automatically opposed to justice, freedom and human rights. These new insights made possible a New Order. But a New Order presupposed New Men, whose minds had been cleansed from all the prejudices and falsehoods of the past. The old, messy, incoherent ideology had to be removed and a new one fitted in its place before the brave new world could be brought into being.

When fifty years later Karl Marx attacked 'bourgeois ideology', it was not these systematic ideologists he had in mind. He was certainly able to demonstrate that their particular interpretation of the Rights of Man, with its emphasis on the individual and his property, served the class interests of the bourgeoisie. But for Marx, 'ideology' did mean *mentalité*; and the *mentalité* of the possessing classes in the early nineteenth century, while it comprised some of the ideas of the revolutionary *idéologues,* included a great deal else besides. It would have had to accommodate the attitudes of unlettered people who had never heard of the Enlightenment and would probably have disapproved of it if they had. It comprehended the whole cast of mind, the Weltanschauung, with which or into which everyone in society, particularly everyone in the huge amorphous social group known as 'the bourgeoisie' had been born. It comprised everything that grew from the soil created by the particular set of economic relations which characterized 'bourgeois society'. For Marx, ideology was not so much *what* people thought as *how* they thought and inescapably thought. There was only a small group of intellectuals who like Marx himself were able, through some Houdini-like trick which has never been explained, to escape from the dark prison of the mind to which history had confined their contemporaries and view the development of mankind in its entirety with minds (like those of the Encyclopaedists) scoured clean from the detritus of the past. Only they, equipped with this knowledge, could open the prison gates and allow the rest of mankind to escape in their turn.

These emancipated minds could now develop a totally fresh ideology, one which would be as deeply rooted in the class interests of the proletariat as that of the Encyclopaedists had been in the class interests of the bourgeoisie. The difference was that, whereas the doctrines of the Encyclopaedists really had developed, naturally and unconsciously, out of the interests and perceptions of the middle and professional classes, those of the Marxists had to be deliberately planted in the mind of a proletariat which was as yet unconscious of them, being still blinded by a 'false consciousness' derived from their bourgeois environment, which it was (and still is) the task of the enlightened to strip away.

So this proletarian, or Marxist, ideology had to be *created.* A new and coherent value-system had to be built up to replace the jumble of ideas and prejudices which clogged the perceptions of mankind in general and the working classes in particular. And this new system of ideas, this new morality, had, once it had been established, to be constantly purged of all divergent views, heretical interpretations and doctrinal disagreements that might sully the purity of the new world-vision and make the new order unworkable. Thus 'ideology' was not seen as something that was *there* already, whether consciously or (more likely) unconsciously. It had to be defined, imposed, and then kept free from taint. Ideology as *mentalité* became ideology as dogma.

What had all this to do with international relations?

The original *idéologues* were not so much international as pre-national. Reason, in their eyes, was uniform and universal; they could therefore speak for all rational men. It is true that almost simultaneously with the appearance of the *Encyclopédie*, Montesquieu had published *L'esprit des lois*, in which he described how historical and geographical circumstances created diversity in human cultures. But even Montesquieu had defined laws as being 'necessary relations arising out of the nature of things';[2] and that 'necessity' had surely by definition to be universal. For the Encyclopaedists, Reason operated as uniformly throughout the world as did the laws of natural science, and all that stood in the way of its universal recognition was ignorance, superstition and the surviving vested interests of the old feudal order. These puddles of obscurantism would quickly evaporate once the healing rays of education (within one's own society) and civilization (applied to other barbarous societies which one had a duty to conquer and rule) could be brought to play on them. But to make that process possible at all, it might be necessary to have revolution at home and wars for liberation abroad. Liberty for oneself was not enough; the duty remained to liberate one's fellows. The world could not survive half slave to superstition and half free from it.

There is something gruesomely familiar about this rhetoric of the Girondins, those early idealists who preached world revolution only to be devoured at home by their own. Here 'the modern age' begins. For it was this rationalist universalism which was, in the twentieth century, to become so characteristic of both liberal democracies and Marxist regimes. In the United States it survived in a particularly untainted form until the era of Woodrow Wilson, and still reverberates strongly, if intermittently, through American presidential rhetoric. All peoples, according to this ideology, are naturally 'good'. If we could only get at them over the heads of their oppressors, we would find them to have the same perception of their needs and values, the same capacity to settle their disputes according to rational principles, and so to live together in peace. All that is needed, therefore, is the universal institution of democracy. Conflicts arise only because of misperceptions, or of the vested, anti-social interests of ruling groups. In 1919 Woodrow Wilson believed that he could achieve a peaceful settlement of European disputes by appealing to peoples over the heads of governments. In the Second World War the belief persisted in liberal circles—and indeed still persists in some quarters today—that if only Hitler and the Nazi 'clique' could have been removed from power by a coup mounted by 'good' Germans, the Second World War might have been avoided or at least brought to an early end. There is a strong school of strategic thought in the United States today which advocates the discriminating use of nuclear weapons to 'decapitate' the Soviet regime; presumably on the assumption that the liberated Soviet peoples would then elect a government truly representative of their values and interests. The question of *why* such naturally good and rational people so often end up with such bad governments is less often addressed.

The liberal *idéologues* thus had, and still have, a 'theory' of international relations. It is based on the assumption that there already exists a natural global community, whether international or supranational, whose interests are harmonious and whose value-system would be generally perceived as universal if only all its members could be reached, liberated and where necessary educated.

In nineteenth-century Europe it was believed that this liberation would take the form of the assertion or fulfilment of a 'national' identity. Once nations had achieved full independence, it was assumed by Mazzini and his disciples, they would co-exist in harmony, each adding the timbre of its particular instrument to the universal concert of mankind whose tones had been blended by a master hand. Nations would accept their role as provinces in a single global society. International relations would then be simply the administration of an essentially homogeneous world community.

This essentially Benthamite view of international relations was inherited by Marx, who substituted the 'proletariat' for the liberal concept of 'peoples'. Like the liberals, the Marxists believed that international conflict existed only because of the vested interests of the ruling classes. But they carried their analysis a stage further. The whole concept of nationality they saw as a bourgeois myth which the proletariat did not share: 'The proletariat [wrote Marx] are in the great mass by nature without national prejudice, and their whole upbringing and movement are essentially humanitarian, anti-national. Only the proletariat can destroy nationality'.[3]

So whereas Mazzini saw the problem of international conflict as one which would be resolved in a natural harmony of nations, for Marx the problem itself would cease to exist. With the triumph of the proletariat the whole illusion of nationality would vanish. Ultimately of course the State itself would vanish with the advent of the classless society and the consequent disappearance of the ruling classes, which Marx claimed used the State as a mechanism for oppression of the proletariat. There would then be no need for international relations at all. Issue a few manifestos, as Trotsky said when he took over the Russian Foreign Ministry, and then shut up shop. But meanwhile, there must be war for the liberation of those people who were still unjustly oppressed, whether by their own ruling classes or by colonialist occupiers. Tomorrow, as Auden wrote during his Marxist phase.

Tomorrow, for the young, the poets exploding like bombs . . .
  Tomorrow the bicycle races.
Through the suburbs on summer evenings: but today the struggle.[4]

So for both kinds of *idéologue,* liberal as well as Marxist, international relations were no more than a temporary and disagreeable necessity, a transitory phase which would, inevitably and properly, be one of conflict ranging from competitive co-existence to full-scale wars of liberation. At the end of this phase there would be peace, which would come about not through the establishment of world empire or even world government, but through the removal of obstacles to the emergence of a world community which was *there* already, and which would begin to function once the operation of Reason, or the forces of History, were given unchecked rein.

This optimism has unfortunately not been borne out by events. Exactly two centuries have passed since the outbreak of the French Revolution— two hundred years of conflict which might lead us to suppose that in the affairs of mankind there is no such thing as progress but that, as in New-tonian physics, action and reaction are equal and opposite. Internation-alism, so far from dissolving nationalism, has provoked it. In the eigh-teenth century within the commonwealth of learning on both sides of the Atlantic the Encyclopaedists were indeed seen as expressing the ideas of all civilized and rational men. The fact that they gave expression to those ideas largely in French was no more an obstacle to their acceptance than had been Aquinas's Latin or Aristotle's Greek to the universal acceptance of their ideas. But the commonwealth of learning was small. Once these ideas became more widely known, and, more important, once they had become associated with the activities and ambitions of Revolutionary France, it was a very different matter. The dawn of the reign of Reason and the establishment of the Rights of Man became widely associated first with ferociously oppressive Jacobinism and then with militarist and expansionist Bonapartism. A few sages like Goethe remained loyal to their ideals, accepting the French *imperium* as an acceptable price to pay for the implementation of the values of the Enlightenment, but they were in a minority. The forces of populist chauvinism proved stronger than those of Reason and Reform.

Arguably, the French Revolution set back the cause of political reform in Britain and Germany by half a century by strengthening not only the fears but also the popularity of the ancien régime. Certainly that Revolution led, not to a new age of peace for mankind, but to an era of escalating nationalism which was to reach a bloody climax in Europe in 1914–18 and whose global reverberations show no signs of dying away. For the nineteenth century witnessed the growth of another kind of ideology: that of the Nation.

It was Rousseau, the progenitor of so many of the ideas which were to come together in the totalitarianism of the twentieth century, who first pointed to the possibility, indeed the necessity, of creating 'nations' by a process of ideological indoctrination: 'It is the task of education [he wrote] to give to each human being a national form, and so direct his opinions and tastes that he should be a patriot by inclination, by passion, by necessity. On first opening his eyes a child must see his country, and until he dies, must see nothing else'.[5]

The same use of education for the process of nation-building was to be urged by Fichte in the aftermath of Prussia's catastrophic defeat at Jena in 1806: 'I propose a total change in the existing scheme of education as the sole means of preserving the existence of the German nation. . . . By means of this new education we want to mould the Germans into a corporate body, which shall be stimulated and animated in all its individual members by the same interest'.[6] Germany would exist, in short, if Germans were brought up to *will* its existence. The same would apply to Italy, Poland, Greece and all other communities aspiring to a national identity; not least to the United States.

As the nineteenth century wore on, these aspirations became reality. New states were created, and old ones consolidated their internal authority. That authority made possible universal, State-directed education, and the requirements of the modern State made it necessary. Education was everywhere used to create national self-consciousness as an essential element in social mobilization. Nationalism was not ideology as dogma; that is, it was not, like Marxism, based on a coherent philosophy. It was rather ideology as *mentalité*; but it was a *mentalité* as artificial and as deliberately created as the 'proletarian' ideology of Marx. National attitudes, myths, beliefs and perceptions had to be inculcated in the minds of the young, and during the nineteenth century schoolteachers throughout Europe and the United States saw it as their function to do precisely that: to plant in the minds of their pupils ideas, myths and attitudes which were specifically English, German, French or American.

The Mazzinian assumption that all this would ultimately result in universal harmony was not generally shared. The perception of Fichte, itself derived from Kant, was a great deal more acute: 'Every nation wishes to spread its own ideas and ways of life as far as it can, and as far as it is in its power, to incorporate the whole of mankind; and this is due to a compulsion which God has implanted into men and on which the society of nations, their mutual friction and development rests'.[7] The result, as most of Fichte's countrymen came to agree, was likely to be not universal harmony but universal struggle, as each nation strove for self-determination at the expense of its neighbours—a struggle willed by God, as Fichte's generation saw it, or by nature, as it was seen once the process of natural selection and evolution had been expounded by Charles Darwin. In the conceptual framework provided by the ideology of nationalism, therefore, international relations was the art of surviving in a jungle of predators in order to preserve one's own superior culture and ultimately to impose it upon inferior adversaries.

Looking back on European nationalism as it developed before 1914 from the perspective given by the experience of two world wars, we are naturally inclined to regard the whole phenomenon as a pathological condition, a sickness which it needed a terrible blood-letting to cure. But we historians know, or should know, that our judgements are themselves culture-bound, an aspect of the *mentalité* of our own times. A Social Darwinian from the 1900s might very plausibly argue that those conflicts were indeed necessary, that the blood-letting was inevitable, so as to determine which of the various competing European ideologies should set the pattern for the future development of mankind. Those who are not willing to fight in order to protect and if possible extend the political and social structures which were created by and which preserve their cultural values, will see those values wither and die, like molluscs deprived of their shells. If the two wars were terrible, it was because both sides so profoundly believed in their ideals. The severity of the ordeal was due not so much to the weapons with which the belligerents fought as to the social cohesion which enabled them to endure for so long. Ultimately, so the Darwinian would argue, only the strongest did survive, as nature had intended; and it has been the ideology, the *mentalité* of those victors which has shaped the world in which we now live.

It is understandable that after 1918 such Social-Darwinian views became unpopular and after 1945 virtually untenable. The wars destroyed, at least among European nations, the frenetic nationalism that had caused them. But although we may regard their destruction with understandable relief, we must take account of two points. The first is that the nineteenth century process of 'nationalization' which was pioneered in Europe is still working itself out in the rest of the world. New states, in order to create and preserve social cohesion, still inculcate in their citizens some measure of national ideology. Unsatisfied aspirants to statehood, be they Basques, Palestinians, Kurds, Sikhs or Tamils, continue to wage their own holy wars for self-determination and bring up their children in the true faith, as did Czechs, Italians, Germans, Poles, Irish, Serbs and Croats in Europe a century and a half ago. These aspirations are unfortunately often satisfiable only at the expense of one another. Europeans may feel blasé about nationalism, but there are many dedicated and violent people in the world who do not.

The second point is that once the genie of national self-consciousness is out of the bottle it is not easy to put it back. There are broadly three ways in which this has been attempted in the post-war era. The first way is represented by the efforts of the victorious powers after the Second World War to extinguish the nationalist ideologies of their defeated adversaries as part of the process of removing their war-making capabilities. But the Japanese have remained firmly Japanese, and the Germans have remained obstinately and consciously German; aware of a common past and a common culture embodied in their language which create among them a truly special relationship cutting across political divisions and differences in ideological dogma. Were the two Germanys to remain separate for generations, then the diversity of their historical experience might indeed create cultural diversity, as geographical separation is gradually creating cultural diversity between the British and the Australians; but then we would see the emergence of two separate nations, each with its own ideological *mentalité*, not of a single 'non-nation'.

A second route to 'denationalization' might appear to lie in the use of the very process by which nationalism was inculcated: education. To a certain extent that is happening in Britain. The kind of 'national' history out of which the 'myth' of the British nation was created by nineteenth-century historians—the history of princes and dynasties, of wars and conquest, even of constitutional and parliamentary evolution—is given decreasing attention in our schools and universities. The evolution of British society in all its diversity is emphasized rather than that of the British State. Further, the cultural values of other societies, primarily those to whose emigrants we are hosts, are often given as much attention as those of our own. The idea that British culture is not only distinctive but *properly* distinctive, something with its own value and legitimacy, is unfashionable, to put it no more strongly, while the whole concept of 'patriotism' elicits suspicion and mockery.

To pronounce judgement on this development is to reveal one's own *mentalité*, or more likely that of one's generation. But it is an open question whether abandonment of traditional methods of maintaining social cohesion, without putting anything in their place, will really produce a higher culture whose diverse elements will successfully blend in a richer synthesis; or whether it is not likely to create a depressed and dispirited society, unsure of its identity, increasingly beset by conflicts of class and race, and less and less significant on the international scene. For unless the enormous power wielded by the modern State is legitimized and made acceptable by the mobilization of some kind of numinous national feeling, unless its guardians can credibly claim to be acting on behalf of a community whose diversities are reconciled in the higher and deeper interest implicit in the term 'the nation', that power will be seen as oppressive and is likely to become oppressive. Politics then degenerate into a dismal cycle of disruption and oppression, which we see in so many Third World countries and which sometimes appear to threaten our own.

The third escape-route from the ideology of nationalism is of course to replace it with the ideology of internationalism. But the record here has not been good either. We must never forget that the primary and instinctive loyalties of human beings are to the small local communities they know best and of which they and their families have always formed part. Parochialism came before nationalism. The creation of national self-consciousness was, for the mass of mankind, a widening of horizons, not a narrowing of them. Progress towards a yet higher ideology, a system of cultural values transcending national boundaries, is possible for a highly-educated minority, but in making such progress that minority is in danger of distancing itself from the mass of its fellow-countrymen, if not of losing touch with them altogether.

Since ideology as *mentalité* is shaped by experience, progress of this kind certainly becomes possible for larger groups in society as communication and travel become easier and as English becomes a lingua franca for international intercourse. Within Western Europe a genuine community may indeed be gradually shaping, as such a community was gradually shaped among the different nations in the United Kingdom. But Western Europe is not the world, and even such limited internationalism is not cost-free. It is often seen, at least initially, as an attempt to inculcate alien values, and the liberation it offers is suspected as a new and unwelcome kind of slavery.

The ideology of the Enlightenment may have been that of all civilized men, but there were a lot of uncivilized people, particularly in Germany, England and Spain, who saw it as an attempt to legitimize a specifically French hegemony. The whole essence of German nationalism, indeed, derived from a sense of outrage at the invasion and pollution of indigenous values by what was widely seen as a specious and debilitating alien creed. A generation later the Slavophile movement in Russia was born of a no less violent reaction against invasion by these alien Western values, and developed its own specific, indigenous ideology in defiant contrast—an ideology which has probably been a great deal more influential in determining the *mentalité* of the Soviet Union today than the formal dogmas of Marxism–Leninism.

Conversely the proletarian internationalism preached by the Soviet Union after 1917 was widely seen, not least among the working classes in Western Europe, as alien, subversive of indigenous cultural and social values, and a flimsy cover for Soviet imperialism. In many influential quarters in the West today the doctrines of Marxism–Leninism are still seen as no more than a programme for Soviet 'world conquest'. In Europe between the wars, Fascism everywhere derived much of its appeal from its hostility to international capitalism on the one hand and to international communism on the other. Both were depicted by Fascists as alien and sinister influences which threatened the capacity of nations to preserve their own values and control their own destinies.

This negative reaction to internationalism is still evident today. If the West fears Soviet-sponsored internationalism as subversive of its values, the Soviets are equally fearful of the disintegrating effect of Western values on their own society and those of their satellites. For many Third World states, 'Western values' derived from the universalism of the Enlightenment are either irrelevant or deeply disruptive, an instrument for ensuring a continuing Western hegemony. It is perhaps only the depth of their impoverishment that keeps them from reacting still more strongly against the ideology of the rich white world; and once that poverty is alleviated we may see yet more violent nationalist reactions. And even within the West, the growth of an internationally-minded 'overclass' with their credit cards, overseas business contacts and holidays abroad, the growing internationalization of their cities, and increased provision for servicing tourism, all combine to leave behind a semi-educated and resentful underclass which defiantly takes as its symbols the national flags abandoned by the élites—the Union Jack, the Stars and Stripes, perhaps even the swastika—and displays them on new and less glorious battlefields. These debased relics of national identity are often all they have left of their self-respect.

So a truly global community still lies a very long way in the future. We are stuck with the reality of international relations: not inter*state* relations but inter*national* relations. And international relations is about *dealing with foreigners*. This is a point that I have made many times before, but it cannot be made too often. In all too many textbooks on international relations, states are treated simply as entities to be assessed in such quantifiable or behavioural terms as economic potential, military power, technological development, internal political structure or geopolitical imperatives. Such treatment is itself the product of a particular culture—a particular ideology in fact: Anglo-Saxon political thought. It is a culture from which we may not ourselves be able to escape, but which we cannot expect other peoples necessarily to share.

The first duty both of the theorist and of the practitioner of international relations, therefore, is *empathy*: the capacity to enter into other minds and understand ideologies which have been formed by environment, history and education in a very different mould from our own. The most direct way of doing this is of course to study the languages which both express and create these differences between nations. For many this will be a counsel of perfection, but at least we should be conscious of our imperfections. To study international relations without understanding linguistic diversities is like studying painting with the handicap of being colour-blind. The fact that an increasing amount of the business of the world is conducted in English is undeniably a functional convenience, but it can be deceptive. English is not the native language of those with whom we are dealing, and is not a natural or effective vehicle for their ideas. It enables them to understand us a little better than we can understand them, but it can give an illusion of mutual understanding where none in fact exists.

Whether or not we possess the key which languages provide to the understanding of other peoples and their ideologies, there is another which lies within the grasp of all of us: the study of their history. If without languages we are colour-blind, without history we are groping in total darkness. History enables us to understand ourselves as well as other cultures. It teaches us what we may and may not expect in our mutual relations. It teaches us our own limitations, and thus a certain humility. In dealing with a multicultural, multi-ideological world, that in itself is not a bad beginning.

10

Churchill

and the

Era of

National

Unity

When nations commemorate great men, they nearly always choose those whose work was significant in the creation of the nation itself. We may count ourselves fortunate when a great artist or scholar or scientist is born an Englishman, but we seldom make it a matter for national rejoicing. When we commemorate a great writer, it is usually one who, like Shakespeare in England or Robert Burns and Walter Scott in Scotland, has by his development of our language or his retailing of our history done something to forge a distinctively national culture. When we revere soldiers or sailors, Wellingtons or Nelsons (to choose no more recent and controversial figures) we do so not just because they were good at their jobs but because their victories were instrumental in preserving and enhancing the national community to which we belong.

So it is with statesmen. However much we admire their skills, whatever they may have done for our national efficiency and well-being, they are accorded the highest honours only if they have contributed in some spectacular way to the building and preservation of the nation as a whole. Sometimes we can identify a personality to whose courage and skill the nation owes its very existence: a George Washington, a Simon Bolivar, a Cavour, a Bismarck, a Gandhi, even in his way a Lenin. Older, more complex societies may excavate quasi-mythical figures—Hereward the Wake or

*Lecture delivered in November 1984.

152

Joan of Arc. And sometimes these older societies conscious of early greatness and later decay or disintegration can throw up a figure who somehow pulls them together, reminds them of past achievements, guides them through present dangers and sets them on their way with new confidence and resolve. One such was Abraham Lincoln. Another was Charles de Gaulle. But pre-eminent among them was Winston Leonard Spencer Churchill.

It is the business of serious historians, not to create comfortable myths but to destroy them; to remind you that the past was not golden, that our ancestors were not geniuses, that previous eras tolerated a degree of inequity, misery and suffering that we would find intolerable in our own societies and are shocked to discover in others; that previous generations blundered their way through problems as blindly as we do today; that historical idols had feet, not perhaps of clay but certainly of flesh and blood. The achievements of Bismarck and Stalin remain a matter of record, but each new generation of historians uncovers horrifying new details of their pettiness or cruelty or vindictiveness. At the other extreme the wisdom and good humour of a Lincoln or a Gandhi is so self-evident that we are often shocked to find that they were highly skilled political operators as well. We can admire all that de Gaulle did for his country without finding it in the least necessary to like him. As for Churchill, he is near enough to us for his faults to be fresh in our minds. He was far too much of a romantic to be a successful politician or indeed a successful strategist. Deprived of power he could be outrageously irresponsible; equipped with it, a merciless bully. In peacetime politics he was not so much out of his depth as floundering in shallows like a stranded whale. In war and the whole business of war he found an uninhibited satisfaction which the High Victorians might have understood (Tennyson and Ruskin would certainly have appreciated it) but which to our own battle-scarred generation seems rather shocking. Robert Rhodes James was quite right in suggesting that, had he died in the 1930s, Churchill would have left a reputation much like that of his father, as a brilliant failure.

But Churchill did not die in the 1930s. He lived to reunite a shaken and divided nation, rally it after defeat, sustain it through ordeals unparalleled in its history and lead it to a victory which seemed to assure its survival as a great world power. That this victory did nothing of the sort; that the world had changed too drastically for Britain to continue to play the role in it which Churchill and his generation had always taken for granted: this was no fault of his.

It is probably as a great war leader that Churchill would wish to be remembered, and it is right that he should be. Ultimately it was he who bore the responsibility for Britain's conduct of the Second World War, for reconciling the differing views and interests of the various Services, commands and theatres and harmonising them with those of our allies. It was he, also, who had to provide a constant fount of encouragement and inspiration to subordinates who, understandably enough under the circumstances, were liable to lapse into inertia and defeatism. All this was more important than his own ideas about strategy, some of which were somewhat bizarre. But more important even than Churchill's conduct of the war was his leadership at home. No amount of strategic skill or managerial competence would have availed if he had not presided over a people who were, almost literally, prepared to bear any burden and make any sacrifice for victory, and to do so without any serious measure of compulsion. It is doubtful whether any other statesman of the time could have provided the quality of leadership which made it possible for the British people to make those sacrifices; which evoked from them efforts of which they had never believed themselves capable. There was, it was true, a grumbling group of Adullamites in the House of Commons who twice forced a vote of non-confidence—on both occasions with derisory results. There were fringe parties of the discontented who contested by-elections and indeed won one or two. But these divisions were negligible compared with those of the First World War, during the first half of which the Conservative Party continued, with massive press support, their attacks on the Liberal Administration of Herbert Asquith, and during the second Lloyd George had to contend against an unholy alliance of Asquithian liberals, conservative back-benchers, discontented generals and the Northcliffe Press.

Churchill was able to unite the nation, as Lloyd George could not, partly through a personal charisma which he could, unlike Lloyd George a generation earlier, exercise through the media of broadcasting and film. He did so also because he kept together one of the most successful political coalitions in our political history. The Conservative Party did not love him: he was after all a political maverick with an appalling record of tergiversation and misjudgements. But they did not have for him that sustained hatred which so many of them had felt for Lloyd George, the enemy and would-be destroyer of their class, throughout the First World War. Many in the Labour ranks *did* see Churchill as the class enemy; the name 'Tonypandy' still awoke a Pavlovian reaction, especially among those who had no idea what had happened there or even where it was. But his very distance from the Conservatives, that Palmerstonian touch of Whig raffishness which set him apart from the sober city bankers and the sombre manufacturers from the Midlands, made Churchill the more acceptable to the Labour leaders; and this was one of those very rare occasions in the party's history when the Labour leaders were more or less in agreement, and the Labour Party was more or less willing to be led.

Certainly no pukka Conservative would ever have entrusted the lion's share of domestic administration, as did Churchill, to his Labour colleagues and left them to create what was effectively a socialist siege economy while he himself got on with fighting the war. Churchill knew that the Labour leadership could communicate with the urban working-class population in a way that the Conservatives could not. The ponderous, and to much of the population largely unintelligible exhortation 'Your Courage, Your Cheerfulness, Your Resolution will Bring Us Victory' came down off the billboards, to be replaced by Herbert Morrison's perky 'Go to it!' (though there were those sardonic spirits who replied to Morrison, 'Come off it!'). The incomparable Ernest Bevin moved in to handle labour problems. Brilliant entrepreneurs like Lord Woolton handled food distribution. That classless enigma Brendan Bracken brought zest and imagination to the underrated but vital job of Minister of Information, making communications snappy, informative and often fun. There developed throughout the land a sense that at the top of the vast grey bureaucracy which issued ration cards and petrol coupons and work-permits and import quotas there were people who understood the problems of ordinary men and women and were working to ease them. So people by and large put up with dangers and inconveniences and got on with the war. But at the same time they formed an overwhelming determination not to go back to the old ways again: a determination which they registered in the election of 1945.

It would be a mistake to paint too golden a picture of this wartime camaraderie. There were labour disputes, strikes and, especially in the grey middle years of the war, grumbling tensions and discontents. Nor was the successful forging of national consensus wholly due to the leadership of Churchill and his colleagues. Hitler's attack on the Soviet Union silenced those Left-Wing elements which, though numerically inconsiderable, were the more dangerous for their readiness, then as now, to exploit social difficulties and tensions in the interests of revolutionary objectives; not only silenced them but brought them into willing if strictly temporary alliance with the capitalist enemy and the moderate Labour leaders, whom they disliked even more. Circumstances created a genuine national unity which excluded only a tiny fringe of Fascist psychopaths. As a result some former communists quietly shed their old allegiances and allowed themselves to be permanently absorbed into the general democratic process. Others did not, and returned to their old allegiances as soon as the war was over. The experts in MI5 are probably still trying to work out which did which.

Behind all this however there were longer-term trends at work; trends which historians are still trying to discover and evaluate. Great Britain on the whole was during the first half of the twentieth century a far more orderly society than it had ever been in the past. The first half of the nineteenth century had seen social disorders throughout the land which had sometimes approached the intensity of civil war. The second half had seen the development of enormous cities in certain districts of which the writ of law did not run; areas of crime and deprivation and squalor from which respectable Victorian society tried to avert its eyes. In the first decade of this century labour disputes in the mines, on the docks and on the railways reached an intensity culminating in violent and sometimes lethal confrontations. Compared with some of those, the clashes between pickets and police today would look like a friendly football match.

Nevertheless it was during that decade that the Liberal Administration in which Winston Churchill started his ministerial career laid the foundations, with its social insurance and pensions schemes, for what was later to be termed 'the welfare state'; a community in which the well-being of the entire population was recognised as being the proper concern of the government. Until then, it is doubtful how far one can speak of Britain as being a 'community' at all, rather than an infinity of differing communities, staggeringly different in their standards of living and often barely able to communicate with one another.

How fast and how far this process would have gone but for the outbreak of the First World War; whether rising expectations would have led to impatience and disruption, to backlash and confrontation as they so often do, it is impossible to say. At all events, that war gave a powerful impetus to this process of community-building. As Lord Beloff has reminded us in the title of his latest book, *Wars and Welfare* have paradoxically gone hand in hand. It was the revelation of the sickly condition of young men called up to serve in the militia in the Crimean and Boer Wars that provided the impetus for the first surveys and provisions for national health services. It was the expectation of war before 1914 that made national 'fitness' a serious political issue. And the war itself, when it came, speeded the development of national community in two fundamental ways.

First, in a conflict whose conduct was so fundamentally dependent on industrial productivity, the labour force had to be conciliated not only with higher wages, but by having their leaders brought into the process of government itself. 'Labour' could no longer be treated as a commodity: it had to be seen as *people,* whose well-being demanded careful attention and who collectively could exercise considerable political power. The extension of the franchise in 1918, perhaps the most important domestic consequence of the First World War, brought the whole of the 'working classes', as it brought the great majority of women, within the pale of the political community for the first time.

Second, the experience of virtually universal military service forged, as it always had in continental conscript forces, a sense of national identity and cohesion far deeper than any political or social programmes could possibly have achieved. Common experiences, broadly shared across barriers of locality and class; common ordeals endured; common memories to be recollected: these were to provide a deep binding force, as effective on the miners of South Wales and Durham as on the countrymen of Wessex or the city dwellers of Liverpool and London. Service with the armed forces in the First World War, as in the Second, did not 'militarize' people, in the sense that it made them amenable to discipline and indifferent to slaughter. But it did 'socialize' them by introducing them to wider communities and giving them broader loyalties than they had known in civil life.

It was not least effective in confronting young men of the wealthier classes with the inequities of their own societies and making them resolve—Major Attlee, Captain Eden, Captain Harold Macmillan, to name only three—to do something about it. And it may have provided a ballast in keeping the country steady during those disturbed post-war years, when the wave of revolution sweeping across Europe lapped the shores of our islands, especially those of the Firth of Clyde; when attempts to restore economic 'normalcy' seemed to threaten everything that the working men had gained during the war; and when firebrands like the young Emmanuel Shinwell had to be imprisoned as dangerous menaces to public order. Television cameras, had they existed, would have recorded scenes on Clydeside and in South Wales in 1919 and 1926 as disturbing as those of 1911 and at least as violent as those of 1984. We remember today that the miners are reliving the very different battles fought for very different purposes by their fathers and grandfathers before them. And after the General Strike of 1926 (as tragically abortive and unpopular as is the miners' strike today) came, for many workers, the cold misery of the slump.

Nevertheless social cohesion held. The frontiers of the welfare state were extended by Mr. Baldwin's Minister for Health, Neville Chamberlain, who, had he died in 1931, might have been remembered as one of the great reforming ministers of the twentieth century. The returning prosperity of the 1930s gradually shrivelled up the worst pockets of misery and improved the living standards of the great bulk of the population. In 1939 the country went into the war once again virtually united.

So Churchill did not have to conjure national unity out of thin air. He had only to sense and evoke it, to find the tones, the style of leadership to which it would respond. And again, war and welfare went hand in hand. Labour leaders, co-opted to a far greater share of power than their predecessors had enjoyed in the First World War, were determined to use it so as to remove for ever the inequities of the old order, and they found willing hands to help them in a civil service educated, over the past thirty years, to a new sense of social responsibility. The fair shares ensured by wartime rationing; the concern for child-welfare and provision for old age; the war-induced sense of belonging to a close and beleaguered community in which no one should prosper at the expense of anyone else; all this became enshrined in wartime legislation carried by universal consent, and was extended by the subsequent Labour Government, many of whose measures enjoyed a broad measure of cross-bench support. With Labour administrations dominated by Attlee and Bevin and Gaitskell and their like; with Conservative administrations dominated by Eden and Butler and Macmillan and *their* like; with Tony Crosland and Roy Jenkins rising fast in the one party and Edward Heath and Edward Boyle in the other, Britain seemed at last to have reached the broad sunlit uplands of which Churchill once spoke. When Churchill himself retired in April 1955, he could look back on fifty years of ever-increasing national consensus in the creation of which he had himself, whether through wars or through welfare, played a highly creditable part.

That is the point at which we would all like to end the story, with the time-honoured sentence 'And they all lived happily ever after'. Alas: only fairy tales end with that sentence, whether they are fairytales told by Hans Christian Andersen or by Karl Marx. In real life the story goes on, providing new tragedies and new challenges. Perhaps it is a blessing for mankind that it should be so, so that there is no temptation for us to fall back into comfortable inertia. If so it is, as Churchill himself once remarked, a blessing very effectively disguised.

The first and most obvious point to be made about the course of events since 1945 is that the degree of national unity which we achieved under the leadership of Winston Churchill has since been steadily eroded; that

that glorious flood tide which swept us all up together in a single national effort has ebbed, leaving a desolate foreshore littered with evil-smelling detritus and decay.

The underlying cause has probably been the fact, so evident to us now but then concealed from all but a very few far-sighted prophets, that the era of national unity was also that of national economic decline. Why this should have been so, and what connection, if any, can be traced between the two phenomena, it would take too long to discuss, and I do not feel myself well equipped to do so.* But the consequence has been that, although the shares of national wealth may have been more equitably distributed, they have been shares of a shrinking cake. At first our economic problems could be attributed to wartime strains and dislocations; only a few prescient analysts realised that they ran far deeper. Only gradually was it appreciated that our problems were more profound; rooted in our history, our social structure, in our very early success; and that their resolution might have to involve precisely those traumatic shocks which we had all prided ourselves on having, unlike less fortunate nations, so successfully avoided. I shall leave it to economists to dispute how far, if at all, the burdens of the welfare state contributed to the decline of our economy. One can only say that they could not have made our recovery any easier.

Then there came 'the oil shock' of the early seventies; that sudden, sharp increase in the price of the staple fuel of the industrialised world which shook even the strongest economies and nearly destroyed the weaker ones. How we would have fared if we had not simultaneously become an oil-producing country ourselves I do not dare to speculate, but for us the effect has been at least cushioned. None the less the era of cheap fuel has gone for ever; at least until the scientists provide us with a source of nuclear or solar energy which is not only plentiful and cheap but quite evidently safe.

The second factor, and one seldom cited in this connection, has been the sexual revolution: the dissemination of cheap and reliable means of birth-control which make sexual intercourse simply a finite and highly enjoyable act without any necessary further consequences. The effect of this on the status of women and on the traditionally central role of the family is self-evident. Less evident, however, is the part this has played, for better or worse, in encouraging a new generation to reject in their entirety the social mores of their parents; or at least to select from among them

*A plausible if sombre explanation is provided by Correlli Barnett in his two works *The Collapse of British Power* (1972) and *The Audit of War* (1986).

those which they find personally convenient. It is arguable that this is only extending to the entire population the freedom which has been available to the 'enlightened' upper classes since the days of H. G. Wells and Bernard Shaw, but the implications for social stability are none the less profound. Societies everywhere have always been held together by a shared continuity of mores, with sexual mores at the very core of them. The new freedom certainly liberates the individual, but it imposes on him, and her, responsibilities whose full implications they may not appreciate until it is too late. The inability of so many people, deprived of traditional guidelines, to cope with these responsibilities has created huge social problems. As for the effect on the cohesiveness of society, on that web of mutual obligations and duties and responsibility which enables it to function at all, once can say only that is is far too early to assess it. What we are witnessing is perhaps the greatest social revolution in the history of mankind.

But of overriding importance is of course what has been appropriately termed 'the third industrial revolution': the first being that in which Britain led the way with coal and iron; the second, pioneered by Germany and the United States, with electricity and petrochemicals; the present one, led by Japan, in computers, microtechnology and robotics. As anyone knows who has had to grapple with the introduction of computers into office management or university libraries, the transformation in our lives is likely in the long run to be as complete as that effected by the transition from the horse and carriage to the automobile. But the social and economic costs are likely to be yet greater. With the whole mode of production being transformed, we are seeing social dislocation, if not suffering, on a scale comparable to that of the early industrial revolution. Communities and social groups whose livelihood depends on obsolescent processes face the prospect of social extinction. It is not just the levels of unemployment resulting from this dislocation which are so disturbing; it is the grim long-term outlook of the labour forces discarded by old labour-intensive industries, with little prospect of being absorbed into the new capital-intensive ones.

Such a situation is bound to produce major social strains. It throws on to the structure of the welfare state a burden such as its architects never conceived it would have to bear; and a generation brought up, rightly or wrongly, to regard the provision made for it by the State as a natural right understandably resents any curtailment of the benefits they receive from it, whether those benefits lie in the area of health, education, amenities, housing or social security. Unions originally formed to protect their members from exploitation at their work, to fight for better conditions and a living wage in an economic climate devoted to the maximisation of profits, now fight to protect the jobs themselves, whether there is an economic need for those jobs or not. Workers always see their jobs less as a way of contributing to national wealth than as a means of drawing on it—the most basic kind of social security; and that goes for university teachers as well as miners. Nevertheless unless people are able to contribute by their work to the functioning of society, thereby acquiring some status within it, they will feel rejected and ultimately alienated. It is bad enough to feel exploited; it is infinitely worse to feel ignored and forgotten. The long-term threat to social stability today arises less from those who feel them-selves unjustly treated than from those, especially the young, who simply do not feel part of society at all and so defiantly turn their back on it. It is among such people that chiliastic and unreasoning mass movements, led by messianic visionaries and dedicated to the destruction of the existing order, have, historically, always found their strongest support.

Developments such as these can impose intolerable strains on the strongest of communities. We must not underestimate the success with which our own society has so far contained them, the extent to which patience, tolerance, good will and mutual understanding have eased nec-essary transitions and defused unnecessary crises. I believe that this success owes a great deal to the habits of mind and sense of community established during that 'era of national unity' of which I spoke earlier. But neither should we ignore the existence of a dedicated minority which does not wish to see those strains contained; whose object indeed is to exacerbate them to the point at which the entire social order disintegrates and a new revolutionary élite can seize power and implement their own ideological objectives. Their strategy was originally conceived by Lenin; the tactics have been conveniently described for us by such theorists and practitioners as Che Guevara, Mariaghella and Regis Debray. Legitimate grievances, especially those not easily remediable, are seized upon and exploited. A confrontation is forced in which the authorities are deliberately provoked to retaliate with violence. That violence is then itself exploited, both to discredit the authorities and to justify further violence on the part of the insurgents. 'Red Guards' are formed, to intimidate potential or actual dissidents and ultimately to displace the incumbent authorities as the ef-fective instruments of government. The mass of the population, wearied and sickened by endemic violence, ultimately accepts the revolution as the only way of restoring some kind of stability and order.

This theory of revolution has been spelled out by the theorists of the Left, whose works were such fashionable reading in the late sixties among students who have now reached positions in society where they may feel able to start putting them into effect. But the practitioners who used these tactics most successfully even before they were formulated were the revolutionaries not of the Left but of the Right; first Mussolini, then Hitler: models whom Left-Wing theorists prefer to ignore, but whose methods, in rising to power, gave rise to scenes very similar to those we have been witnessing in this country over the past few months. But whether it comes from revolutionaries of the Left or of the Right, the threat to our society remains the same. It must be identified, it must be resisted, and it must be denounced. Those who out of compassion with the grievances which are being so skilfully exploited fail to do so, however great their political or ecclesiastical eminence, are at best naïve, and at worst willing dupes.

The tactics of dealing with such revolutionary manoeuvres demand courage, intelligence, patience, and above all invincible good humour. The strategy must of course be to remove the sources of grievance, which is a great deal more easily said than done. Ultimately it can be achieved only by the creation of national wealth, both for investment to create further employment, and for public expenditure on the level needed to sustain the welfare state. That wealth, as we all now know quite literally to our cost, cannot be created by printing money. High-minded adjurations as to how wealth should be redistributed are of very little help if the wealth is not there to redistribute. As to how that wealth is best created we look to the economists for guidance, but it has always seemed to me to have been a sad day when the subject ceased to be called 'political economy' and became simply 'economics'. Classicists will remind us that the term in Greek means 'the management of a household', but it is too easy to forget that economics is a branch of politics rather than of mathematics, and that households consist of people rather than of account books.

There is probably no way in which the transition through which we are passing can be managed without hardship, and if these are really the only alternatives it may be that some short-term, local hardship, if properly alleviated, may in the long run be better than widespread and growing pauperisation. But the greater that hardship, the greater the need for evident and genuine public concern, for a sense of compassion to be radiated from the top, perhaps for some sumptuary taxation to be levied on conspicuously-displaced wealth, above all for encouragement to see light at the end of the dark tunnel. The criticism seems to me to be well founded, that key members of the present government appear to see their function to be that of managing an economy, or indeed running a business, rather than that of caring for a community. Indeed (speaking as a drop-out from a long line of businessmen) I don't see how you *can* effectively run a business unless you are seen by the work-force as caring for their welfare. In political as in military leadership, the way in which things are done is no less important than what is done. The tougher the going, the greater the hardships demanded, then the greater the need for resolution at the top; but the greater the need for evident compassion as well.

This brings me back to the concept of the nation as a focus of communal loyalty. Nostalgia is the worst imaginable guide in politics, and there was much in old-fashioned patriotism of which we should be glad to see the end. Too often national unity has been purchased at the price of international disunity, and we must not forget that the era of national unity which I have described was the era of the most terrible wars in the history of mankind; wars in the creation and continuation of which fanatical dedication to a national ideal played a dominant and sinister role. Patriotism is the close ally of xenophobia, if not of racial arrogance. But a proper pride in the community to which one belongs, an awareness of how it has developed in the past and the problems which it has confronted and overcome, an understanding of the tasks which confront it today and the opportunities which await it in the future, above all a shared appreciation of the values for which it stands or should stand in the international community; all this seems to me an essential framework to enable our society to function at all.

For national feeling is like the devil in the gospel in whose place, once it was cast out, seven devils entered in. Loyalty, or what sociologists call 'group cohesion', is a fundamental instinct in mankind, and national loyalty only gradually developed out of a mass of small, conflicting, more immediate loyalties. The abandonment of the nation as a focus for loyalty means that loyalties focus not at a higher level, but at a lower; upon class, or regions, or sects (or indeed sex), or on race, or simply upon gangs; groups in continual and often murderous conflict with one another. National feeling is what makes community-building possible: the sense that, in a fundamental way, we belong to one another.

Clearly it is desirable, so far as possible, to continue this move from lower to higher loyalties, from Britain to Europe or to Commonwealth or the Atlantic Community; ultimately to the Planet Earth. But this can be done effectively only if the roots of national loyalties are well nourished, and that higher loyalty carries the whole nation with it: not just the intelligent and educated few. Otherwise national unity can be disrupted and nothing gained in its place. It is all too possible in seeking unity with other peoples, to lose touch with one's own. There is much satisfaction to be gained by feeling oneself a good European or a good Atlanticist; as much at home in Brussels or Paris, or Washington or New York, as one is in London; but it is not so good if one is not equally at home in Scunthorpe or Rhondda Valley and is in consequence perceived in those areas as a member of an alien international élite, which neither understands their problems nor shares their loyalties. It is all very well creating a great international trading community, turning one's back on protection and currency restrictions, but not so good if as a result British industry is starved of investment and funds are channeled instead into more lucrative enterprises overseas. It is all very well improving productivity and profitability by international mergers; but not so good if as a result the fate of entire British communities is determined in Essen or Tokyo or Detroit.

My point is this. Internationalism, or rather supra-nationalism, is all very well if it is based on strong, coherent national entities. But the greater the opportunities it seems to offer, the greater is the need to promote *national* consensus. Otherwise the élites who participate in these supranational enterprises, be they politicians, industrialists, financiers or intellectuals, will be seen as out of touch with and irrelevant to the needs of the ordinary people at the grass roots; people who may eventually turn to other leaders rather nearer home, more closely in touch with their concerns, speaking with accents they find more familiar: leaders who will seem to stand very much more unequivocally for what *they* perceive as being the national interest.

I noted above the rise of Fascism and the lessons we should learn from it. Do not let us forget the extent to which European Fascism was legitimised by a nationalistic backlash against internationalism; especially against an international capitalist system whose apparently arbitrary operations enriched the few—a few who spent their wealth in insolently conspicuous display—but created enormous pockets of misery about which democratically elected leaders apparently could or would do nothing.

The concept of national unity took centuries to develop. The danger today is not so much that it will fail to develop yet further to embrace higher loyalties, as Lionel Curtis and Alfred Milner hoped that it might with the Commonwealth, or as Jean Monnet hoped that it might with Europe; but rather, that it will gradually disintegrate, leaving a country divided, impoverished and virtually ungovernable; a country at the mercy of fanatics and ideologues who are quite prepared to use violence to achieve their ends. National unity cannot be preserved by governmental action alone. There must be a realisation on the part of us all that Britain is a Commonwealth; a society in which the enrichment of the few contributes little if anything to the national well-being but the deprivation of a substantial minority impoverishes us all.

Should we wish that Winston Churchill were alive to lead us today? Frankly, I do not think so. After all, the Churchill of 1940 was also the Churchill of 1911 and indeed of 1926. He was a warrior whose joy in battle often overrode any desire for conciliation and who itched for the opportunity, as he once phrased it, 'to put these grave matters to the proof'. I suspect that the present crisis would find him in the police control rooms, devising new strategies, new tactics and even new weapons to beat the pickets; in the intervals of making speeches which delighted a part of the population as much as they infuriated the rest. The genius required to lead a united people is not necessarily that best attuned to nursing a community through a period of deep internal division and social stress.

But from that protean character we can none the less learn lessons of abiding relevance for all of us. It was Churchill's firm vision of a united nation transcending all barriers of party, region and class, a vision rooted in his understanding, as a historian, of how that unity came to be created and his confidence, as a statesman, that in spite of all dangers threatening from outside and within it could yet be enhanced and preserved, that made him so universally acceptable as a national leader. The problems which confront us today are far more complex and the dangers are no less great than those which we faced forty years ago. They demand a different style of leadership and a rather different blend of resolution, compassion and sheer political skill. But without that vision of transcendent national unity, the British people, as a people, will quite assuredly perish.

11

War and

Social

Change

The vital questions which confront not only students of war but all concerned with peace and security are, why wars happen; how, if necessary, they should be fought; and above all how they can be prevented.

At one level of analysis the answer to the first question is simple. Wars occur when the established order, the status quo, is forcibly challenged, and the status quo powers react. In 1939 the established order in Europe was challenged by Nazi Germany. In 1941—or indeed earlier, in 1937—the order in Asia was challenged by Japan. Even so, war would not have occurred in either instance if the status quo powers had not defended themselves. As Clausewitz put it, 'War takes place mainly for the defender: the conqueror would like to enter our country unopposed'. There was no war in Europe in March 1939 when Hitler destroyed Czechoslovakia; there was one in September when he attacked Poland and Poland resisted. There was no war in Asia in 1931 when Japan engulfed Manchuria, and no world war when she attacked China in 1937. There is no war without resistance; but without resistance, and the possibility of resistance, there is no international order. All States, however revisionist or revolutionary, have an interest in their own self-preservation and maintain armed forced with that end in view. One of the basic foundations of the international order is the perceived capacity of States to protect themselves, or to persuade others to do it for them. That remains unaltered in the nuclear age.

I know that this explanation for the phenomenon of war is superficial and simplistic, but it provides a sufficient basis for the operational doctrines of the military, as the simple need to preserve domestic law and order provides a sufficient basis for the operations of the police. It is not for the military to ask why the security of their country is threatened: their task is to identify the threats and counter them. Defences are therefore kept up and soldiers trained to repel 'aggression'; forcible threats to the international order. But a deeper level of social and political analysis should increase our understanding of what threats to anticipate, what kinds of wars to expect, and if not how to prevent them, at least how most effectively to fight them. Such an understanding is impossible without some insight into the way in which societies have developed in the past, and with them their cultures and their value-systems.

Many, perhaps most, of the cultures of which we have a historical record have been warrior societies. Their survival and growth depended upon military effectiveness, if only because territory was the only basis for wealth. War was normally a simple contest for the extension and preservation of control over land. Peace was preserved only so long as the strongest ruled: but since rule in such societies was highly personalised and even the strongest ruler was mortal, peace rarely lasted for more than a generation, and every succession was likely to be disputed by force. Not only was war a highly effective instrument of policy: it was what the ruling élites were for. Their capacity to conduct it legitimised their authority. Prolonged peace was often for them a disaster. So for a thousand years after the fall of the Roman Empire in the West warrior families in Europe squabbled bloodily over the succession, and the values they developed during this millennium—the equation of warfare with nobility, the ideal of the warrior hero, the moral superiority of the fighter over the trader, war as the noblest destiny of mankind—lived on long after the social basis of their power had been undermined by the rise of commercial wealth and the coming of industrialization. The interesting question to ask about Europe and much of the rest of the world before the eighteenth century is not, why were there so many wars, but why was there ever any peace?

With the coming of industrialization, and the social and political transformation which this brought about in Europe (and we must now add North America) values began to change. Philosophers and social scientists like Jeremy Bentham and Herbert Spencer in England, St. Simon and August Comte in France, argued that as the basis of wealth changed from land to commerce and to industry, warrior societies would become obsolete, and war itself would eventually disappear.

The growth of urbanization and the decline in the wealth and power of the landed classes did indeed change the structure of the ruling élites in Europe, and the attitude of many of them to international affairs. The growth of international communications and of commerce in the nineteenth century created 'peace movements', which achieved a significant breakthrough in the Hague Peace Conferences of 1899 and 1907. But these movements polarised European élite opinion. Developments which liberals saw as leading to peace, progress and international harmony were seen by the burgeoning Right Wing political movements as symptoms of degeneracy and decadence. These groups contrasted what they called the 'flabby' talk about peace and arbitration in Europe with the magnificent performance in Japan, a society where the old warrior values remained intact, in defeating the Russians in 1904–5. But it was not only members of the old ruling élites who held such views. The extent to which 'bellicist' values extended was demonstrated by the enthusiasm with which European youth, irrespective of class, went to war in 1914. A study of the literature of this era reveals the need which many of the literate classes felt to show that they were still *men,* that the old heroic values still survived in them, and that in spite of the transformation that had occurred in their societies they were still worthy of their warrior forbears.

That a belief in the moral benefits of war and the primacy of warrior values could survive into industralised societies, was shown not only by the First but by the Second World War. Indeed Fascism, an ideology which, between the wars, infected all Europe and dominated its most powerful and highly industrialised State, Germany, was based upon a specific renunciation of the pacific doctrines now accepted by the Western democracies, and a revival of historic ideals of war and conquest. The collapse of liberal democracy and the triumph of Fascism in Europe was mirrored by developments in Japan, where the rapid onset of industrialization had not affected the prevalence of the old *samurai* spirit and the dominance of the warrior caste. Germany and Japan provided such hideously difficult adversaries to defeat in the Second World War because they presented a unique combination of modern industrial and scientific expertise with the old barbaric warrior virtues. Only total defeat and occupation made possible the transformation of their societies. Those who survived in both countries were under no illusion that war, in the industrial age, was hell. It hardly needed Hiroshima and Nagasaki to drive home the lesson.

Thus war as an institution outlived the warrior societies of which it had formed so intrinsic a part, and survived—and still survives—in a very different social climate. The establishment of the United Nations in 1945 did not, any more than had the establishment of the League of Nations a quarter of a century earlier, mark the end of war. Why not?

There is one very simple explanation. War as an activity was still *functional.* It still enabled states to maintain or extend control over territory. After 1945, in the aftermath of the collapse of the European and Japanese colonial Empires, as in the aftermath of the collapse of all Empires, a new political order had to be forged. Conflicts over the succession, over rival claims to legitimacy, could in many cases be resolved only through war. War established the State, and settled the borders, of Israel. War confirmed the independence of South Korea and destroyed that of South Vietnam. War defined the frontiers of India and Pakistan, and more recently has confirmed the frontiers of Iran and Iraq. More recently still, war has established the continuing independence of Afghanistan. So long as there are conflicting claims to territory, war remains a possibility—as we British discovered, to our amazement, in the case of the Falkland Islands in 1982.

For although territory is no longer the sole or even the main basis of national power, it still has value. First, the space it provides may have strategic importance: the determination of the Soviet Union to retain control of Eastern Europe, in spite of all the political problems involved;* the comparable determination of the United States to exclude the Soviets from exercising influence in Central America; the determination of Israel to retain control of the Left Bank of the Jordan; all show how much importance States still attach to the control of space. Second, the resources such territory contains may be deemed vital to economic survival. The one place in the world today where a global conflict might still conceivably originate is the Persian Gulf, without whose oil resources the West would be economically crippled.

But in very few parts of the world today can territory be thought of purely in terms of space and resources. Territory contains people; and today people are more important than the land they inhabit.

This is the great social transformation that has occurred since the days of the warrior societies. In the feudal age people belonged to the land as unquestionably as did the animals or the crops. In a world whose horizon was bounded by the village and foreigners began over the hill, a change in ruler might pass unnoticed, unless he increased taxes or altered religious observances. It was only in the early modern era, as prosperity and commerce developed, that this situation began to change. Political self-consciousness and self-awareness followed in the wake of economic development. The French Revolution of 1789 both gave expression to and accelerated these changes, and its effects have been transforming the world ever since.

The change which the Revolution brought about in the nature of warfare was discerned by a brilliant contemporary, Carl von Clausewitz, but

*Written in 1988.

its full significance was to be spelled out only a century and a half later by the Chinese strategist Mao Tse-tung. There could be no effective territorial conquest, taught Mao, without population control. If you could conquer the hearts and minds of the people, whether by persuasion or intimidation or both, the land would follow. If you could not, possession of the territory could be more trouble than it was worth. Ever since the French Revolution wars have been increasingly 'People Wars', fought not so much to protect or extend control of territory as to change or preserve the structure or the ideology of entire societies.

The ideology introduced by the French Revolution was *nationalism*. It has remained dominant ever since. National self-consciousness, far more than any aspirations towards social justice or economic equality, has fuelled international conflict in the nineteenth and twentieth centuries. National wars did indeed sometimes originate, both in Europe and elsewhere, as revolts against the old ruling élites. The leaders of the French Revolution identified the French 'nation' in distinction to the monarch and aristocracy who had oppressed it. Where the ruling classes could be identified as foreigners as well, as they could in the colonial territories of the Third World, class consciousness and national self-consciousness combined to create a very powerful motivation indeed. Revolution and war then became indistinguishable. But in all such wars, success depended on the ability of those conducting them to mobilise popular enthusiasm and secure mass participation. Often a 'nation' was created through the sheer process of fighting. The French nation as a politically self-conscious entity was created, not by the declarations of a few politicians in 1789, but by the twenty-five years of war that followed. The Germans became conscious of their nationality, and created their political unity, in their struggles against the French, as did the Italians during the wars of the Risorgimento against Austria. Even the Russian Empire, the most absolute of all States, acquired a degree of popular legitimacy through its struggle against France in 1812, against the Ottoman Empire in 1877 and against Germany in the First World War; as its successor the Soviet Union did, again against Germany, in the Second. As for the experience of Poland, where national identity was forged through generations of struggle against alien adversaries both East and West, it is hardly necessary for me to speak.

The French Revolution and all those which followed in imitation have been categorised by Marxists as 'bourgeois revolutions' and nationalism itself dismissed as a bourgeois creed. In a certain sense this was true. The leaders of revolutions, almost without exception, have been educated members of the middle classes, neither workers nor peasants, though they occasionally numbered disaffected or opportunistic members of the old feudal aristocracy in their ranks. For many of them the 'nation' they represented did not include the illiterate masses, whether peasants or proletariat. But they quickly discovered that their revolutions would fail, or their nations would be defeated, if they did not enlist the support of those masses, through propaganda, indoctrination and education. Italians, Frenchmen, Germans, even Poles, had to be *created* out of peoples whose political consciousness was often limited to the valleys they inhabited. Later, Nigerians, Indians, Chinese and Vietnamese had to be created as well.* Of course this could not be done unless there existed already some common culture or sense of identity, embodied in historical memories of shared experiences. The 'bourgeois' leaders had to make themselves acceptable to the people as a whole in order to consolidate their power. If a nation was to be successfully created, the people had to identify themselves with the concept and be willing to fight and if necessary die under its flag. The First World War, with its millions of casualties, was to show how gruesomely successful this process of 'nation-building' had been.

That war showed also how badly the early Marxists had gone astray in their analysis. They had dismissed nationalism as a purely bourgeois phenomenon, which would not affect the working classes. In due course, they believed, the bourgeois societies created by the bourgeois revolutions would be replaced by the proletariat, as economic processes continued to father political change; and because the nation-state was, in their view, simply an instrument of bourgeois domination it would ultimately disappear, and wars would disappear with it. The revolution of the masses would thus inevitably lead to peace; so those who fought to promote such revolution were true 'fighters for peace'. International relations themselves would wither away.

It did not work out like that. English, French, Russian and German workers throughout the First World War remained true to their national loyalties. When the revolution came in Russia in 1917 and in Germany a year later, it was only as a result of war weariness among the people and loss of nerve on the part of the government. These revolutions were not manifestations of proletarian internationalism; indeed they were to be followed in Germany and elsewhere a few years later by a backlash of the most ferocious nationalism the world had ever seen.

Indeed it can now be stated with reasonable certainty that it is only

---

*I mention neither the British nor the Japanese, nations whose insular position had already given them a sense of separate identity and a unique degree of social cohesion.

when they are able to exploit nationalist feeling, usually as a result of war, that the revolutionary regimes are able to secure any degree of popular legitimacy. The Russian Civil War of 1918–21 enabled Lenin to don the mantle of a national hero and legitimised his revolutionary doctrines by identifying them with Russian nationalism. Twenty years later Stalin in his turn was able to consolidate his increasingly precarious regime by fighting what is still known in the Soviet Union as the 'Great Patriotic War'. Mao Tse-tung established his credentials as a national leader, first by the effectiveness of the resistance he organised to the Japanese occupation, and then through his resistance to American and Soviet pressures alike. In Vietnam Ho Chi Minh first emerged as a national leader against the French colonialist government and his status was increasingly enhanced as his rivals in Saigon became ever more dependent on American help. The same has been true of every revolutionary leader who has emerged in the Third World, from Castro to Gaddafi. Nationalism remains, even after two hundred years, by far the most effective instrument of social mobilisation—and so a most effective tool of war.

It is interesting to consider how this situation came about. The Marxist analysis of the situation had been correct enough. Economic and industrial development, above all urbanisation, certainly destroyed traditional social structures. It dislocated societies, eroded ancient legitimacies and created new élites. It did not take much insight, in nineteenth-century Europe, to observe this process at work. In the twentieth century the same process was to spread to the rest of the world. Throughout the old colonial Empires economic development, and with it rising political self-consciousness, produced alienation from traditional authority, and rival groups disputed succession to the power which the old order could no longer wield. But in their prognosis the Marxists were mistaken. They had thought that the new forces which they termed 'capitalism' would in turn cease to correspond to social needs and be destroyed, as they had destroyed the feudal order of society. That destruction, they believed, would be hastened by the increasing misery which the new ruling classes were inflicting on the workers as they fought ever more desperately for profits among themselves. From their ruin a new classless society would arise, social justice would reign and both internal and international conflict would come to an end.

But the workers under capitalism did not grow increasingly miserable. They grew richer. If some sank into a lumpen proletariat, others rose into the ranks of the petty-bourgeoisie and adopted the values of their masters.

They were not alienated from the power-structures. They were enfranchised, and became part of the political process.

Emancipated from their old feudal obligations and restraints, precipitated into the confusion and anomie of the new great cities, the working classes were ripe for nationalist indoctrination by a state-controlled education system and a mass-circulation press. National self-consciousness gave them status. When war came they supported it with enthusiasm and fought it to the bitter end. Thus, the social developments of the nineteenth century, so far from making war obsolete, had made it yet more ferocious and destructive; and revolution, when it came, resulted only in a continuation and intensification of the nationalism which had caused those wars.

Lenin and his colleagues explained the unexpected and unwelcome success of capitalism in Europe by arguing that the growing misery foreseen by Marx himself had in fact been exported to the colonial possessions of the European nations, where a new 'external proletariat' had been called into being and was being exploited by white workers and capitalists alike. It was on the rising of the 'world proletariat' that Marxist-Leninists in the early twentieth century pinned their hopes of revolution. Once again, their analysis was correct. The initial impact of industrial change and the dislocation of the old regional economies caused major social and economic disruption with consequent misery and alienation in Asia and Africa as it had in Europe a century earlier. Further, in colonial territories those problems were exacerbated, as we have seen, by the fact that the ruling élites consisted either of foreigners or of local groups closely associated with them who had adopted their attitudes and life-style. National self-consciousness and resentment of foreign occupation could thus be harnessed to economic discontent. When it became clear after the Second World War that there was no longer any prospect of a revolutionary situation developing in Western Europe, Marxist-Leninist leaders both in the Soviet Union and in the People's Republic of China, turned their attention to the Third World; with, they hoped, better prospects of success.

But European colonialism, like European capitalism, contained its own self-correcting mechanism. The leading colonial states, France, Britain and the Netherlands, were also those where the groups brought into power by industrialization and social change were most deeply affected by democratic beliefs and unease about the ethics of colonial rule. Domestic pressure in the metropolis was thus added to the indigenous discontent and to the disruption caused by European military defeat, to ensure that European Empires did not long outlast the Second World War. As a result, indigenous Asian and African élites, often educated in Britain, France or the United States, found themselves in power, often without having to fight for it. Even where a war of national liberation was necessary to dispose of colonial rule, as in Indonesia and Algeria, the new leaders eventually found that their interest lay in close economic co-operation with the West—or were replaced by those who did. The most remarkable example of this tendency was of course the People's Republic of China; which having first set itself up as the standard-bearer of world revolution, in rivalry with the Soviet Union, is now competing with the Russians in a very different fashion—to attract investment from and establish friendly relations with their old adversaries, the capitalist West. The inevitable conflict between the socialist and capitalist worlds foreseen and prepared for by Lenin and Stalin seems ever less likely to take place.

That is not to say that all was well in the Third World. As in all new States, political turbulence meant that its leaders have often been faced with a choice between political instability and repression. Further, continuing dependence on Western technology, expertise and finance has created a situation sometimes described as 'neo-colonialism' in which the new States have found Westerners still socially and economically dominant even if they no longer exercised direct political power and enjoying a life-style to which very few of their own citizens could aspire; a life-style which has become increasingly evident and potentially divisive with the advent of mass communications and mass tourism. The contrast between the extremes of wealth and poverty, which had been so ugly a feature of early capitalism in Europe and North America—and, in so many of their cities, still is—has become a characteristic of the whole world scene.

As a result, nationalism in the Third World remains a highly disruptive force. Further, even within developed societies, however great their degree of cultural community, nation-states remain artificial political structures with a greater or lesser degree of heterogeneity among their members. Even within Britain, Irish, Scots and Welsh are to some degree discontented, while in Eastern Europe and the Soviet Union examples of such minorities multiply. In the rest of the world Palestinians, Kurds, Sikhs, Tamils, Tibetans and many other such groups compete for attention with their demands for national autonomy as Serbs, Bulgarians, Croats and Czechs did in Europe a century ago. When this sense of political alienation is sufficiently reinforced by economic deprivation, overpopulation and large-scale unemployment, these groups may mobilise enough support to wage a sustained conflict—even indeed a civil war. If they cannot, they may turn, as they have turned for the last hundred years, to the strategy of despair: terrorism.

Terrorism is in fact the form of war which has over the past decade or so caused the authorities in the West the most direct concern. Even in societies as stable as Britain it can compel an allocation of resources to combat it on a scale quite out of proportion to its significance. Its most serious effect is to force governments in less stable societies, especially in Latin America, to take repressive measures and delay the broadening of their social and political base which alone can ultimately ensure their stability. And as we all know the attempts of terrorists to intimidate the international community by hijacking and hostage-taking has made life uncomfortable, if not dangerous, for us all.

Nationalist discontent, often intensified by religious fanaticism, is thus likely to be a continuing feature of the world scene as political self-consciousness develops throughout the Third World, fuelling both terrorist activities and regional conflicts. It is bound to make the preservation of peaceful order a delicate and difficult business for the indefinite future. It was precisely dissident nationalism of this kind that provided the detonator for war in 1914, when Bosnian terrorists assassinated the Archduke Franz Ferdinand at Sarajevo.

But the analogy is not exact. That incident occurred in a highly volatile international community whose people were, in every sense, ready for a war which many of them saw as being necessary and most of them believed they could win. Today the kind of frenetic 'bellicism' which made both the First and the Second World Wars possible and which characterised societies in process of anguished transition from agrarian to industrial economies has largely disappeared from the developed world, however stubbornly it may survive elsewhere. Experience of two world wars, dread of a third fought with nuclear weapons, and above all a consciousness of the need for interdependence to ensure stability have become general throughout both socialist and Western societies. The atavistic movements which at the beginning of this century denounced peace movements as degenerate and welcomed war as a symbol of national health have, as we have seen, destroyed themselves. Today everyone in developed societies belongs to 'the peace movement', even those who, in the name of stability, are most zealously building up their national armaments. The socialist world needs capitalism too much to aim any longer at its destruction: a major crisis of capitalism on the scale of 1929 would be a global catastrophe as disastrous for socialist countries as for everyone else. The capitalist world decreasingly sees socialism as a 'threat', whether in the Soviet Union or in the Third World, and is concerned rather to use its wealth to promote a global stability in which it can continue to prosper. The major powers, in consequence, have a deep interest in the preservation of peaceful order which shows no signs of abating.

This makes me believe that in the long run those optimistic philosophers of the nineteenth century were probably correct: industrialization, in spite of all the alienation and suffering it causes, ultimately produces very unwarlike societies dedicated to material welfare rather than heroic achievement. It is a development which some, especially the idealistic young, will condemn as moral decadence. Reaction against such materialism fuelled Fascism in the 1930s, and more recently the romantic anarchism of the 1960s. It has played a part in the Moslem fundamentalism, the reaction against the West, which has disturbed so much of the world since the 1970s. We may see further such convulsive reactions all over the world as modernization proceeds at an inevitably uneven pace. But as modernization does proceed, the groups who hold such views are likely to find themselves increasingly marginalised. Heroic revolutionary leaders are usually followed by highly pragmatic successors, as we have seen both in the Soviet Union and the People's Republic of China; technocrats concerned not with ideology but with making their societies work and trying to match promise with performance.

Such people are not bellicose. War is not, for them, a preferred option, and large-scale war a disaster. Gradually they swell the ranks of those who are prepared to work within, and strengthen, the framework of the status quo. In consequence it is quite possible that war in the sense of major, organised armed conflict between highly developed societies may not recur, and that a stable framework for international order will become firmly established. Nevertheless violence will continue to erupt within developed societies as well as undeveloped, creating situations of local armed conflict often indistinguishable from traditional war and requiring the continuing exercise of military skills. We have, for better or worse, not yet reached a state of social development when the soldier will find no opportunity to exercise his profession and warrior values have become obsolete.

12

Military

Experience

in European

Literature

Arma virumque cano: arms and the man I sing. And if I were to take the term 'military experience' to comprehend all mankind's action in war, my topic would be even less manageable than it already is. For until the sixteenth century at least—comparatively recently in the history of civilized man—the overwhelming bulk of Western literature that was not concerned with religion was concerned with war. Much of it was concerned with both. Europe was a militant society. Personal relationships existed within an inescapable martial environment. The world of chaotic violence depicted by the Icelandic sagas hardly indeed deserves the description 'martial', which implies a degree of cohesion, organization and dedication which was notably absent from that aimlessly ferocious experience.

It is in the *chansons de geste* that we first find the experience of war as we can still dimly comprehend it, being digested and presented in literary form: the experience not only of conflict but of suffering, not only of antagonism but of friendship, not only of the splendours but of the miseries of war. Roland and Oliver, Carlon and Marsilion, Ganelon and Naimon are not pasteboard heroes and villains but men who love and hate one another in a disquietingly convincing way. And they are men who, for all their mighty acts, cannot control their destinies. You remember that astounding last stanza of the Song of Roland when Charlemagne, Roland at last magnificently avenged, seeks rest:

The Emperor now has ended his assize
With justice done, his great wrath satisfied . . .

177

The day departs and evening turns to night;
The King's abed in vaulted chamber high;
St. Gabriel comes, God's courier, to his side:
'Up Charles! assemble Thy whole imperial might;
With force and arms unto Elbira ride;
Needs must thou succour King Vivien where he lies
At Imphe, his city, besieged by Paynim tribes;
There for thy help the Christians call and cry?
Small heart had Carlon to journey and fight;
God!' says the King, 'how weary is my life!'
He weeps, he plucks his flowing beard and white.

Here ends the geste Turoldus would recite.

This sense of tragic destiny ennobles the best of medieval literature; all
too much of which admittedly is on the level of boys' adventure stories,
sometimes almost strip cartoons, as is to be expected of an art form designed to entertain not very highly educated audiences through the long
winter evenings. They are adventure stories which reach magnificent peaks
of sophistication and excitement in *Gawain,* in Ariosto and Tasso, and by
then romantic love has appeared to add zest to the martial adventures. By
the end of the Middle Ages an awareness is developing that men, even
heroes, could lead other lives than war, that there can be deep conflicts
between private affection and public duty: something unthinkable in the
days of Roland, but which was to become the staple fare of West European
literature from that day to this.

Medieval literature is fundamentally melodramatic since it depicts a
ceaseless conflict between the forces of wrong and right, evil and good,
Paynim and Christian. Even in the kind of domestic conflict described by
Malory, fought within Christendom, the adversaries, the false knights, are
etched all the more black and villainous because they had betrayed the
oaths which held their society together. The traitor was infinitely more
dangerous than the honest enemy, the Paynim, to whose skill and courage
one could pay respect, with whom indeed one could recognize a certain
comradeship in arms even though one regarded the prospect of his ultimate victory as a catastrophe on an unimaginable scale. Mordred is the
figure of darkest evil to emerge from medieval literature: not such weak
figures as the Saracen king Marsilion, who could not be expected to know
any better.

It was the tradition of classical literature which came gradually to hu-

manize this stark black-and-white picture; the tradition above all of Homer, for whom the Trojan wars were tragic because they were civil wars,
ironic because they were unnecessary. Greeks and Trojans were tragic because they were cousins, members of the same culture, sharing the same
ideals and the same gods, closely interrelated—too closely in the case of
Menelaus and Helen. The irony, as Homer's successors saw it, lay in a
conflict to the death between such mighty heroes as Hector and Achilles
over so absurd a quarrel. The hero is not contending with villains or aliens:
he is fighting antagonists as worthy and virtuous as himself because of the
caprice of the gods, and win or lose he is their victim. This is the tragic
approach which underlies all the greatest military literature: the hero cannot win. Either he dies miserably in battle or he triumphs at a cost, or
perhaps in a cause, which calls in question the whole value of his victory.
In Shakespeare's *Troilus and Cressida* the irony becomes almost too bitter
to stomach. Greeks and Trojans alike are contending teams of louts. Cressida is a whore. Achilles is a cowardly villain. Men kill and are killed for
the meanest of objects, or for no object at all. The gods are not even
capricious: they are dead. It is an approach we shall meet again, nearer
our own times.

This bitterness is not typical of Shakespeare's approach to war. The
speeches of Henry V, paeans of martial ardour which still have power to
stir us, are no less deeply felt, even though Henry was fighting in a cause
no more serious than that which led to the burning of the 'topless towers
of Ilium'. But with Shakespeare and most of his generation war is becoming increasingly a background, a context within which the real drama, the
conflict and development of his characters, can be enacted. Macbeth's defeat in battle is only the nemesis invoked by a hubris itself the result of an
inner weakness which provides the core of the plot. Othello's mighty deeds
are likewise chronicled to provide a lamentable contrast with his weakness
and gullibility. So with Antony, the sweet war man in a play which cari-
catures almost to the point of absurdity the conflict between public duty
and private appetite and obsession. And finally in *Hamlet,* Fortinbras and
his armies are marched almost wantonly across the stage as if to set off,
like a distant battle glimpsed through a window in a painting devoted to
some personal confrontation between adversaries, the fundamentally *un-
military* and personal nature of the problem which Hamlet has to solve in
a world whose values, as he ruefully had to confess, remained fundamentally military.

Yet there is another aspect of Shakespeare's work which is even more
illuminating for our topic. He shows how in his time 'the military expe-

rience' was beginning to be a specialized affair, involving only those who deliberately sought it out. The remnants of the old shire levies and the feudal obligations of the gentry responsible for them are made a matter of good-natured mockery, at the same time as the world of Don Quixote was being urbanely escorted by Cervantes to the lumber-room of history. Falstaff was a knight who made a more successful transition to a world without honour. But in place of honour there was appearing a new standard of behavior no less rigorous: military professionalism, 'the discipline of the wars'. We meet for the first time not knights but professional soldiers: Corporal Nym, Lieutenant Bardolph, Captains Fluellen and Mackmorrice, Ancient (that is, Ensign) Pistol. With their conversation we become initiated into that world of campfire and billets, of military technique and technology, of rank and subordination which was henceforward to set the soldier apart from the civilian: a world not notably different from that of Kipling's *Soldiers Three*.

But it was a world which contained few men of letters to experience and describe it. The gradual professionalization of arms in the seventeenth and eighteenth centuries, the drawing apart of the professional soldier from the rest of society, resulted in a paucity of military literature. If one was unfortunate enough to be caught up in the mindless bestiality of the Thirty Years War in Germany, as was Grimmelshausen, then one could describe the result, as he did, with a deadpan irony worthy of the sagas. But by the eighteenth century war was an activity which the man of letters (and by now there *were* men of letters) could ignore and despise. Soldiers, if they appeared on the scene at all, did so as ignorant louts. The heroes of picaresque novels could, like Candide, get caught up in war for a few chapters. It was something about which the Uncle Tobies could reminisce. But one could say with only mild exaggeration that in the eighteenth century military experience lay almost outside the range of literature—and so remained until the great wars of the French Revolution forcibly brought it back inside again.

When it did come back, it was as part of the tempestuous literature initiated by the Sturm und Drang movement which upset the polite surface of European society towards the end of the eighteenth century, evoking romantic martial ardour rather than exploring the vicissitudes of the military life. Young Frenchmen followed Napoleon as if he were some kind of barbaric warrior chief, and he was resisted as if he was an emanation from the Dark Ages. Much of the literature of the Napoleonic Era— certainly the German literature of the time, the work of Fichte and Arndt—is that of tribal heroism. Stendhal was at once infected by the disease but sufficiently cool to analyze and mock the infection. The Stendhalian hero is engaging but absurd. The attempts of Fabrice in *La Chartreuse de Parme* to find and take part in the battle of Waterloo, his bewildered bumbling around the edges, his naive inquiry, 'Have I taken part in a real battle?' are comic. Stendhal's description of Waterloo, the diminution of a huge conflict to a series of random and faintly ludicrous adventures, has sometimes been seen as an appropriate debunking of the military experience. It is nothing of the kind. Had Stendhal made his hero a member of the Young Guard involved in the desperate fighting in the centre of the battlefield, he would have painted a very different picture of Waterloo. But that would hardly have suited his literary objective, of showing the contrast between the romantic aspirations of his hero and the flatness of reality. Like Shakespeare he sang of Arms only the more effectively to sing of the Man.

For a convincing evocation of the Napoleonic Wars we have to turn to Tolstoy. In *War and Peace* Tolstoy is concerned to capture the military experience, not of an individual or even a group of individuals but of a nation—and a nation made conscious, by that experience, of its nationhood. For Tolstoy the war was no mere background to his characters. At times indeed his characters are little more than devices to enable us to observe the climactic events of the war. He does not have Pierre bumbling ineffectively around the outskirts of the battle of Borodino: he places him (perhaps a shade unconvincingly) in the middle in the central redoubt. Prince Andrei roved conveniently at will over the battlefield of Austerlitz. And Tolstoy had them observe not only the horrors of the battlefield, the sufferings and the heroism, but the military mechanics which governed the action—the technical framework binding the innumerable small actions on whose almost random outcome the course of history depended. (Solzhenitsyn in our own day has done the same with the battle of Tannenberg in his novel *1914*.) They did not have to ask whether they had 'assisted at a battle'. Tolstoy made them see war clearly as the thing it was—and is. It was, as Prince Andrei described it on the eve of Borodino, 'not a polite recreation but the vilest thing in life, and we ought to understand that and not play at war. Our gratitude to the stern necessity of war ought to be stern and serious. It boils down to this: we should have done with humbug and let war be war and not a game'.

The Napoleonic Wars thus broke down the barriers between soldiers and the rest of society. Writers and intellectuals found themselves immersed in the military experience, and the continuation of conscription in the nineteenth century, first in vestigial and ultimately in absolute form, meant that they never entirely shook themselves free. They became aware that professional soldiers were not total barbarians; or even if they were, as Alfred de Vigny put it, 'the most melancholy relic of barbarism (next to capital punishment) that lingers on among mankind, yet . . . there is nothing more worthy of the esteem and affection of the nation than this family of victims whose sacrifice occasionally wins for it so much glory'.

De Vigny indeed found the military life fascinating, not because of its excitement but, more perceptively, because of its fundamental *boredom:*

> Merely to glance at a body of troops is to see that the general characteristics of the military expression are boredom and discontent. . . . Nevertheless a quality common to them all often lends this band of grave men a majesty of bearing; and this quality is Abnegation . . . which . . . together with the constant and careless expectation of death, the complete renunciation of all liberty of thought and action, the delays suffered by a limited ambition and the impossibility of acquiring riches, all produce virtues which are much rarer among those classes of men who remain free and independent.

One cannot generalize too widely from de Vigny's experience of the post-Napoleonic French Army to other professional armies. 'Abnegation' was certainly not a characteristic of the German Army between 1870 and 1914, and *gravitas* was hardly a characteristic of the soldiers described by Kipling. None the less there was a common structure of professionalism, a cadre with which some writers were to become increasingly familiar and by which some of them, not least Marcel Proust himself, were to become fascinated. This immersion of men of letters in a military environment, which reached its peak in the Great War, produced the kind of military experience which I want to spend the rest of this article discussing.

In this experience, three elements interact. One is the military environment I have sketched, the disciplined activity, the routine, the drill, the organisation, the administration, the training—'the discipline of warres'. This has the fascination of all professional activity, and perhaps because it is more than any other a *total* activity, creating a complete and self-contained world, it can become in a perverse way almost compulsive. Certainly hardly an English writer who served during either world war remained unaffected by it. Robert Graves and Evelyn Waugh delighted in regimental minutiae. David Jones recreated in *In Parenthesis* the rhythm and chores of trench warfare. Ford Madox Ford showed how the workings of the reinforcement machinery at a base depot became more significant in the life of his hero Tietjens, than the unhappiness of his disastrous marriage.

Anthony Powell went into almost obsessive detail in describing the functioning of a divisional staff. This is after all what most soldiers, even in
wartime, spend most of their time doing: making the machine work.
Fighting is brief, unpredictable, intermittent. Of the totality of military
experience it is a small even if a colourful part.

The second element is made up of human relationships; and it is this
that constitutes the most moving aspect of literature of the Great War,
perhaps more than any other conflict before or since. In war men discover
a comradeship which, as Frederick Manning put it in *The Middle Parts of
Fortune,* 'rises on occasion to an intensity of feeling which friendship never
touches'. The comradeship of the trenches was clearly something almost
incommunicable. Charles Carrington wrote of it in his book (published
under the pseudonym Charles Edmonds) *A Subaltern's War.* So did Guy
Chapman in his glowing study *A Passionate Prodigality* and his posthumous
biography *A Kind of Survivor,* quoting with approval Montherlant's description of the war as 'la plus *tendre* experience humaine qu'il eut vécu'.
Edmund Blunden apostrophised the men he commanded: 'Man, ruddy-
cheeked under your squat chin-strapped iron helmet, sturdy under your
leather jerkin, clapping your hands together as you dropped your burden
of burning-cold steel, grinning and flinging old-home repartee at your pal
passing by. . . . It is time to hint to a new age what your value, what your
love was'. But most convincing of all were the words of Frederick Manning,
who did not command men but served among them and observed how
they endured the ordeals to which they were subjected:

> These apparently rude and brutal natures comforted, encouraged and
> reconciled each other to a fate with a tenderness and tact which was
> more moving than anything in life. They had nothing; not even their
> own bodies, which had become mere implements of warfare. They
> turned from the wreckage and misery of life to an empty heaven,
> and from an empty heaven to the silence of their own hearts. They
> had been brought to the last extremity of hope, and yet they put
> their hands on each other's shoulders and said with a passionate
> conviction that it would be alright, though they had faith in nothing,
> but in themselves and each other.

Finally of course in this trinity there were the ordeals of the military
experience, the fatigue, the hardship, the danger, the horrors: ordeals
which the disciplined structure existed to enable the men to face, but which
comradeship alone made possible—and which also in return strengthened
that comradeship to endure yet worse ordeals. This was the aspect of war

literature which became dominant in the 1930s, the aspect stressed in the poems of Sassoon and Wilfred Owen, in the work of Erich Maria Remarque and Céline. It was in fact treated soberly and somberly, without hysteria or self-pity, by the overwhelming majority of war writers: by Edmund Blunden and Robert Graves, by Charles Carrington and Guy Chapman, by Frederick Manning and David Jones.

On the Western Front in particular the powers of endurance of troops on both sides were tested almost to breaking-point. Only very rarely did they break: for the most part men found resources of whose very existence within themselves they were unaware which enabled them to survive the ordeal. It is this endurance, this response, rather than the ordeal that evoked it, that has provided us with the finest literature of that war. The worst, the almost unendurable test, was to be found not in one's own suffering but in the death of one's comrades, the destruction of that link which alone made endurance possible.

So had it ever been since the days of Patroclus and Achilles. One of Frederick Manning's inarticulate soldiers saw his mate shredded to bloody pieces by shellfire before his eyes. When his companion tried to comfort him by saying that the victim could have felt nothing he replied simply, 'I don't know what he felt. I know what I felt'. It is the deepest ordeal that warriors have had to endure since fighting began. It was what Roland felt for Oliver in the pass of Roncesvalles when his friend, mortally wounded, slipped from his horse, made his confession, invoked God's blessing on his country, his lord, and his friend, and died: 'The valiant Roland weeps for him and laments, / No man on earth felt ever such distress'.

It is perhaps easier to endure such ordeals and even to take pride in them if one is conscious that there is nothing new in having to do so; that men of earlier generations have faced and overcome them and gained well-deserved renown as a result. That is why military units, and militant societies, lay so much more emphasis on their past, and why military history more than perhaps any other branch of historical studies is so liable to falsification. In a most interesting, if occasionally obtuse study, *The Great War and Modern Memory* (1975), an American scholar, Paul Fussell, made the point that the British people in 1914 were soaked in memories, folk-memories as well as literary ones, of their cultural past; that, well-read men of letters apart, there can have been few people of any class whose minds had not been affected by the imagery of the Bible and *The Pilgrim's Progress* with their emphasis on endurance, sacrifice, martyrdom. Britain was a far less militant society than most in Europe, but the roots of its culture, like those of all European cultures, lay in a bellicist past which the peaceful fashions of the last hundred years had done little to erode. Literary memory provided a dimension for military experience, and the deeper one's literary culture, the more profound this dimension became.

I will quote only one example: from David Jones's narrative poem *In Parenthesis,* which in its blending of past and present, of historical memory and shrewd observation, of high poetic diction and demotic slang, seems to me the most remarkable work of literature to emerge from either world war. He is describing that awe-ful moment on the morning of July 1, 1916, when the British army rose from its trenches in the valley of the Somme and stood exposed to the fire of the Germans on the chalk uplands above: only to go the way of so many warriors before them:

By one and one the line gaps . . . who impinges on less space

sink limply to a heap
nourish a lesser category of being
like those who fructify the land
like Tristram
Lamorak de Galis
Alisand le Orphelin
Beaumains who was the youngest
or all of them in the shaft shade
at strait Thermopylae;
or the sweet brothers Balin and Balan
embraced beneath their single monument.
     Jonathan my lovely one
on Gelboe mountain
and the young man Absalom.
White Hart transfixed in his dark lodge.
Peredur of steel arms
and he who with intention took grass of that field to
be for him the Species of Bread.
     Taillefer the maker,
and on the same day,
thirty thousand other ranks.

It was a tradition at once terrible and comforting; and it was one which perhaps died on that very day at the hands of the German machine-gunners. Not even the *ghosts* of Roland and Oliver, of Balin and Balan, of Taillefer and Peredur could ever ride again.

One does however catch a glimpse of this tradition in the work of some of the slightly older generation of Englishmen caught up in the Second World War—Anthony Powell, for example. Powell's hero, Nick Jenkins, on enlistment recalled his military ancestors, 'forerunners of the same blood [who] had set out to become unnoticed officers of Marines or in the East India Company', and remembered more remote forbears still: 'A pale, mysterious sun opaquely glittered on the circlet of gold round their helmets, as armed men, ever fainter in outline and less substantial, receded into the vaporous shining mists towards intermediate, timeless beings, at once measurably historical, at the same time, mythically heroic'. Evelyn Waugh's Guy Crouchback, also joined up in a consciously crusading mood, wearing a holy relic and fighting for Christendom like his ancestors before him. But Powell's hero suffered no ordeals to make him evoke traditional heroism in his aid. As for Guy Crouchback, what he witnessed in Crete was the end of a tradition. Both the professional soldier, Major Hound, and the elegant aristocrat, Ivor Claire, collapsed in abject cowardice. The figure who endured and who enabled Crouchback himself to survive was the enigmatic Corporal-Major Ludovic, classless and epicene; darkly foreshadowing the social confusion into which post-war England was to fall.

Younger British writers in that war called up no literary memories. Their attitude was that of Prince Andrei, bleakly unromantic in face of a 'stern necessity' which they hated. Their poetry was dry, sparse, ironic, their prose economically descriptive and understated. But they remained within a European literary tradition, in that they did accept war as a grim necessity and remained conscious of the need for self-respect in the conduct of it.

The degree to which they did so can be seen by comparing the work of such writers as Keith Douglas with the more spectacular American writings on the topic: Norman Mailer's *The Naked and the Dead*, Joseph Heller's *Catch-22*, Kurt Vonnegut's *Slaughterhouse Five*. In such works, all trace of the European idea that in the endurance and overcoming of suffering there is something that is ennobling, an idea that had reconciled the Christian and the warrior ethic since the end of the Dark Ages, together with the yet older tradition of the classics that man should maintain dignity and serenity in spite of the wildest caprice of the gods—all this has disappeared. We are back to the godless, chaotic world of Troilus and Cressida, enhanced by the mindless barbarities of Grimmelshausen. When, in *Slaughterhouse Five*, the American hero and his companion arrive at a German prison camp and meet British soldiers who had maintained discipline, cleanliness, cheerfulness and morale and who regarded the ordeals of war as a challenge to be overcome, their reaction is one neither of admiration nor of hostility. It is one of blank astonishment. These were beings from another planet. It was pointless even to try to understand or communicate with them.

Paul Fussell suggests at the conclusion of his book that the entire European literary tradition was in fact simply a narcotic, masking the essential obscenity of war. Many people in this country would probably now agree with him; and there would be few—or I hope there would be few—to dissent from Prince Andrei's verdict, that it is 'the vilest thing in life'. Yet one does not have to make a value judgement about war itself to accept that the whole corpus of European literature suggests that military experience, by deepening men's understanding and widening their knowledge of themselves and one another; by enhancing their perceptions both of torment and of ecstasy; by confronting them with novel impressions, terrifying, sickening, tedious, occasionally delightful; by creating for them new relationships and new challenges; has, when it has been properly understood and interpreted, immeasurably enriched that understanding of mankind, of its powers and its limitations, of its splendours and its miseries, and not least of its relationship to God, which must lie at the root of all societies that lay any claim to civilization.

13

Structure

and Process

in History

Eight years have passed since I gave an Inaugural Lecture in these Schools, and expressed my views as to why history should be studied and how it should be taught. It was a fairly routine apologia and a declaration of intent which I have since done all too little to implement.

It is not my purpose in this Valedictory Lecture to give an account of my stewardship, nor to provide yet another justification for the study of history. I want rather to consider why the study of history *has* been seen, throughout the evolution of Western society, as an intrinsic and essential part of the education of all civilized men and women, and what they have expected to acquire from that study.

Today most of us would argue that only a knowledge of the past enables us fully to understand the present, and that a failure to read the past correctly warps our capacity to act intelligently in the contemporary world. But for most of the past millennium, expectations of what historians can contribute to the common weal have been even higher. The study of history has been believed to provide a guide, not simply to passive understanding of the world, but to active political and moral action within it. Today few of us—certainly few non-Marxists—would have the temerity to make such a claim, but it was not always so. For the best part of a thousand years Western man has studied the past in the expectation that he would receive both political and moral guidance from doing so, and historians have been on the whole only too happy to oblige.

Almost from earliest times history was expected to 'teach lessons'; to provide guidance as to how to act or not to act; to furnish examples of virtue rewarded and evil punished. The laws of moral and political be-

A Valedictory Lecture given in the University of Oxford, May 1989.

haviour were generally regarded as immutable and invariable in all ages and all societies. Each new generation was joining in an activity, of which the rules were well established and whose skills could only be learned by studying the techniques of past masters. Even in the picture of the past painted by medieval scholars, directed though this was to depicting God's eschatological purposes for mankind, both Old and New Testaments are used to define patterns of behaviour and provide examples of virtue rewarded and evil punished—and the need for remaining virtuous even if, in the unknowable purposes of God, good behaviour was not rewarded but resulted, as it did for most of mankind throughout most of its history, only in suffering; the reward for which lay in the hereafter and whose purpose would be understood only in the fulness of time.

For the humanists of the Renaissance and the classical historians on whom they commented, virtue was not necessarily rewarded either: only *virtù*, which was a very different matter. History was a manual of statecraft. But it was also a guide to conduct. It was defended, in the 1579 translation of Plutarch's *Lives,* as 'a certain rule and instruction which by examples past, teacheth us to judge of things present and to foresee things to come, so as we may know what to like of and what to follow, what to mislike, and what to eschew'. Thucydides had already made the same point nearly two thousand years before: history was 'philosophy teaching by example'. What was exemplified were the challenges which all generations had in turn to confront in conducting their affairs; and the qualities required to meet those challenges—courage, equanimity, moderation, loyalty, magnanimity, foresight, all the prudent skills of the statesman and the warrior—were considered to be as 'relevant' for the moderns as they had been for the ancients. Gentlemen in the eighteenth century filled their libraries with the classics and sent their sons to the universities to read 'more humane letters' in the belief that these still provided the best preparation for public, as the study of the Scriptures provided the best preparation for private life.

The impact of the Enlightenment strengthened this belief in the uniformity of human behaviour with its assumption that man governed his own destiny by the use of his own judgement and reason, and that, in all ages, rational and intelligent behaviour led to felicity, and foolish passion or unreasoning superstition to disaster. The past was to be studied in the same spirit, and for the same reasons, as scientists studied the natural world. The chief use of historical study, taught Hume, 'is only to discover the constant and universal principles of human nature'; and in the eighteenth century historians maintained that only such history should be studied as did possess such utility. Anything that was not so relevant was simply antiquarianism; a respectable enough way of passing the time, but an activity that had little in common with the writing of history. No utility was seen, in that pre-romantic era, in studying the past 'for its own sake'. The men of the Enlightenment therefore read history to find not, as in the Renaissance, models for appropriate behaviour, but illustration of the natural laws which governed the conduct of mankind.

This mechanistic view did not satisfy, among others, Immanuel Kant. For Kant, man did not simply govern his own destinies by rationally observing and applying static universal principles. For one thing 'nature' was not static, a kind of arena within which successive generations played out their destinies in accordance with an unchanging set of rules. It was dynamic and evolving; and that dynamism, that evolution, consisted of the actions of men whose rational decisions were part of the process whereby nature's purposes gradually unfolded themselves. History was the record not of random human activities but of the self-fulfilment of Reason itself.

For Kant, each human act created a new set of circumstances and new problems which created a further need for judgement and decision. The process was one that would continue over countless generations and involve unremitting struggle. It had been a long march, with many setbacks, from the Greeks through the Romans to the Barbarians and modern times, but always breaking fresh ground. 'A seed of enlightenment always survived', declared Kant hopefully, 'developing further with each revolution, and prepared the way for a subsequent higher level of improvement'.

Kant's formulation was too subtle to make the same political impact as did Rousseau's simplistic cry for instant liberation from the trammels of the past, or Condorcet's infectious belief in the imminent victory of Enlightenment and Reason. But his *Idea for a Universal History* (1784) established the pattern of historiography for the next hundred years. For the great majority of historians in nineteenth-century Europe, history was to be precisely 'the story of liberty'; an unfolding process directed by some teleological force towards a great and glorious goal. Over how that goal was to be defined, and how 'liberty' was to be understood, opinions differed, among philosophers and historians as among politicians; but the function of the historian was generally seen as being to chart the progress of mankind towards that goal, to show how far he had come and to point the way for his onward journey. History was not so much prescriptive as indicative.

For virtually all British historians—Macaulay, Froude, Freeman, even

Stubbs—that goal was the continual perfection of that system of representative government in which freedom had broadened down from precedent to precedent and in which Britain served as a model for mankind. With this there usually went a belief in the mission of the British to spread their beneficent power throughout the world and the duty of historians to chart and encourage that process. 'I do not pretend to impartiality', remarked, with engaging frankness, my predecessor in this Chair, James Anthony Froude; 'I believe the Reformation to be the greatest event in English history, the root and source of the expansive force which has spread the Anglo-Saxon race over the globe'. Hegel and his Prussian disciples, from Sybel to Treitschke, were yet more explicit: the goal of History was the State itself which, because it embodied freedom, was 'the absolute, final aim . . . All the worth which the human being possesses, all spiritual reality, he possesses only through the State'. Further, explained Hegel, the State was 'moral—virtuous—vigorous—while it is engaged in realizing its grand objects and defends its work against external violence during the process of giving to its purposes an objective existence'; that is to say, while it was fighting. Careful scholars though they were, the Prussian historians of the nineteenth century were in no doubt that they owed their primary duty to the State and that by their writings they should urge this duty on their pupils; a duty which would find its highest fulfilment, so Treitschke, in particular, argued, in war.

We must not allow the excesses of this specifically German patriotism, especially in its final debased form of Nazism, to blind us to the extent to which by the end of the nineteenth century in all European countries— and not only European—historians were depicting historical progress and the moral imperative to co-operate with it as indistinguishable from the power and greatness of their own nation and the moral imperative to serve it. Before and during the First World War, indeed, historians became little better than recruiting-sergeants, explaining to their fellow-countrymen that their nation embodied the concept of freedom in a unique and irreplaceable way and that in dying for it they would be serving the highest good. At best they can be seen as priests, tending that sacred flame of nationalism which was to exact such horrendous sacrifices between 1914 and 1918.

The tragic outcome of that conflict did much to discredit the concept of nationalism and perhaps even more to discredit that of progress. For most established historians the post-war environment was significantly less agreeable than had been that before 1914. The events of the war and its aftermath offered little evidence that Reason was inexorably unfolding its purposes within the phenomenal world. Rather they suggested that European civilization had reached its peak in the nineteenth century as other civilizations had peaked before it, and like those civilizations was now entering a period of degeneracy and decay. Toynbee, Spengler and their imitators became fashionable between the wars; historians who discovered in the rise and fall of civilization a rhythm as inevitable, and as purposeless, as the rise and fall of the ocean tides. There was a *process* in history, perhaps, of a purely cyclical kind, but no progress. Historians could no longer deduce from the pattern they observed in the past any guide to moral or political conduct. At best they could give explanations of the crises which were shaking Western civilization, and which people had to endure as best they could. More and more, however, they were content to turn to the archives to seek not an explanation of the troubled world outside but a refuge from it; to study the past 'for its own sake', as a matter not of public duty but for private scholarly satisfaction.

To this generality there was a significant exception. One group of thinkers saw no cause to abandon their belief in history as progress and in the duty of historians to expound it: the Marxists. The First World War, and the turmoil that succeeded it, had done nothing in their view to invalidate the analysis, and the prognosis, of Marx and Engels. Indeed it had done much to revitalize them after the growing prosperity of pre-1914 Europe had led so many of the fainter hearts among their followers to despair of the inevitability of revolution.

Marx had taken the Kantian teaching about the evolution of Reason and the self-liberation of mankind through conflict, as modified by Hegel's concept of the dialectic; removed the metaphysics; replaced them with positive scientific laws based on the careful observation of social and economic phenomena, in the best traditions of the Enlightenment; and produced a creed which combined the assurance of scientific Truth with Messianic promise of an earthly paradise, as the culmination of the historical process to be achieved virtually within the lifetime of his disciples.

Events did not turn out as he had predicted. The Russian Revolution of 1917 occurred neither in the place nor for the reasons he had expected. It was indeed hardly a 'revolution' in the Marxian sense of the rule of one class being replaced by that of another, but a combination of insurrection and coup d'état, skilfully legitimised by Marxist ideology. But for many Western intellectuals the Soviet Union—or what little they knew of it—provided exactly that evidence of historical progress which the liberals could not: assurance that history really was the story of evolving freedom and that under the Soviet banners the toilers of the world could unite to achieve the final liberation of mankind. And again we must not allow our after-knowledge of the squalid end of those hopes, as vile in its way as that of the Nazis—the mass starvation, the lies, the purges, the massacres, the oppressions, above all the sheer monstrous *inefficiency* of a system against which the Soviet people themselves have now revolted—to blind us to the plausibility, between 1917 and, say, 1947, of the claim that 'the Soviet experiment' represented the last, best hope of mankind: a claim that seduced some of the brightest and best of our intellectuals and idealists—not excepting some of our historians—between the wars.

By the second half of the twentieth century, however, even the Marxist God had clearly failed. Where Marxism survived it was as a wholly admirable passion for social justice and a valuable tool for social analysis, rather than as a creed with predictive powers based on a unique insight into the historical process. There was not by then much left of the concept of history as process, much less as progress. But the reaction against that concept had already been gaining strength for a hundred years.

The belief that the past should be studied in its own right and on its own terms, without distorting its significance by forcing upon it a pattern of development involving selectivity in the treatment of evidence and insensitivity to values other than our own; this reaction dated back as far as the eighteenth century and the pioneering studies of Giambattista Vico and Johann Herder. For Herder indeed the understanding of each epoch of the past as, in its own way, one form of human perfection, was itself a contribution to understanding the process of history and indeed of understanding oneself: everything in history was both means and end, to be studied both as part of a process and in its own right. That view would probably be endorsed by most professional historians working today.

But the complex techniques required to understand the traces left by the past—philology, paleography, diplomatic, documentary analysis—and the growing number of tools placed in the hands of historians by their colleagues in the fields of archaeology, anthropology and the social sciences, increasingly emphasised the latter task at the expense of the former, the understanding of the nature of the past rather than of the historical process. It was a development that reached its climax with the great school of French historians founded by Marc Bloch and publishing largely in the periodical *Annales*; a school immensely influential among British historians today. These scholars consciously and deliberately studied the past, not as process but as *structure*. They were concerned not so much to trace the causes and consequences of events as to explain them in their context: to see them, not as links between what went before and what came afterwards, but as part of a system complete in itself and to be recreated in its entirety.

Some of them indeed regarded the study of actual *events* by which the process of history can be charted—the wars, the power-struggles, the political changes, the revolutions—as being almost as pointless as studying the patterns made by foam on an ocean wave. What mattered were the deep, slow-moving ocean currents. For radical historians indeed, *Histoire évènementielle,* because it chronicles the activities of élites (and largely male élites), is politically suspect. Yet if we study the past primarily in order to understand its structures, then the concept of process and development, the expounding of which was once regarded as the historian's premier task, is downgraded where it is not lost to sight altogether.

It is strange that this should be so, for the whole concept of structure, of the interrelationship of all the phenomena of a given epoch, is central to Marxism, and many of the most distinguished of our structuralist historians have been Marxist or Marxisant. The study of the past 'for its own sake' is normally a characteristic of conservative rather than of radical historians. Traditional Marxist history and morality were impregnated with the sense of the historical process: those elements which 'objectively' forwarded that process were applauded (as Marx applauded British rule in India); those who stood in its way or did not contribute to it were condemned. But today the criteria are reversed. Distinguished Marxist historians like E. P. Thompson and Christopher Hill reserve their sympathy for the losers, the little men whose values and livelihood were swept away by the power structures of the time; basing their value-judgements not on any objective assessment of the historical process but on older and more enduring concepts of equity and social justice with which most of us would have considerably more sympathy.

But such value-judgements, much as we may share them, are suspect by many professional historians. They involve taking a stand *outside* the period we are studying and judging it by extrinsic standards which historians nowadays are trained to suppress. We are told that it is no business of historians *qua* historians to pronounce value-judgements on the societies they study, any more than it is the business of anthropologists. Our own values, we are reminded, emanate from the structure of our own late twentieth-century white, male-dominated European society. It would be anachronistic to apply them to the twelfth century, or the seventeenth. In the twelfth century they burned heretics. In the seventeenth century they burned witches. It is the task of the historian to *empathize*, to understand and explain why they did so; not to engage in otiose moral condemnation.

That is all very well. But does the same apply to the mid-twentieth century, when the Nazis gassed and burned several million Jews?

There are various answers one can give to this question, none of them very satisfactory. One is that because the Nazis belonged to our own culture we can judge them by our own moral standards in a way that we cannot judge the burners of witches. But the Nazis did *not* belong to our culture: they consciously and deliberately turned their backs on 'bourgeois' culture—that amalgam of Christianity and the Enlightenment which still distinguishes Western civilization—and created a very different and very nasty one of their own with its own distinct value-systems. Another answer is, yes, we must judge, but not as historians: we should appeal to moral absolutes, whether divine or human, which somehow transcend history. This was the line so firmly taken and proclaimed by Lord Acton when he exhorted his audience 'never to debase the moral currency or lower the standards of rectitude, but to try others by the maxim that govern your own lives'. But why were such maxims and standards not apparent to those profoundly devout Christians who burned heretics and lonely old women, or to the respectable, Mozart-loving bureaucrats, with their happy family lives, who presided over the concentration camps? Or finally there is the entirely consistent but to most of us unacceptable answer: historians should describe and explain what happened at Auschwitz as dispassionately as they describe and explain the burning of martyrs at Smithfield in the sixteenth century: describe, explain, and not judge.

This is the position in which we find ourselves if we reject that whole school of historical thought, from Kant to Marx, which saw history not only as process but as *progress*; if we do not believe that in spite of all set-backs, 'a seed of enlightenment' does survive and prepare the way for continual improvement, so that the standards by which we judge ourselves and others are, in a sense at once absolute and historical, an improvement on those which prevailed in the past; standards which entitle us to condemn slavery or persecution or torture or genocide wherever or whenever we find it, however justifiable it appeared to other ages or other cultures. If we really cannot make any such claim, all moral judgement sinks to an undifferentiated level of cultural relativism, in which we have no 'standard of rectitude' to judge, either the past, or the present.

To accept such a position seems to me perverse. The fact of the historical process over the last two hundred years is self-evident, whether or not we regard it as 'progress'. Fernand Braudel, that great architect of historical structures, could in his giant study *Civilization and Capitalism from the 15th to the 18th Centuries* take a *longue durée* of three hundred years in which the structure apparently remained stable and change incremental. He might for an earlier epoch have chosen an even longer period. But from the end of the eighteenth century until our own day we have been witnessing the progressive and infectious *disintegration* of traditional social structures, and history has become the record of ever more rapid and bewildering change throughout the world. That change has been discontinuous and uneven, faster and earlier in some areas than in others, and it is precisely the contrast in the speed and the incidence of that change that has caused most of the social and political tensions which have underlain the very *évènementielle* history of the past two centuries. (And if anyone tries to write the history of the twentieth century without dealing with 'events', I can only say, good luck to them.)

Earlier generations had no hesitation in describing as 'progress' or 'the march of civilization' that process of economic transformation which, originating in Britain in the eighteenth century, spread to the whole of Europe and North America in the nineteenth century, and the rest of the world in the twentieth. Later, less loaded words were used: 'industrialization', or more often 'modernization'. Now I think that the accepted term is 'development'; one which, interestingly, returns to the original Kantian concept of the unfolding of potential, of seed germinating and growing towards fulfilment.

It is this process of modernization that confounds purely cyclical theories of history. It is indeed possible that agrarian societies were constrained by the structural limitations of their environment to follow certain common patterns of growth and decline; but the chain-reaction of modernization has transformed the range of opportunities available to mankind, creating a situation for which there exists literally no historical parallel.

The benefits of this process are easy to list. The increase in life-expectancy, of surviving beyond childbirth and infancy and living to see one's fiftieth, even one's eightieth birthday; the elimination of the plagues and famines which so regularly decimated the population of Europe; the drastic reduction in the incidence of *pain*—that pain which had accompanied men, and even more, women, like an evil shadow throughout their brief lives; emancipation from the bonds of law or custom that had bound men to their masters or to the soil for so many centuries; the alleviation, through the application of technology, of the day-long, year-long, back-breaking toil in field or factory that made a mockery of political freedom; the increase in the universal provision of the necessities of life, and of luxuries that rapidly came to be regarded as necessities—necessities not just for the rich but for the entire population, not just for developed countries but increasingly for the entire world; the growth of literacy and with it access to knowledge, and with knowledge, power. The list is infinite and the process far from complete. We are indeed quite properly conscious of how much further we have to go rather than how far we have already come. But the distance that we have already travelled during the past two hundred years, especially in the Northern Hemisphere, is already so great that it is not surprising if we have to study the earlier history even of our own societies as if it were that of some remote age in the past. Is it really so naive to call this process 'Progress'?

But if there has been such progress, why has the history of the twentieth century been so generally frightful: so replete with wars, massacres, revolutions, tyrannies and now the ever-present threat of annihilation? Does not this record cancel out all those benefits and invalidate the optimistic assumptions of the Enlightenment and its heirs, whether Liberal or Marxist?

It has certainly invalidated one expectation: that Liberty and the rule of Reason would of itself bring happiness, and that after 'liberation' mankind would live in universal and perpetual harmony. The assumption of the Enlightenment was that man was corrupted only by his institutions or the social structure, and that once these were reformed he would recognise his best interests and act rationally. A hundred years later Lenin had to recognise that this corruption might have penetrated so deeply, even into the minds of the proletariat, that a 'vanguard' had to be created of those with a true insight into the historical process, who would use whatever measures might be necessary to obtain power and then exercise it, in order to fulfil the task entrusted to them by 'History'.

For in addition to their simplistic views about the nature of Man, the Enlightenment and its heirs committed one appalling methodological error from which not even Kant was immune. They *reified*, first 'Nature', then 'Reason', and finally History itself; and in so doing they *deified* them. It was understandable. If a personal God was no longer recognised as the prime mover and demiurge of the Universe, if events had instead to be explained or justified in terms of the unfolding of Reason, or the self-realisation of the World Idea, or the processes of the Historical Dialectic, then these abstractions took the place vacated by God and inherited the reverence and obligations previously due to him. In particular they inherited a priesthood, an intellectual élite trained to discern their purposes and transmit them to the laity, teaching it to think the right kind of thoughts and eliminating those refractory spirits unwilling to do so. The consequences were evident in the French Revolution for a few terrible months at the hands of Robespierre and St. Just: we have watched them operating in the totalitarian societies of the socialist world for the past seventy years.

But Reason is not a Thing, or a Person, much less a God. It is an *activity*, and a highly individual one. It is *people* thinking and judging: more, it is individual *persons* thinking and judging. Neither is History a Thing: it is what people think, write and believe about the past. A knowledge of the past is essential in making political or moral judgements, but 'History' as such does not judge. That is done by people; and best done by people free to think, read, inform themselves and debate before they decide; and having decided, be free to change their minds. They may be free to do so only within the constraints imposed by historical structures; but those structures are themselves created by human thoughts and actions, and are constantly being modified by them.

Free people can make wrong, foolish and even wicked decisions. That is something which the heirs of the Enlightenment tended to forget. Kant himself did not: 'Nothing straight', he warned, 'can be constructed from such warped wood as man is made of'. André Gide put it rather differently: '[T]o free oneself is nothing: to live in freedom, that is the difficulty'. For modernization, if it has brought undreamed-of opportunities, has also brought undreamed-of problems. The crumbling of traditional structures led to conflict, bewilderment, *anomie*. Increase in population, and perhaps more important the growing *mobility* of population, has created economic, social and alas racial tensions. Freedom of political choice has opened the way for mountebanks and fanatics to seize power. Is it surprising that there have been those who viewed the whole process with horror, and longed for the old order in which nothing very much happened and everyone knew their place?

But these problems are ineluctably part of a learning process. As Kant indicated in his *Idea for a Universal History*, it is out of the very nature of man as a social and political animal, and the tensions which this engenders, that there come these continual conflicts to exercise our intellectual and moral faculties. The solutions we find to them, themselves partial and incomplete, create further and greater problems which pose even greater challenges; but only in meeting these challenges can our faculties mature and develop.

They will not necessarily do so: people may simply reject the burden, imposed on them by freedom, of exercising judgement and choice. Nor will their judgement, however wisely used, necessarily have the expected and desired results. Further, as by the free use of his reason man accumulates more power, the greater becomes his capacity to do evil as well as good. There is no certainty of a happy ending; only of continual challenge, response and with it at least the opportunity for growth.

Such a perspective at least provides us with a framework for moral judgement which is not divorced from history but derived from our understanding of it. It rescues us from, on the one hand, the desert of sterile cultural relativism and arid professional 'neutrality', and, on the other, the lush self-indulgence of escapist nostalgia—'the Heritage Industry'. It is rooted in a perception of history as a continual movement from the realm of necessity to that of choice, and a belief that the growth and diffusion of knowledge increasingly equips us with the opportunity, and the capability, to make those choices.

This movement, this historical dynamic, consists of freely-willed human activities. It engenders both its own criteria for judgement and its own imperatives for action. These enable us, however successfully we may 'empathise' with past generations, to judge them if necessary with Actonian rigour. They lead us in our own generation to favour political regimes in which free discourse is favoured and encouraged over those in which it is not. They further lay on us the continuing obligation to ensure that nowhere in the world should poverty, illiteracy and grinding hardship deprive peoples of those opportunities for physical improvement and moral growth which the historical process has provided for the fortunate societies of the West.

This imperative provides indeed the real justification for the study of history as process; for it is only from that study that we can discover what we have been, understand what we are, and gain intimations of what we might become. The study is not comforting. It holds out hope of nothing but continuing problems, continuing conflicts—conflicts which may become yet more bitter as more of mankind become conscious of the gap that separates potential from fulfilment, aspiration from achievement, and, once they have achieved their immediate goals, reach out for more. But it is only by such conflicts that growth can take place at all and that mankind can move on to higher levels of aspiration and achievement.

There is, as I have said, no assurance of a happy ending: all may disintegrate into ruin and chaos on a scale never before seen. But whether it does so or not depends not on any abstract concept of historical development, nor on the random play of chance, nor on the providence of an almighty God. It depends on our skill in using that capacity for reason and judgement which has already brought us so far; reason and judgement both educated and *created* by historical experience. On the whole we have done quite well in avoiding or recovering from catastrophe, but we must continue to do well: *for ever.* We have no justification for looking forward to a time when we can sit back and say, 'That is it: now we are safe: now there is peace'. If such a time were indeed to come it would be the end of history, since we would all be dead.

Let me in conclusion again quote Kant: 'Nature does not seem to have been concerned with seeing that man should live agreeably, but that he should work his way onward to make himself by his own conduct worthy of life and well-being'. That is what we have continually to do. The historical process, through the very challenges it poses and the responses it evokes, itself creates the morality of mankind. That seems to me a very good reason for studying it.

Attributions

"The Lessons of History" was given as an Inaugural Lecture at Oxford on March 6, 1981

The Yigal Allon Memorial Lectures were given in the University of Tel Aviv in March 1982

"Prussia in European History" was delivered as a lecture to the *Stiftung Preussische Kulturbesitz* in September 1983

"Empire, Race and War" is printed in H. Lloyd-Jones, V. Pearl and B. Worden, *History and the Imagination: Essays in honour of H. R. Trevor-Roper* (London, 1981)

"The Edwardian Arms Race" is printed in Donald Read, ed. *Edwardian England* (London, 1982)

"Men against Fire" is reprinted from *International Security* 9, no. 1 (Summer 1984)

"Europe on the Eve of the First World War" was delivered as a lecture in Oxford in October 1984, and is printed in R. J. W. Evans and H. Pogge von Strandmann, eds., *The Coming of the First World War* (Oxford, 1988)

"1945—End of an Era?" was delivered as the Huizinga memorial lecture in the University of Leiden in December 1985 and is printed in *Alle Cultuur is Streven: de verzamelde Huizin-galezingen* (Amsterdam, 1987)

"Ideology and International Relations" was delivered as the E. H. Carr memorial lecture in the University of Wales at Aberystwyth in March 1988 and is printed in *The Review of International Studies* 15 (1989)

"Churchill and the Era of National Unity" was delivered as the Churchill Lecture for the English-Speaking Union in November 1984

"War and Social Change" was delivered as a lecture in the University of Warsaw in December 1988

"Military Experience in European Literature" was delivered as the Tredegar Memorial Lecture to the Royal Society of Literature in October 1976

"Structure and Process in History" was given as a Valedictory Lecture at Oxford on May 19, 1989

Notes

Chapter 2 Empires, Nations and Wars

1. J. A. Hobson, *Imperialism: A Study* (London, 1952).
2. A point made most persuasively by J. A. Gallagher and R. E. Robinson in *Africa and the Victorians* (London, 1961).
3. Michael Howard, *The Continental Commitment* (London, 1972), 71.
4. Alfred, Viscount Milner, *England in Egypt* (London, 1893), 40.
5. Theodore Herzl, *Diaries,* ed. M. Löwenthal (New York, 1962), 382.
6. Elie Kedourie, *Nationalism* (London, 1960), 12.
7. Ibid., 15.
8. L. B. Namier, *The Revolution of the Intellectuals* (Oxford, 1946), 88.
9. Kedourie, *Nationalism,* 94.

Chapter 3 Prussia in European History

1. Law No. 46, Allied Control Council, February 25, 1947.
2. *Oeuvres de Mirabeau,* 5:413 (Paris, 1822).
3. Heinrich von Treitschke, *Origins of Prussianism,* trans. E. Paul and C. Paul (London, 1942), 19.
4. Quoted in Paul Kennedy, *The Anglo-German Antagonism* (London, 1980), 18.
5. Ibid., 20.
6. Heinrich von Treitschke, *Politik,* 2 vols. (Leipzig, 1899), 2:307.
7. Ibid., 1:105.
8. Ibid., 1:34.
9. Ibid., 1:30.
10. Ibid., 1:74.
11. Ibid., 1:76.
12. Andreas Dorpalen, *Heinrich von Treitschke* (New Haven, 1957), 237.
13. Gerhardt Ritter, *Staatskunst und Kriegshandwerk* (Munich, 1960), ii, 142.
14. Friedrich von Bernhardi, *Germany and the Next War* (London, 1912), 6.
15. Ibid., 27.
16. Ibid., 39.
17. Ibid., 113.
18. Ibid., 156.
19. Parliamentary Debates lxxx (1916), 736–7.

Chapter 4 Empire, Race and War in pre-1914 Britain

1. George Nathaniel, Marquess of Curzon, *Subjects of the Day* (London, 1915), 5.

2. C. S. Goldman, ed., *The Empire and the Century* (London, 1905), 1.

3. John Ruskin, *Lectures in Art delivered before the University of Oxford in Hilary Term 1870* (Oxford, 1870).

4. Lewis Michell, *The Life of the Rt. Hon. Cecil Rhodes* (London, 1910), 68.

5. Quoted in R. Koerbner and H. D. Schmidt, *Imperialism* (Cambridge, 1964), 192.

6. L. S. Amery, *My Political Life* (London, 1953), 1:145.

7. Goldman, *The Empire and the Century*, xix.

8. Quoted in Bernard Semmel, *Imperialism and Social Reform: English Social and Imperial Thought 1895–1914* (London, 1960), 85.

9. Michell, *Life of Cecil Rhodes*, 2:61.

10. Quoted in Semmel, *Imperialism and Social Reform*, 62–3.

11. H. B. Gray, *The Public Schools and the Empire* (London, 1913), 3.

12. Evelyn, Earl of Cromer, *Political and Literary Essays 1908–1913* (London, 1913), 3.

13. Marjorie Perham, *The Colonial Reckoning* (London, 1961), 32.

14. Benjamin Kidd, *Social Evolution*, 2d ed. (London, 1896), 46, 70, 266, 295, 299.

15. Vladimir Halperin, *Lord Milner and His Empire* (London, 1952), 195.

16. Alfred, Viscount Milner, *England in Egypt* (London, 1893), 40.

17. Frederick, Lord Lugard, *The Dual Mandate in Tropical Africa* (London, 1972), 318.

18. Cromer, *Political and Literary Essays*, 12.

19. Ibid., 27–8.

20. *The Nineteenth Century* 45 (May 1899): 692.

21. J. A. Cramb, *Reflections on the Origins and Destiny of Imperial Britain* (London, 1915), 89.

22. Quoted in Semmel, *Imperialism and Social Reform*, 41.

23. Kidd, *Social Evolution*, 39.

24. George Bernard Shaw, *Fabianism and the Empire* (London, 1900), 41–2.

25. Rudyard Kipling, *The Army of a Dream* (London, 1904), passim.

26. Reginald, Viscount Esher to R. de Havilland Esq., June 23, 1909, Esher Papers, Churchill College, Cambridge.

27. Spenser Wilkinson, *The University and the Study of War* (Oxford, 1909).

28. Colonel F. N. Maude, *War and the World's Life* (London, 1907), vii, 244, 249, 252.

29. H. G. Wells, *Mr. Britling Sees it Through* (London, 1916), 237.

30. *The Times*, June 28, 1909.

Chapter 5   The Edwardian Arms Race

1. Lord Grey of Falloden, *Twenty Five Years* (London, 1925), 1:91–2.

2. J. A. Spender, *The Life of the Right Hon. Sir Henry Campbell-Bannerman* (London, 1923), 2:208.

3. Elie Halévy, *History of the English People in the Nineteenth Century*, vol. 6: *The Rule of Democracy* (London, 1952), 1:11.

4. B. R. Mitchell and Phyllis Deane, *Abstract of British Historical Statistics* (Cambridge, 1962), 398.

5. See e.g. J. T. Walton Newbold, *How Europe Armed for War 1871–1914* (London, n.d.), G. H. Perris, *The War Traders* (London, 1914), Philip Noel-Baker, *The Private Manufacture of Armaments* (London, 1936).

6. A. J. A. Morris, *Radicalism against War* (London, 1972), 151.

7. See Paul Kennedy, *The Rise of the Anglo-German Antagonism* (London, 1980), passim but esp. 291–440.

8. The article is reprinted in full in Spender, *Life of Sir Henry Campbell-Bannerman*, 2:328.

9. Halévy, *History of the English People*, 222.

10. E. L. Woodward, *Great Britain and the German Navy* (Oxford, 1935), 135.

11. Ibid., 155.

12. Quoted in Morris, *Radicalism against War*, 85.

13. H. W. Nevinson, for example, describes W. T. Stead at the Hague Conference as being 'exuberant for peace, and in the end calling for as many battleships as we could possibly build'. *Fire of Life* (London, 1935), 219.

14. E.g. Jonathan Steinberg, *Yesterday's Deterrent* (London, 1955); Walter Hubatsch, *Die Aera Tirpitz* (Göttingen, 1955); V. R. Berghahn, *Der Tirpitz Plan* (Düsseldorf, 1971); E. Kehr, *Battleship Building and Party Politics in Germany* (Chicago, 1973).

15. A. T. Mahan, *Retrospect and Prospect* (London, 1902), 165–6.

16. G. P. Gooch and H. V. Temperley, *British Documents on the Origins of the War 1908–14* (London, 1930), 6:184–90. See also the reports from the British naval attachés in Berlin quoted in A. J. Marder, *From Dreadnought to Scapa Flow* (London, 1961), 1:147–9.

17. Woodward, *Great Britain and the German Navy*, 1:170–2.

18. Quoted in ibid., 98. For other statements to the same effect see ibid., 160–2.

19. A. J. Marder, ed., *Fear God and Dread Nought: The Correspondence of Lord Fisher of Kilverstone* (London, 1956), 2:91.

20. See V. R. Berghahn, *Germany and the Approach of War in 1914* (London, 1973), 54–66.

21. Woodward, *Great Britain and the German Navy*, 153 ff. A. J. Marder, *Dreadnought to Scapa Flow*, 136.

22. Quoted in Marder, *Dreadnought to Scapa Flow*, 148.

23. Martin Gilbert, *Winston Churchill*, vol. II, Companion volume 2, p. 937.

24. Hansard, *Parliamentary Debates*, 5th series, vol. iii, Commons, 1909, cols. 39–146.

25. John Ellis's Diary, quoted in Morris, *Radicalism against War*, 157.

26. Winston Churchill, *The World Crisis*, abridged ed. (London, 1931), 39.

27. Berghahn, *Der Tirpitz Plan*, 84.

28. *Die grosse Politik der europäische Kabinette 1871–1914*, 31:188–9. See also Woodward, *Great Britain and the German Navy*, 352.

29. Hansard, *Parliamentary Debates*, 5th series, vol. xxii, Commons, 1909, cols. 1977–1992.

30. *Die grosse Politik*, 28:397.

31. Woodward, *Great Britain and the German Navy*, 305.

Chapter 6   Men against Fire

1. Jean de Bloch, *Is War Now Impossible? The Future of War in its Technical, Economic and Political Relations* (London and Boston, 1899).

2. Ibid., xi.

3. Ibid., xxviii.

4. Ferdinand Foch, *The Principles of War* (New York, 1918), 362.

5. Ibid., 365–66.

6. Bloch, *Is War Now Impossible?*, xxvii.
7. Ibid., xvii.
8. Ibid., xlvi.
9. Ibid., 30.
10. Ibid., 335, 314.
11. George F. R. Henderson, *The Science of War* (London, 1905), 411. It is ironic to read in an article which Henderson had written shortly before the war: 'Neither smokeless powder nor the magazine rifle will necessitate any radical change. If the defense has gained, as has been asserted, by these inventions, the plunging fire of rifled howitzers will add a more than proportional strength to the attack. And if the magazine rifle has introduced a new and formidable element into battle, the moral element still remains the same'. Ibid., 159–60.
12. *Journal of the United Services Institution*, 15:1316–44, 1413–51.
13. G. F. R. Henderson had been writing and lecturing on the American Civil War well before 1899 and Lord Roberts was to acknowledge the influence of those writings on his own operational planning in South Africa. After 1901 the Civil War became the main topic for historical study at the British Army Staff College at Camberley. Jay Luvaas, *The Military Legacy of the Civil War* (Chicago, 1959), 229.
14. Friedrich von Bernhardi, *On War Today* (London, 1912), 1:192.
15. Quoted in Luvaas, *Military Legacy of the Civil War*, 107.
16. Major General E. A. Altham, *The Principles of War Historically Illustrated* (London, 1914), 92.
17. Bernhardi, *On War Today*, 2:337.
18. Wilhelm Balck, *Tactics*, 4th ed. (Fort Leavenworth, 1911), 2:383.
19. Altham, *Principles of War*, 80.
20. Balck, *Tactics*, 1:373.
21. Charles Ardent du Picq, *Études sur le combat: Combat antique et moderne* (Paris, repr. 1942), 110.
22. Ibid., 87.
23. Eugène Carrias, *La pensée militaire française* (Paris, 1960), 276.
24. Henderson, *Science of War*, 135–40.
25. Ibid., 373–75.
26. Carrias, *La pensée militaire française*, 290.
27. Douglas Porch, *The March to the Marne* (Cambridge, 1981), 214–20.
28. 'The steadily improving standards of living tend to increase the instinct of self-preservation and to diminish the spirit of self sacrifice. . . . The fast manner of living at the present day undermines the nervous system, the fanaticism and religious and national enthusiasm of a bygone age are lacking, and finally the physical powers of the human species are also partly diminishing'. Balck, *Tactics*, 1:194. For equally gloomy British assessments see T. H. E. Travers, 'Technology, Tactics and Morale: Jean de Bloch, the Boer War, and British Military Theory 1900–1914', *Journal of Modern History* 51, no. 2 (June 1979): 264–86. This article is of seminal importance in showing the connection between tactical doctrine and national morale before 1914.
29. General François de Négrier, *Lessons from the Russo-Japanese War* (London, 1905), 69.
30. Altham, *Principles of War*, 295–6, 302.

31. General A. N. Kuropatkin, *The Russian Army and the Japanese War* (London, 1909), 2:80.

32. Major General Sir Ian Hamilton, *A Staff Officer's Scrapbook* (London, 1905), 1:10–13.

33. Quoted in Travers, 'Technology, Tactics, and Morale'.

34. R. B. Haldane, Introduction to Sir Ian Hamilton, *Compulsory Service*, 2d ed. (London, 1911), 38.

35. Quoted in Fritz Fischer, *War of Illusions* (New York and London, 1975), 395.

36. Eugène Carrias, *La pensée militaire allemande* (Paris, 1948), 1:319.

37. Joseph Joffre, *The Personal Memoirs of Marshal Joffre* (London, 1932), 1:27ff.

38. Quoted in Henri Contamine, *La revanche 1871–1914* (Paris, 1957), 167.

39. Eugene Weber, *The Nationalist Revival in France, 1905–1914* (Berkeley and Los Angeles, 1959), 93–105.

40. Contamine, *La revanche*, 276.

Chapter 7   Europe on the Eve of the First World War

1. The information in this paragraph comes from W. S. T. Stallybrass, 'Oxford in 1914–1918', *Oxford* (Winter 1939); H. W. B. Joseph, 'Oxford in the Last War', *Oxford Magazine,* May 22, 1941; and from researches for the History of the University currently being carried out by Mark Curthoys, to whom I owe a great debt of gratitude.

2. Carl von Clausewitz, *On War,* trans. M. Howard and P. Paret (Princeton, 1976), 89.

3. V. R. Berghahn, *Germany and the Approach of War in 1914* (London, 1873), 185.

4. E.g. Arno J. Mayer, *The Persistence of the Old Regime* (London, 1981).

5. A. J. A. Morris, *The Scaremongers* (London, 1984), passim.

6. Henri Contamine, *La Revanche, 1871–1914* (Paris, 1957), 195.

7. See D. C. B. Lieven, *Russia and the Origins of the First World War* (London, 1938), 78.

8. Alfred von Schlieffen, *Gesammelte Schriften* (Berlin, 1913), 1:17.

9. J. C. G. Röhl, 'An der Schwelle der Weltkriege', *Militarische Mitteilungen* 1 (1977); Fritz Fischer, *War of Illusions* (London, 1975), 161.

10. This is the thesis expanded and documented by Fritz Fischer in *Germany's Aims in the First World War* (London, 1967).

11. Lieven, *Russia and the First World War,* 139–57.

12. John F. Keiger, *France and the Origins of the First World War* (London, 1983), 153ff; Douglas Porch, *The March to the Marne* (Cambridge, 1981), 227.

13. Zara S. Steiner, *Britain and the Origins of the First World War* (London, 1977), 242ff.

14. See Röhl, 'An der Schwelle der Weltkriege'.

15. J. de Bloch, *La Guerre future aux points de vue technique, économique et politique,* 6 vols. (Paris, 1898), trans. and summarised as *Is War Now Impossible? The Future of War in its Technical, Economic and Political Relations* (London and Boston, 1899).

16. Rudyard Kipling, 'The Islanders', in *Rudyard Kipling's Verse* (London, 1982), 301.

17. E.g. R. Wohl, *The Generation of 1914* (London, 1980) and Roland N. Stromberg, *Redemption by War: The Intellectuals and 1914* (Lawrence, Kansas, 1982).

18. A. C. F. Beales, *A History of Peace* (London, 1931).

19. See the contrasting studies by Roger Chickering, *Imperial Germany and a World Without War* (Princeton, 1975), and *We Men Who Feel Most German: A Cultural Study of the Pan-German League 1886–1914* (London, 1984).

Chapter 9   Ideology and International Relations

1. John Plamenatz, *Ideology* (London, 1970), 15.
2. Baron de Montesquieu, *The Spirit of the Laws,* trans. Thomas Nugent (New York, 1949), 1.
3. Quoted in V. Kubálková and A. A. Cruickshank, 'A Double Omission', *British Journal of International Studies* 3 (1977): 292.
4. W. H. Auden, *Collected Shorter Poems 1930–1944* (London, 1950), 191.
5. Quoted in K. R. Minogue, *Nationalism* (London, 1969), 41.
6. Quoted in E. Kedourie, *Nationalism* (London, 1960), 83.
7. Quoted in Hans Kohn, *Prelude to Nation-States: The French and German Experience 1789–1815* (New York and London, 1967), 235.

Index

Act of Union (1801), 31
Acton, Lord, 195, 199
Adullamites, 154
Afghanistan, 24, 42, 169
Agadir crisis (1911), 59, 94, 120
Alembert, Jean Le Rond d', 140
Alexander II, 3
Algeria, 42, 174
Allied Control Council, 49
Allon, Yigal, 21, 36, 48
Amery, Leopold, 66, 67
Anarchism, 176
Angell, Norman: *The Great Illusion*, 119
Arms race, 11, 81, 82, 96; expenditures,
   82, 83, 84–86, 89, 90, 93, 94, 95; fire-
   power in, 98–99; misperceptions in, 92
Arndt, Ernst Moritz, 32, 39, 54, 55, 58
Arnold, Thomas, 7
Asquith, Herbert, 60, 82, 91, 92, 116,
   125, 154
Attlee, Clement Richard, 157, 158
Auden, W. H., 144
Australia, 65, 132
Austria, 43, 44, 45, 51, 55, 56, 118, 122

Baader-Meinhoff Gang, 44
Baker, Philip Noel, 92
Balck, Wilhelm: *Tactics,* 104
Baldwin, Stanley, 158
Balfour, Arthur, 125
Balkans, 44, 45, 116, 117, 118, 131
Baluchistan, 24
Battleships, 87, 88, 90
Bayonet warfare, 103–4, 105, 106, 108,
   114, 123, 136–37; by Japanese, 108–9
Beaverbrook, Lord, 80
Becker, Jean-Jacques: *1914: Comment les
   Français son entrés dans la guerre,* 124
Beloff, Max, Lord: *Wars and Welfare,* 156
Bentham, Jeremy, 143, 167
Berchtold, Leopold von, 117

Bergson, Henri, 125
Berlin, 54, 55, 56, 57, 117, 118, 133
Bernhardi, Friedrich von, 59–61, 103,
   124; *Germany and the Next War,* 59
Bethmann-Hollweg, Theobald von, 93, 94,
   95, 96, 116
Bevin, Ernest, 155, 158
Bible, 184, 189
Bismarck, Prince Otto von, 56, 60, 67,
   153
Bloch, Ivan (Jean de), 97–101, 107, 111,
   193; *Is War Now Impossible?,* 98; *La
   guerre future . . . ,* 97, 101, 121; on
   modern weapons, 121
Blücher, Gebhard Leberecht, 55
Blunden, Edmund, 183, 184
Boers, 67, 74, 101, 102
Boer War, 75, 107, 110, 114, 123, 156
Boileau, Nicolas, 32
Bonapartism, 145
Bosnian nationalism, 45, 117, 175
Bourgeoisie, 141, 195
Boyen, Hermann, 55
Boyle, Edward, 158
Bracken, Brendan, 155
Braudel, Fernand: *Civilization and Capital-
   ism . . . ,* 196
Bright, John, 81, 85
Britain, 47, 119, 127, 156; economic de-
   cline, 159; empire, 64–67, 132; national
   unity, 158–59, 161; naval power, 84–88;
   welfare state, 156, 157, 158, 159
British Army Staff College, 122
British Expeditionary Force, 121
Brockway, Fenner, 92
Bruck, Moeller van den, 50
Bulgaria, 45
Bülow, Bernard Heinrich Martin Karl, 93
Burckhardt, Jakob, 11, 18
Butler, Richard Austen, 158

209

Campaign for Nuclear Disarmament, 2

Campbell, Thomas, 64

Campbell-Bannerman, Henry, 81–82, 84–85

Canada, 65, 132

Candide, 180

Capitalism, 4, 5, 22, 149, 164, 172, 173, 175; Lenin on, 173

Carlyle, Thomas, 64

Carrington, Charles (aka Charles Edmonds), 184; *A Subaltern's War*, 183

Catherine II, 3

Catholic church, 3, 31, 126

Cavalry, 102–3, 108

Cavour, Camillo, Count, 67

Cawdor, Earl of, 89

Cecil, Robert, 24

Céline, Louis-Ferdinand, 184

Central Powers, 46, 80, 118

Cervantes, Miguel de, 180

Chamberlain, Houston Stewart, 71

Chamberlain, Joseph, 68, 69

Chamberlain, Neville, 15, 18, 158

Chapman, Guy, 184; *A Kind of Survivor,* 183; *A Passionate Prodigality,* 183

Childers, Erskine: *The Riddle of the Sands,* 86

China, 166, 174, 176; nationalism of, 36

Churchill, Winston, 91, 92, 121, 127, 153–55, 165; leadership, 154, 158, 165; *The World Crisis,* 93

Civil war, 174, 179; American, 98, 102, 122

Class, Heinrich, 59, 124, 126

Class/classless society, 143–44, 148, 157; overclass/underclass, 150

Clausewitz, Carl von, 1, 47, 58, 166; *On War,* 77; trinity of war, 115–16

Cobden, Richard, 81, 85

Colonialism, 29, 37, 41–42, 73, 173, 174

Colonial life, 25–26

Committee of Imperial Defence, 86

Committee on the Present Danger, 2

Communism, 131, 136, 149, 156

Comte, August, 167

Condorcet, Marie Jean, Marquis de, 140, 190

Cory, William Johnson, 64

Council of War (1912), 117, 120

Cramb, J. A., 59, 75

Crimean War, 3, 156

Cromer, Evelyn Baring, Lord, 69, 73

Crosland, Anthony, 158

Cultural equality, 25

Cultural purity, 34, 36, 37

Cultural relativism, 72, 80, 195, 199

Cultural superiority, 26–27, 42, 58, 77–78, 80

Curtis, Lionel, 164

Curzon, George Nathaniel, Lord, 63

Czechoslovakia, 45, 46, 166

Dahlmann, Friedrich, 55

Darwin, Charles, 70, 75, 76, 132, 146

Davis, Charles, 8

Deakin, Alfred, 79

Declaration of the Rights of Man (1789), 30, 32, 54, 141, 145

Deeds that Won the Empire, 75

Democracy, 143, 173

Despotism, enlightened, 73

Deutschtum (Germanness), 59

Diamond Jubilee (1897), 66, 67

Diderot, Denis, 140

Dilke, Charles: *Greater Britain,* 65

Diversity, contribution of, 37–39

Douglas, Keith, 186

Dragomirov, M. I., 104, 105

Dreadnought (battleship), 78, 88–90, 91–93

Dreyfus case, 107, 111

Droysen, Johann Gustav, 50, 55, 56

Dual Alliance, 118, 119, 120

Economic development, 4, 29, 68, 169, 172; east/west co-operation, 174

Economic imperatives, 23

Economic reductionism, 22

Economics, 162

Eden, Anthony, 157, 158

Edmunds, Charles (Charles Carrington), 184; *A Subaltern's War,* 183

Education, 142; contemporary British, 148; nationalism and, 34, 35, 145, 147, 173

Edwardian era, 64, 69, 74, 123; militarism, 75, 77, 78

Egypt, 24, 27, 29, 36, 43, 72, 74, 102

El Salvador, 45

Emigration, 4, 23, 35, 68

Empathy, 150, 195

Empires, 22–29, 33, 67, 74, 79; concept, 65; decline, 80, 168–69

Encyclopaedists, 140, 141, 142, 144

Engels, Friedrich, 192

England, 51, 52. *See also* Britain

Enlightenment, 52, 130, 135, 141, 145, 149, 192, 195; history in, 189–90; and belief in human progress, 27, 197

Equality (concept), 71

Erhebungzeit (era of Liberation of 1813–15), 55

Esher, Reginald, Lord, 64, 76, 79

Ethnocentrism, 15, 16, 17, 18–19

Europe: centrality of, 133–34; U.S. in, 136, 137

Fabian Society, 28, 76

Falklands campaign, 4, 30*n*, 169

Famine: war and, 99–100

Fascism, 149, 155, 164, 168, 176

Fichte, Johann Gottlieb, 32, 39, 54, 58, 145, 146, 180

Firearms, 98–99, 103, 105; in Russo-Japanese War, 107, 110–11; in South Africa, 101–2

Firth, Charles, 8

Fischer, Fritz: *Griff nach der Weltmacht*, 128, 129

Fisher, John, 89, 90

Foch, Ferdinand, 98, 99

Ford, Ford Madox, 182

France, 40, 46, 51, 79, 111, 119, 122, 132; in Algeria, 42; and French aristocracy, 52; colonialism of, 134; military in, 105, 182; nationalism of, 170; Three-Year Law, 119

Franco-Prussian War, 98, 102

Franz Ferdinand, 114, 175

Frederick the Great, 50, 51, 53, 58, 60

Frederick William (Great Elector), 50, 51, 52–53, 58

Frederick William I, 51, 53

Frederick William III, 54, 113

Frederick William IV, 54

Freedom, 198–99

Freeman, Edward, 7, 190

French Revolution, 30, 53, 54, 130–31, 133, 138, 198; effect of, 145, 169; literature, 180; nationalism and, 170

Froude, James Anthony, 64, 66, 190, 191

Fussell, Paul, 187; *The Great War and Modern Memory*, 184

Gaitskell, Hugh, 158

Galbraith, Vivian, 8, 12

Gaulle, Charles de, 153

General Strike of 1926 (Great Britain), 157

German language, 57

Germany, 32, 35, 49, 54, 76, 160; France and, 83–84, 118; hegemonic goals, 128–29, 133, 149; militarism, 60, 76–77, 87–88, 120, 132–33, 168; military service, 116, 182; nationalism, 54, 56, 58, 131, 133, 147, 149, 170, 171; Naval Law of *1900*, 89; peace movement, 126; Prussia and, 55, 56, 57, 60; revival, 127–28; Right Wing, 128; wars, 40, 45, 46, 56, 58, 121, 123, 127

Ghana, 26, 42

Gide, André, 198

Girondins, 142

Gladstone, William Ewart, 27

Gleichschaltung (integration), 49

Gneisenau, August von, 54, 55

Gobineau, Joseph-Arthur, 71

Goethe, Johann Wolfgang von, 145

Gorbachev, Mikhail, 2, 3–4

Grandmaison, Louis de, 111

Graves, Robert, 182, 183

Grey, Edward, 81, 85, 88, 92, 94, 96

Grimmelshausen, H. J. C. von, 180, 186

Habsburg Empire, 38, 46, 132

Haggard, H. Rider, 74

Hague Conferences, 84, 90, 101, 126, 167–68
Haldane, Richard B., 86, 94, 110
Halévy, Elie, 82, 85
Hamilton, Ian, 109–10
Hardinge, Charles, 88
Hart, B. H. Liddell, 21, 106
Haüsser, Kaspar, 55, 56
Health, 156, 196–97
Heath, Edward, 158
Hegel, G. W. F., 39, 58, 75, 76, 191, 192
Hegemonial states, 128–30, 149
Heller, Joseph: Catch-22, 186
Helvetius, Claude-Adrien, 140
Henderson, George F. R., 101, 106
Henry, G. A., 74
Herder, Johann, 32, 54, 193
Heroes, 152, 179, 180–81
Herzl, Theodore, 29, 35
Hill, Christopher, 194
Hindenburg, Paul von, 61
Histoire évènementielle, 194, 196
Historians: bias, 2, 20, 195; function, 12
Historiography, 190
History: comprehending, 14–15, 189, 193; concept of, 197–98, 199; context of, 2, 20; contribution of, 9, 16, 151, 188–89, 199; as cyclical, 196; ethnocentrism in, 15, 16, 17, 18–19; as "Heritage Industry," 199; lessons of, 5, 10–11, 13, 18, 19; military, 19, 41, 184; myth and, 39–40, 153; nature of, 11–13, 189–91; as process, 192, 193, 194, 195; as progress, 191, 195, 196, 197; as structure, 193–94, 196; teaching of, 8–9, 16–17, 18
Hitler, Adolf, 13, 14, 61, 128, 130, 136, 143, 155, 162, 166; on U.S., 38
Hobson, J. A., 22; Imperialism, 22
Ho Chi Minh, 172
Hodgkin, Thomas: Italy and Her Invaders, 69
Hohenzollern dynasty, 49, 50, 51, 52, 54, 55
Holbach, Paul Henri Dietrich d', 140
Holocaust, 37
Holy Land: as British Empire, 66, 67

Homer, 179
House, Edward M., 133
Housman, A. E., 121
Howard, Michael: Studies in War and Peace, 1–2; The Causes of War, 2
Hume, David, 189
Hungary, 46

Idéologue, 139, 140, 141, 142, 143, 144
Ideology, 170; bourgeois, 141, 143, 170, 172; term, 139–40, 142
Imperial Federation League, 65, 66
Imperial General Staff, 79
Imperial Institute, 65
Imperialism, 22, 26–27, 29, 63, 69, 75, 80; British, 65, 68; justification, 22, 68, 72, 73; socialist, 28; Soviet, 149
Imperial Race, 63, 69, 80
Imperial War Museum, 80, 124
Independence, 27, 32; nonviolent, 41–42
India, 23, 25, 28, 43, 74, 80, 132; independence, 134; Marx on, 194; nationalism in, 36; war and, 169
Industrialization, 1, 3, 167, 173, 196
Industrial revolution, 160, 176; third, 160
Intermediate Range Nuclear Forces, 2
Internationalism, 144, 148–49, 150, 164; opposition to, 149, 164; proletarian, 149
International Peace Conference (1899), 101
International relations, 143, 146, 150, 171
Invincibles (battle-cruisers), 90
Ireland, 31, 45, 116
Islamic world, 30
Israel, 35–36, 38, 47, 48; claims, 30, 45, 169; independence, 21, 24, 35, 169
Italy, 44, 46, 126, 127, 131, 132, 170

Jacobinism, 145
Jahn, Friedrich, 50
James, Robert Rhodes, 153
Japan, 111, 166, 168; army, 107–8; bayonet warfare, 108–9; cavalry, 108; morale, 109, 110, 123; nationalism, 147; technology, 160; U.S. popularity, 137
Jaurès, Jean, 126

Jenkins, Roy, 158
Jews, 37, 127; anti-Semitism, 35, 59, 61
Joffre, Joseph J., 110–11
Jones, David, 184; *In Parenthesis,* 182, 185
Junker families, 59

Kadavergehorsamkeit (obedience), 49
Kant, Immanuel, 146, 190, 192, 196, 197, 200; *Idea for a Universal History,* 190, 198
Kenya, 42
Kidd, Benjamin, 77, 125; *Social Evolution,* 71–72, 75
Kingsley, Charles, 64
Kipling, Rudyard, 64, 66, 74, 123–24, 182; *The Army of a Dream,* 76; *The Islanders,* 76; *Recessional,* 66; *Soldiers Three,* 180; *The White Man's Burden,* 70
Kitchener, Herbert Lord, 117, 125
Knox, W. G., 110
Kuropatkin, A. N., 109

Labour: dislocation, 160; seen as people, 157
Language, 18; common, 31–32; empathy and, 150; nationalism and, 34
Laurier, Wilfrid, 79
League of Nations, 168
League of Peace, 82, 84
Lehár, Franz, 125
Lenin, 135, 152, 161, 172, 173, 174, 197
Liberation, 142–43
Lichnowsky, Prince Karl Max, 113
Literature: medieval, 178; war in, 177–85
Lloyd George, David, 82, 90, 92, 154
Louis XIV, 130
Louis Philippe, 55
Low, Sidney, 75, 125; *The Nineteenth Century,* 75
Loyalty, 163–64
Lugard, Frederick, 73, 80

Macaulay, Thomas Babington, 190
McKenna, Reginald, 91
Mackinder, Halford, 67
Macmillan, Harold, 157, 158
Magic Flute, The (Mozart), 140

Mahan, Alfred Thayer, 85, 86, 87
Mailer, Norman: *The Naked and the Dead,* 186
Malaya, 42
Malory, Thomas, 178
Manchuria, 107, 108, 109, 123, 166
Mandate of Heaven, 26
Manifest destiny, 26, 67
Manning, Frederick, 184; *The Middle Parts of Fortune,* 183
Mao Tse-tung, 170, 172
Marder, Arthur, 91
Marx, Karl, 141, 143–44, 192, 194
Marxism-Leninism, 3, 23, 27, 28, 139, 141, 142, 146, 149; history in, 194; nationalism and, 171, 172; on progress, 192; post-war, 193; prospects of, 138. *See also* Proletariat
Maude, F. N., 78, 125; *War and the World's Life,* 77
Maurras, Charles, 59, 124
Mayer, Arno: *The Persistence of the Old Regime,* 120
Mazzini, Giuseppe, 39, 44, 45, 143–44, 146
Meinecke, Friedrich, 61
Mentalité, 140, 141, 142, 146–47, 148
Metternich, Klemens, 56, 88, 92
Middle East, 22–24, 118
Militarism, 47, 52, 58, 63, 74; British, 76, 78–79; German, 60, 132–33
Military, 166–67; professionalism, 180, 182; service, 157, 181, 182, 183–85, 191
Military history, 41; revisionism, 19, 184
Milner, Alfred, 72, 74, 78, 164; *England in Egypt,* 27, 72
Mirabeau, Honoré Gabriel, Comte de, 50
Mitteis, Ludwig, 113
Mobility, 4, 198
Modernization, 196, 198
'Moltke, Helmuth von, 61, 110, 120
Monarchies, 30, 40
Monnet, Jean, 164
Montesquieu: *L'esprit des lois,* 142
Montherlant, Henry de, 183

Moral absolutes, 195. *See also* Value-
  judgments
Morale, 106, 107, 109, 110, 111, 123,
  124
Morocco, 84, 116
Morrison, Herbert, 155
Moslem fundamentalism, 176
Mukden, battle of, 108
Multi-ethnicity, 37–39, 135
Music, 125
Mussolini, Benito, 162
Myths: historian and, 153

Namibia, 45
Napoleon, 55, 129, 180
Napoleonic wars: in literature, 181
Nation, 29–39, 145, 163, 170–71; defini-
  tion, 31
Nationalism, 4, 27, 33–37, 44, 111, 130,
  133, 135, 145–46, 170; contemporary,
  147, 149–50; counter, 36, 136; effects
  of, 37, 130, 145, 147, 191; Soviet, 135;
  supra-, 164; Third World, 174; U.S.,
  135
Nationalization, 145–46; de-, 147
National Service League, 78, 79
National Socialism, 49, 61, 133
National unity, 158, 163–64
Naval Defence Act (1889), 86
Nazi-Soviet Pact (1939), 136
Nazism, 15, 42, 127, 133, 139, 191, 195;
  Prussianism and, 49–50, 61. *See also*
  Hitler, Adolf
Netherlands, 130, 134, 173
New Order, 141
New Zealand, 65, 80, 132
Nicholas II, 101
Nietzsche, Friedrich, 125
Nigeria, 37, 42
Nkrumah, Kwame, 26
Norway, 39
Nuclear weapons, 47–48

Objectivity (of historian), 195
Offensive, doctrine of the, 122
Officer Training Corps (OTC), 114
Oil crisis, 159

OTC. *See* Officer Training Corps
Ottoman Empire, 24, 36, 80, 97, 170
Overpopulation, 174
Owen, Wilfred, 184
Oxford, University of, 113, 114; History
  School, 8, 15–16, 17, 76

Palestine, 21, 23, 24, 27, 35, 36, 174
Pan-German League, 126
Panic, Great (of 1909), 91, 92
Parochialism, 148
Patriotism, 4, 163, 191; as suspect, 148
Peace, 85, 90, 167; lobby, 85, 90, 92
Peace movements, 95, 126, 167, 175
Pearson, Karl, 75
Péguy, Charles, 124
People are good (ideology), 142–43
Perham, Marjorie, 71
Persian Gulf, 169
Philip II (Spain), 129, 130
Philippines, 69
Picq, Charles Ardent du; *Études sur le com-
  bat,* 105
Pilgrim's Progress, 184
Plamenatz, John: *Ideology,* 139
Plutarch: *Lives,* 189
Poland, 42, 166, 170
Potsdam, 61
Powell, Anthony, 183, 186
Power, 53–54, 60; *Macht,* 58
Powicke, Maurice, 8, 19
Preussentum (Prussianism), 55–56, 57, 61,
  132
Progress, 27, 28, 191, 192, 197
Proletariat, 141, 143–44, 146, 171, 172–
  73; corruption in, 197
Protestantism, 52, 126
Proust, Marcel, 182
Prussia, 47, 49–61, 132, 145, 191; milita-
  rism of, 132–33; as military monarchy,
  51, 133; name, 51; power, 52, 58, 60;
  virtues, 61
Pusey, Edmund, 7

Racism, 63, 69–73, 77; white man's burden, 69, 70, 72–73. *See also* Cultural superiority; Jews; Social Darwinism

Rationalism, 140, 142, 144–45, 189–92, 197, 198

Reductionism: economc, 22

Reformation, 191

Reichstag, 90, 94, 95

Reification, 197–98

Religious motivations, 131, 132, 175

Remarque, Erich Maria, 184

Revisionism, 19, 184

Revolution, 142, 161, 170–72, 173, 192

Revolutionaries, 32, 162, 176

Rhodes, Cecil, 66, 68, 113, 132

Roberts, Frederick, Lord, 78, 102, 125

Roland, Song of, 177–78, 184, 185

Romanov Empire, 46, 51

Rome, 69, 73

Roosevelt, Franklin D., 18

Rosebery, Lord, 64, 66, 68

Rousseau, Jean-Jacques, 145, 190

Rumania, 46

Ruskin, John, 64, 153

Russia, 46, 51, 74, 83, 84, 94, 116, 170; army, 105, 107, 118; Britain and, 79; Civil War, 172; Great Patriotic War, 172; Great Programme, 120; morale of, 109, 110; rearmament, 118; revolution, 171, 192; Slavophile movement, 149; World War I, 119, 122, 170; World War II, 127, 170. *See also* Soviet Union

Russo-Japanese War (1904–5), 87, 107–8, 109, 110, 111; weaponry, 121, 123

Russo-Turkish War (1877–78), 98

Sacrifice, supreme (in war), 123

St. Simon, 167

Salisbury, Robert Anthony Cecil, Lord, 23

Sarajevo, 114, 175

Sassoon, Siegfried, 184

Saxe-Coburg-Gotha, Duke of, 113

Scharnhorst, Gebhard von, 54, 55

Schlieffen, Alfred von, 110, 117

Schoenberg, Arnold, 125

Schrift, 57

Second Reich, 95, 132

Security, 22, 23–25, 47

Seeley, J. R., 66, 67; *The Expansion of England,* 65

Self-determination, 39, 43–45, 146, 147. *See also* Nationalism

Self-government, 27, 29–30, 36, 43, 80

Serbia, 45, 117, 118

Sexual revolution, 159–60

Shakespeare, William, 179–80, 181; *Henry V,* 179; *Troilus and Cressida,* 179

Shaw, George Bernard, 160; *Fabianism and the Empire,* 76

Shinwell, Emanuel, 157

Shipbuilding, 88–93, 94

Siéyès, Abbé, 31, 32

Slavs, 117, 118, 128, 131, 132, 149

Smith, Adam, 46

Smith, Goldwin, 7

Smuts, Jan Christiaan, 21

Social change, 29; disintegration, 196

Social Darwinism, 58, 71–72, 75, 120, 123, 125, 126, 132; nationalism and, 146–47

Socialism, 5, 175–76

Soldiers, 181–83; profile (WWI), 120

Solzhenitsyn, Aleksandr, 181

South Africa, 45, 65, 67, 75, 104, 106; modern weaponry in, 101–2, 123

Southey, Robert, 64

South Korea, 137, 169

Sovereignty, 30

Soviet Union, 2, 3–4, 46, 136, 193; communism and, 131; expansionism of, 22; ideology, 149; leadership, 176; nationalism, 135, 136; and U.S., 135. *See also* Russia

Spain, 25n, 33, 51, 130; peace movement, 126

Spencer, Herbert, 167

Spengler, Oswald, 192

Sputnik, 93

Stalin, Joseph, 130, 153, 172, 174

Stanley, Lord, 56

State (the), 58, 191

Stead, W. T., 98

Stein, Karl von, 54

Stendhal, 181; *La Chartreuse de Parme,* 181

Stolypin, Count Peter, 3

Strauss, Richard, 113, 125

Structural historians, 194
Stubbs, William, 7, 190
Sturm und Drang movement, 180
Sudan, 27, 102
Suez crisis (1956), 134
Sullivan, Arthur, 65
Superpowers, 65, 67, 128, 134, 135
Supplementary Law (Novelle), 89, 90
Sybel, Heinrich von, 56, 191

Tennyson, Lord, 65, 153
Territorial Army (England), 78
Territory: war and, 168–69, 170
Terrorism, 175
Teutonic Knights, 50, 53
Third Reich, 49, 127, 129. See also Nazism
Third World, 5, 149–50, 170, 172, 173;
    nationalism, 174, 175; U.S. in, 137
Thomist Christianity, 139
Thompson, E. P., 194
Thucydides, 189
Tirpitz, Alfred von, 59, 87, 90, 92, 93, 94,
    95, 128
Tocqueville, Alexis de, 65, 134
Togo, Admiral, 87
Tolstoy, Leo: War and Peace, 181
Totalitarianism, 145, 198
Tout, T. F., 8
Toynbee, Arnold, 192
Treitschke, Heinrich von, 50, 55, 56, 58,
    59, 61, 191
Trevor-Roper, Hugh (Lord Dacre), 8, 18
Trotsky, Leon, 144
Tsushima, Battle of, 89
Tweedmouth, Lord, 91
Two Power Standard, 89

Uganda, 37, 42
Unemployment, 4, 160, 174
Uniforms (military), 108
Unions, 161
United Nations, 137, 168
United States, 38, 134, 137, 138; in Eu-
    rope, 136, 137; nationalism, 135; popu-
    larity, 137; and Soviets, 135; wars, 40,
    42, 134
Urbanization, 167, 172

Value-judgments, 194–95, 199
Vico, Giambattista, 193
Victorian England, 26–27, 64, 75, 78, 156
Vienna, 117, 118
Vietnam, 42, 169, 172
Vigny, Alfred de, 182
Virtue, 189
Volk, 54, 58, 131
Vonnegut, Kurt: Slaughterhouse Five, 186

Wallenstein, Albert, 53
War, 39–41, 63, 74–75, 123, 167; as func-
    tional, 168–69; glorification of, 58, 60,
    75, 77, 120, 125, 133, 167, 168, 186–
    87, 191; governments and, 115–17; in-
    dustrial base for, 121; inevitability of,
    75, 120–21; legitimacy of, 42; in litera-
    ture, 177–85; losers in, 40–41; modern,
    47; motivations for, 131, 166, 170;
    Movement, 125–26; nationalism and,
    42, 44–47, 58, 131, 170–73; as para-
    doxical trinity, 115–16; people's support
    of, 115, 124–26; readiness for, 132; as
    suicidal, 98, 111; welfare and, 156, 158
Warfare, 169; strategies, 99, 101–6, 110,
    121, 195. See also Bayonet warfare; Cav-
    alry; Firearms; Weapons
Warrior societies, 167, 168, 169, 176
Waterloo, Battle of, 181
Waugh, Evelyn, 182, 186
Wealth, basis of, 167
Weapons, 121, 123; spade as, 107. See also
    Firearms
Weber, Max, 9
Webern, Anton von, 125
Weizmann, Chaim, 24
Welfare: war and, 156, 158
Welfare state, 156, 157–58, 159, 160,
    162
Wells, H. G., 160; Mr. Britling Sees it
    Through, 78
Weltanschauung, 140, 141
Weltmacht, 83
Wermuth, Adolf, 93, 94
West Africa, 72, 73
White man's burden, 69, 70
Widenmann, Captain, 95

Wilhelm II, 88, 91, 113, 128
Wilkinson, Spenser, 79, 114
William I, 54, 55
Wilson, Woodrow, 142, 143
Woodward, Llewellyn, 91
Woolton, Lord, 155
World War I, 35, 45, 46, 79, 157, 191;
  motivations, 132, 171; opposition to,
  125; start of, 114, 117–22, 156
World War II, 35, 41, 45, 127, 136, 143,
  173; causes, 166; United States in,
  134
Württemberg, King of, 113

Ypres, First Battle of, 114

Xenophobia, 163

Zeitgeist, 55, 126
Zollverein, 68